SuperBo

Tom Stevenson has been writing on 1970s. He conceived the *Sunday Telegraph Good Wine Guide*, and his highly praised *Champagne*, winner of four awards, established him as one of the country's leading wine authors. His *Sotheby's World Wine Encyclopaedia*, published in 1988, won five more awards and *Wines of Alsace* (Faber and Faber, 1993) won the Veuve Clicquot Wine Book of the Year Award in the USA. In recent years Tom Stevenson has been voted both 'Wine Writer of the Year' and 'Wine Trade Writer of the Year'. He is currently working on a completely revised and substantially expanded edition of *Sotheby's World Wine Encyclopaedia* (due to be published in autumn 1997) and *The World Encyclopaedia of Champagne and Sparkling Wine* (due to be published by Absolute Press in autumn 1998). His first edition of *SuperBooze* was published by Faber in 1995.

OTHER BOOKS ON WINE FROM FABER

Bordeaux (new edition) by David Peppercorn
Burgundy (new edition) by Anthony Hanson
French Country Wines by Rosemary George
Haut-Brion by Asa Briggs
Sauternes by Stephen Brook
Sherry (new edition) by Julian Jeffs
The Wines of Alsace by Tom Stevenson
The Wines of Australia (new edition) by Oliver Mayo
The Wines of Greece by Miles Lambert-Gocs
The Wines of the Loire by Roger Voss
The Wines of New Zealand by Rosemary George
The Wines of the Rhône (new edition) by John Livingstone-Learmonth

SuperBooze 1997
The Definitive Guide to Supermarket Drink

TOM STEVENSON

ff

faber and faber

LONDON · BOSTON

First published in Great Britain in 1996
by Faber and Faber Limited
3 Queen Square London WC1N 3AU

Typeset by Parker Typesetting Service, Leicester
Printed in England by Mackays of Chatham plc, Chatham, Kent

A CIP record for this book
is available from the British Library

ISBN 0–571–17975–4

10 9 8 7 6 5 4 3 2 1

Contents

INTRODUCTION

Bigger, better and even more user-friendly

As I travelled about the country last year, going from bookshop to bookshop, presenting tastings and signing copies, it was encouraging to see so many people welcome the innovations that *SuperBooze* is bringing to consumers of supermarket wines and beers. It did not surprise me to discover how much the little details were appreciated, such as:

- How easy it is to find your way around the book.
- What a relief real prices are compared to those price bands others guides use.
- The value of buying a book full of recommendations instead of half full of what to avoid.

A couple of suggestions did, however, surprise me:

- There was huge interest in the own-label beers listings wherever I went, and repeated requests to expand these to encompass all branded beers.
- I was also asked about future coverage of regional supermarket groups such as Morrisons, Booths and Walter Wilson – and some readers in Liverpool even regarded Littlewoods as a local, if not exactly regional, supermarket.

As you can see, I have heeded your suggestions: the second edition has been expanded to include all beers, not just own-label, and the supermarkets covered now includes Morrisons, Booths and, even though it is a group of department stores rather than supermarkets, Littlewoods. As I told some of you on my rounds, Morrisons and Littlewoods had in fact been approached to participate in the first edition and although both expressed interest, neither managed to do so. This year they did. I heartily welcome them and look forward to reviewing their products on a regular basis. Walter Wilson was also enthusiastic to participate, but was carrying out a radical review of its drink range, which has continued throughout 1996; thus they felt it inappropriate to take part, but hope to do so next year. A similar situation prevented London's Europa group from participating this year (regional supermarket groups are not exclusive to the north), but I am assured they will make an appearance in the third edition.

Last but not least in terms of extended coverage, Co-operative Pioneer now has its own fully fledged entry. If you're not clear about the difference between the various Co-op groups, you're not alone, but the brief introduction to each entry explains it all. Suffice it to say that although there is some overlap, they basically sell different products, which is why *SuperBooze* treats them separately and tastes each range – something no other guide does.

If your local supermarket is not currently covered by *SuperBooze*, but you would like it to be and it belongs to a group with at least twenty branches (ask the manager if you're not sure), please send brief details to me c/o Faber and Faber and help make this guide even bigger and better.

The humble hop

The second edition sees the expansion of *SuperBooze* beer coverage from last year's exclusively own-label tastings to include all branded brews. You won't catch me waffling on about fancy Belgian beers, which is what most wine writers seem to do when they dip their quill into the beer writer's domain. I'll taste them and I can appreciate what they are supposed to be, but to tell the truth I do not particularly like most of the more exotic brews: beer for me comes in a pint pot or a nice bottle, and I aim to find the nearest thing to it that I can keep in my fridge.

It seems a nonsense to me that beer and wine writers should go on so much about fruit beers, wheat beers and (much more enjoyable but just as expensive) Trappist beers, which in total account for less than 0.01 per cent of the beer consumed in this country, yet ignore the can and despise the widget, which most people purchase every day. I would like this country to move away from its 'tinnie' culture, as there is no comparison in taste between a canned beer and the same brew in a bottle, but I cannot ignore canned beers. In fact, the more that people drink canned beers the more incumbent it is upon consumer journalists to test them. I cannot help but let my personal view colour what I write, but I must always remember that I am writing for you, not myself.

I also have strong views about the widget, that it suits some beers (stouts) better than other (bitters and lagers) and that it is not being fully or even correctly utilized – it should also be applied to milds and porters, and even bitters could be improved if the brewers made 'widgetized' beers far more bitter than they do, so that a hint of this bitterness could be detected through the widget's creamy mask – but I do not dismiss the gadget out of hand, as some of my more sniffy colleagues do.

Beer recommendations: an explanation

While there is some overlap of wine products throughout the various supermarket groups, it is far less significant than the overlap of branded beers. Most groups stock a fairly large range of branded beers that are common to all retailers.

However, if a particular brand has not been submitted for tasting by a supermarket, it will not be included in that supermarket's *SuperBooze* entry. You can find which supermarket does include an entry on that brand by looking under the **Beer Rankings** at the back of the book.

Unfortunately, although many supermarkets stock as many as 150–350 beers, most do not possess a full price list. Compiling a comprehensive list of brands stocked by each supermarket has, therefore, proved impossible.

More user-friendly

With wines and beers listed under each supermarket in ascending price order in just six sections (Red, White, Rosé, Sparkling, Fortified and Beers), *SuperBooze* is by far the easiest guide to find your way around. If you want to know the best-value products for a particular supermarket, just look up its entry in the **Supermarket Directory**. If you want to know the best-value product sold by all the supermarkets at a particular price-point for a specific type or style (such as Chardonnay, Shiraz or Pilsner), then look up that category in **The Wine & Beer Rankings**. This year all the products for each category are listed, not just the medal-winners. They are in price order, not medal order, making this section far more useful in discerning how the wines, beers and indeed supermarkets have performed in each tasting. Furthermore, they are listed in columns, making it far easier to run your finger down the products, retailers, supermarkets or prices to find exactly what you want.

Each category heading is now listed in the contents at the front of the book, making it easier still to find the type of product you're after.

STOCK ME AND BUY ONE

Each supermarket* has pledged that at least 80 per cent of all wines and beers submitted to *SuperBooze* will be available in at least 80 per cent of its branches. On the one hand, this guarantees that most recommendations will be available to most readers most of the time, while on the other hand it provides a certain flexibility, enabling supermarkets to show at least some products of a more limited production.

What if you want a product that turns out to be one of the 20 per cent and your store does not stock it? Or what about the old fact of life whereby the more a product is hyped up, the sooner it will sell out?

This is where the **Stock Me and Buy One** scheme comes in. In the past, no matter how confident a supermarket was about having sufficient stocks to last the duration of a guide's recommendation, it was impossible to predict what the surge in sales would be or where those who will want specific products live. The new *SuperBooze* scheme does not offer a complete answer – nothing could, short of supermarkets overstocking every line in all its branches and having to dump the leftovers – but **Stock Me and Buy One** comes as close as I can think to making every single recommendation available to every single reader.

If you want a recommended product from a supermarket bearing the **Stock Me and Buy One** logo, but cannot find it in your local branch, just ask the manager (or owner in the case of a symbol group such as Londis). He or she will be authorized to order it in if it is still in stock within the

*This does not apply to symbol groups or the Co-op, owing to the individual ownership of the former and the great variation in branch size of the latter.

company. Some supermarkets will even try to track down an out-of-stock item throughout the group by seeing if any branch has some left. You do not have to commit yourself to anything more than a single bottle or can (unless it happens to be a four-pack, six-pack, etc). The manager (or owner) is not obliged to provide this service, but has the discretion to do so; his or her group will possess the ability to respond and must do so if requested by one of its managers and stocks remain.

What is the shelf-life of *SuperBooze*?

This was the question I was most often asked on my promotional tasting tour last year. As I said earlier, the more a product is recommended, the sooner it will sell out, so the purpose of any guide is in a very real sense self-defeating. That said, the UK has had fifteen years' experience of shop-by-shop, shelf-by-shelf wine guides (although only one of a wine and beer guide – however, beers do not normally change vintage or run out), which makes British consumers the most sophisticated in the world when dealing with the realities of such publications. Most readers know the problems, accept that imperfect guides are better than no guides at all, and try to grab the best bargains as quickly as their finances and thirst allow.

No matter how hard a supermarket tries to ensure the shelf-life of their products, absolute guarantees are a pipe dream, and although it is obviously in a supermarket's interest to make sure that all the products I rave about will be available, some supermarkets try harder than others. Every supermarket has the opportunity to submit new lines and forthcoming vintages right up to two weeks before my copy deadline, but not all of them take advantage of this. Each year I hope to push, nudge and bully more supermarkets into helping themselves by submitting more long-term future lines as late as possible, even if it does complicate the tastings and give my computer database a headache.

All blind-tasted by price-point

SuperBooze is unique in tasting all products blind, which means that the bottles are covered to prevent my knowing their identity. *SuperBooze* is also unique in tasting like with like within the same price category. It is simply not possible to taste the same style and price category of wine in different places at different times and make accurate comparative judgements. This has nothing to do with any lack of skill in the taster; no supermarket buyer, however brilliant a taster he or she may be, would contemplate making a decision while going from cellar to cellar tasting. They bring home samples of all the most promising wines within a set budget and taste them together, sometimes blind, sometimes not, in order to decide which is best. If it's a good enough method for supermarkets to buy their wines by, it's good enough for me to taste them by.

Because I taste everything blind, my notes relate to a bottle number only and are entered into the computer in ignorance of the name of the actual wine or beer. There are two rounds of tastings, with all potential medal-winners subjected to a second test. This is necessary for two reasons. Firstly because in the largest categories there can be as many as forty wines or beers at roughly the same price, and as I taste in flights of twelve (usually eight flights a night), potential medal-winners can be tables apart. Secondly because, although potential medal-winners stand out from the rest of the field, the test is much tougher if they are in each other's company, and it is thus easier to distinguish between the different medal levels. These notes are entered into the database together with the medal status, the computer performs the super-selection process – whereby the lowest tranche of wines and beers I though worthy of recommendation are ruthlessly discarded – and then feeds the data into my word processor. It is only at this point that I see the identity of the products. I often add comments pertaining to that particular wine, beer or appellation, but I do not materially alter my description, as can be discerned from those notes where I freely admit to guessing wrong. When late submissions of new lines and forthcoming vintages arrive, they usually go straight into the potential medal-winner tasting. If this has already finished, my tasting co-ordinator consults the database to identify a bronze medal product of the same style and price category. This is then purchased to serve as a yardstick against which to taste the late arrival.

I taste alone and in the seclusion of a professionally equipped tasting room where I cannot be disturbed. The wines and beers are in this book because that's where I want them to be, not because I have arrived at some compromise with a partner, and not because I tasted the wine in a room full of other journalists whose vociferous support or rejection of a wine has swayed me (if anyone tries to tell you that two or more people can taste together and not have their opinion influenced from time to time, do not believe them). The comments, medals and awards are therefore all my own. They have been arrived at through quiet deliberation and if I think that tasting them again with food might affect how they perform, I take them back for supper. It's a hard life . . .

Acknowledgements

My thanks to my agent Michael Sissons, who is one of the best in the business and deserves his ten per cent. To my editor Belinda Matthews for using more carrot than stick. To Joanna Mackle, Publishing Director at Faber and Faber, for supporting *SuperBooze* to the hilt. To Ian Bahrami, the only person I have worked with who has smoothly interfaced between my computer system, the publisher's and the printer's without the slightest hitch (and I've been working on books typeset directly from disk since 1984). To Alan Dingle and Justine Willett for the patience and understanding all copy-editors should have. Others at Faber I must also thank include Will Atkinson, Ron Costley, Tim Davies, Susan Law, Clare Lawler, Angela Smith and, although departed to other pastures, Jonathan Tilston.

My gratitude for making the tastings possible and for an unending supply of information must go to Nick Dymoke-Marr, Kevin Williams and Aiden Roach (Asda), Chris Dee (Booths), Dacotah Renneau and Tracy Fraser-Stansby (British American), Tony Finnerty and Rod Alexander (Budgens), Angela Muir MW and Deborah de Groot (Cellarwood International), Arabella Woodrow, Gwyneth Smedley, Paul Bastard and Elaine (Co-op), Christine Sandys (Co-operative Pioneer), Annie Todd (DSA), Richard Graves and Justin Addison (Kwik Save), R. A. Willett, Ian Duffy, Liz Curphey and Sharon Kirkpatrick (Littlewoods), Gary Maloney (Londis), Chris Murphy and Angela Johnson (Marks & Spencer), Stuart Purdie (Morrisons), Rosamund Hitchcock (R&R Teamwork), Elizabeth Robertson MW and Victoria Molyneux (Safeway), Allan Cheesman and Dorcas Jamieson (Sainsbury's), Angela Mount and Naomi Clark,

Lucy Clayton and Carmel Giblin (Somerfield), Liz Aked and Ray Donelan (Spar), Stephen Clarke and Nicki Walden (Tesco), Julian Brind MW and Joe Wadsack (Waitrose) – with apologies for anyone inadvertently missed out. To Martin and Mark at Zedcor for taking in deliveries during our absence, to all the Zedcor fork-lift drivers for keeping an eye on things. To Cherry Pattison for indispensable logistical support, and lastly to Pat, my wife, who ran the primary database and co-ordinated all the tastings.

Carry On Christmas with the SuperBooze *Roadshow Wines*

I have selected the following nine wines to promote *SuperBooze* at tastings in bookstores throughout the country. They are all under-a-fiver gold medal winners and represent some of the greatest bargains in the book; five are, in fact, under £4 and one is just £2.55!

Even if you already have the 1997 edition, you are welcome to attend any tasting sessions in your locality. They are very informal; a chance to ask questions and taste the wines from my special selections, which are presented here, in the order in which they will be tasted, along with what to drink them with over the festive period.

WINE NO. 1 – SPARKLING

Waitrose Cava Brut NV Castellblanch
Waitrose, £4.95
If you can face breakfast on Christmas Day, then this is the fizz to wash it down with; otherwise just keep it on ice for when family and friends arrive. And don't forget to keep Mum's glass topped up in the kitchen!

WINE NO. 2 – RED

Ramada NV Vinho de Mesa Tinto
Co-op, £2.89
Although this can easily be drunk on its own, its not-quite-dry finish makes it very useful for those who like cranberry sauce with their turkey. Even the sharpest cranberries contain a surprising amount of sugar, which can make many red wines taste austere, even metallic, but the Ramada will

taste wonderfully fruity. Its exotic spices also make this a perfect accompaniment to various vegetarian dishes. Whether roast or roots, if you have any wine buffs coming to dinner, I suggest you pour it into an empty *cru classé* bottle, sit back and enjoy!

WINE NO. 3 – RED

Domaine des Bruyère 1994 Côtes de Malepère
Kwik Save, £3.49
The Best Value Red Wine of the Year, so this should be good and is, in fact, sublime with turkey and home-made chestnut stuffing. Or just keep it for the roast chestnuts later in the day.

WINE NO. 4 – RED

Pepperwood Grove Cabernet Franc 1994 California
Budgens, £3.99
If you do not like sweet wines and don't want to spoil your palate with a dessert, this is the wine to retire with after lunch. While someone else herds the horde of screaming kids as far away as possible, put Mahler's 5th on the CD, sit in your favourite chair, put your feet up and relax with a glass of this: sheer bliss!

WINE NO. 5 – DRY WHITE

Posta Romana Classic Gewurztraminer 1993 Transylvania
Co-operative Pioneer, £2.79
You have to enjoy pungently spicy Gewurztraminer to appreciate this and if you do, it will take the richest-flavoured dishes normally associated with red wines. Alternatively, if

you don't want to go to bed, it should perk up the turkey and stuffing sandwiches late at night.

WINE NO. 6 – DRY WHITE

Santa Carolina 1995 White Wine
Booths, £2.99
Tesco, £3.29
This easy-drinking Chilean wine with its ripe, peachy fruit makes a superior party wine, is a very handy aperitif and can cope with those who want 'white wine only' at the table.

WINE NO. 7 – DRY WHITE

Kaituna Hills Sauvignon Blanc 1995 Marlborough, St Michael
Marks & Spencer, £4.99
While the Santa Carolina is very flexible and *can* be used as an aperitif, this is the *ideal* aperitif. Keep pouring if you are starting off with fresh, imported green asparagus. Otherwise keep it for spring and summer.

WINE NO. 8 – ROSÉ

Breakaway Grenache 1996 Stratmer Vineyards
Safeway, £4.99
This claims to be a 'light red wine' on the back label, but it's much nearer to rosé than red and I believe in calling a spade a spade, although I recognize that term on the front label would put some people off. If, on the other hand, all rosé was as good as this, it would not have such a poor reputation. A party wine, aperitif, with food or for relaxing with afterwards, this fresh, flavoursome rosé is up to it all and then some.

Wine No. 9 – Sweet Slightly Sparkling White

Moscato d'Asti 1995 Le Monferrine

Safeway, £3.29

Superb with fresh fruit, but Christmas pudding would destroy the fragrance of this wine, although it would go well with plum pudding soufflé and oodles of cream. This is another wine that you should sit back and relax with, only unlike the Pepperwood Grove, it won't matter if you have had a dessert.

The 1997 SuperBooze Awards

The supermarket awards are based entirely on the rankings found in the table following the awards. When Chris Dee of Booths saw the rankings, he phoned me up and asked in a bemused way, 'Well, does that mean we've won?' I knew what he meant – and if you look up the ranking table, so will you!

National Supermarket of the Year

Safeway

Regional Supermarket of the Year

Booths

I retasted fresh examples of all the gold medal wines and beers to decide on the following top awards.

Red Wines of the Year

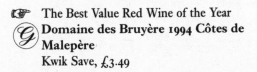

☞ The Best Value Red Wine of the Year
Ⓖ **Domaine des Bruyère 1994 Côtes de Malepère**
Kwik Save, £3.49

☞ The Best Quality Red Wine of the Year
Ⓖ **James Halliday Coonawarra Cabernet Sauvignon 1992 St Michael**
Marks & Spencer, £11.99

White Wines of the Year

☞ The Best Value White Wine of the Year
Ⓖ **Posta Romana Classic Gewurztraminer 1993 Tarnave Region, Transylvania, Blaj Winery**
Co-operative Pioneer, £2.79

☞ The Best Quality White Wine of the Year
Ⓖ **Lindemans Padthaway Chardonnay 1994 South Australia**
Sainsbury's, £7.95

Rosé Wines of the Year

☞ The Best Value Rosé Wine of the Year
Ⓖ **Breakaway Grenache 1996 Stratmer Vineyards**
Safeway, £4.99

☞ The Best Quality Rosé Wine of the Year
Ⓖ **Breakaway Grenache 1996 Stratmer Vineyards**
Safeway, £4.99

Sparkling Wines of the Year

☞ The Best Value Sparkling Wine of the Year
Clairette de Die Tradition 1993 Comtesse de Die, Première Cuvée
Waitrose, £6.45

☞ The Best Quality Sparkling Wine of the Year
Champagne Cuvée Orpale Blanc de Blancs Brut 1985 Union Champagne
Marks & Spencer, £22.50

Fortified Wines of the Year

☞ The Best Value Fortified Wine
Muscat Petits Grains 1993 Vin de Pays des Collines de la Moure
Booths £2.99 (half-bottle)

☞ The Best Quality Fortified Wine of the Year
Lustau Old East India Sherry NV Emilio Lustau
Booths, £9.89

Beers of the Year

☞ The Best Value Bitter of the Year
Black Sheep Ale Paul Theakston
Booths, Morrisons, Safeway, Tesco
Per pint: £1.31–£1.58

☞ The Best Quality Bitter of the Year
Spitfire Bottle Conditioned Bitter
Shepherd Neame
Booths, Budgens, Londis, Morrisons, Safeway, Tesco
Per pint: £1.53–£1.81

☞ The Best Value Light Beer of the Year
Pilsner Urquell
Asda
Per pint: £1.27

☞ The Best Quality Light Beer of the Year
Grolsch Premium Lager
Safeway, Sainsbury's, Somerfield
Per pint: £2.13

☞ The Best Value Dark Beer of the Year
Draught Guinness
Budgens, Co-operative Pioneer, Littlewoods, Somerfield
Per pint: £1.29–£1.52

☞ The Best Quality Dark Beer of the Year
Draught Guinness
Budgens, Co-operative Pioneer, Littlewoods, Somerfield
Per pint: £1.29–£1.52

The Supermarket Rankings

There was no award last year because it was such an uneven playing field. It always is for the first edition of any annual guide – as I know only too well, having launched three such publications over the last fifteen years. Any reader of last year's guide would have realized that had there been an award, Waitrose would have run away with it. That supermarket has again excelled, even if it has not grabbed the number one position.

Which supermarket did come out on top? A good question. When my computer churned out the following results, I was as confused as some of this year's readers might be. Obviously it was a choice between Booths and Safeway, but both had a commanding lead depending on which way you work it out: the number of golds or the weighting.

In the end I decided to award Safeway the *SuperBooze* National Supermarket of the Year Award and Booths the *SuperBooze* Regional Supermarket of the Year. What on earth I will do next year if the same situation occurs between two national groups I have no idea!

Retailer	Gold	Silver	Bronze	Total	Weighting
1. Booths	13	18	16	63	180 (3rd)
2. Safeway	7	17	49	93	211 (1st)
3. Sainsbury	7	15	18	56	139 (8th)
4. Waitrose	6	26	27	78	187 (2nd)
5. Tesco	6	16	35	68	165 (5th)
6. M&S	6	14	30	73	161 (6th)
7. Morrison	6	6	22	48	112 (10th)
8. Somerfield	5	14	37	80	170 (4th)
9. Budgen	5	6	18	36	91 (12th)
10. Co-op	5	5	18	42	95 (11th)
11. Asda	4	13	22	61	129 (9th)
12. Co-op Pioneer	4	12	35	69	148 (7th)
13. Kwik Save	1	8	11	35	67 (14th)
14. Londis	1	7	18	37	74 (13th)
15. Littlewoods	1	2	17	29	55 (15th)
16. Spar	0	1	6	15	23 (16th)

Weighting involves a graduated points system which favours gold medals, but takes more account of the total number of wines and beers recommended:

One point for each wine or beer recommended
Extra 1 point for each bronze
Extra 2 points for each silver
Extra 5 points for each gold

Weighting has more statistical validity than a straightforward gold-first ranking (what if Booths, for example, had had eight gold medals and nothing else – where would you place it in the ranking?), but it is not so easy to explain and everyone is happier with the gold-first principle. Positions by weighting are in brackets.

SUPERMARKET DIRECTORY

The following supermarket entries encompass more than 10,000 superstore, supermarket and convenience store outlets in England, Scotland, Wales and Northern Ireland.

Under each category (Red Wine, White Wine, Rosé Wine, Sparkling Wine, Fortified Wine, Beer) products are listed in ascending order of price. Thus the first medal-winner you find will be the best value, while the last will probably be the best quality, although it can never be as precise as that. Still, that's the theory, and it's easy to remember.

Unless otherwise stated, the price of each wine is for a full 75 cl bottle. If it is a half-bottle, litre, magnum or whatever, this will be indicated.

Beer prices are given at the end of each entry, just before the country of origin, as can and bottle sizes vary so much and many beers are priced for a multipack. For easy comparison, you will find the equivalent price per pint immediately following the name of the beer.

For every supermarket I have selected the Best Value red wines, white wines and beers, which are indicated by a pointing finger (☞), and this is also used to highlight the Wines of the Year and Beers of the Year.

Prices

Prices were correct at the time of tasting. You should expect some changes due to exchange-rate fluctuations, prices rising at source, possible increases in VAT and other variables, but these should be within reason, and the historical price in this book will help you to spot any excessive increases.

Please note that prices were not updated prior to publication because all the wines and beers were tasted within their own price category and to change that would be to make a mockery of the blind tasting, the notes made and the medals awarded.

Different Vintages

Wines recommended in this book are specific to the vintages indicated. Follow-on vintages might be of a similar quality and character, but are likely to be either better or worse. Wines of real interest are seldom exactly the same from one year to the next. Cheap fruity wines, whether white or red, are often better the younger they are, and the difference between vintages is generally less important for bulk wines produced in hotter countries, but even these will vary in some vintages. The difference in vintage is usually most noticeable in individually crafted wines produced the world over. Don't be put off a wine because it is a different vintage, as you could be missing an even greater treat, but do try a bottle before laying out on a case or two.

Is a £3 Gold medal as good as a £6 Gold medal?

It *is* possible, and no doubt there are some in this edition – but remember that a medal is awarded for style and price category, thus the higher the price the harder it is to earn one and the probability of a significantly cheaper product being just as good is a slim one.

ASDA

Number of stores *207*
Opening hours *Monday–Saturday 9a.m.–8p.m.,*
Sunday 10a.m.–4p.m.
Maximum range *346 wines, 205 beers, 146 spirits*
Alternative methods of payment *Cheque with card, Switch and Delta debit cards, Access, Visa*
Local delivery *Not provided, but will help carry goods to car if requested*
Discounts *Yes, on mixed cases, but percentage not specified, so try haggling*
Other services *Free loan of glasses, sale or return, tutored wine and spirit evenings (check with your local store for details)*

Comment Asda, which amongst supermarkets vies with Safeway for the third-largest share of the market, stands for Associated Dairies. This company pioneered the superstore retailing concept in the UK as early as 1965; all its branches are now superstores. Although initially a northern-based group, with a strong presence in Scotland, Asda started moving south in the early 1980s, and it is probably no coincidence that this was when the group first began to take wine seriously.

In more recent years, Asda's flamboyant young wine buyer (sorry, wine category manager, as I was corrected last year!) Nick Dymoke-Marr has built up something of a reputation for cutting out the dross. He also tends to focus on what he believes to be the best-value wine for each particular style rather than offering a huge choice, which he personally finds more bewildering than helpful.

Asda has many brilliant bargains, but with better-thought-out submissions and more notice taken of the guidelines provided, I'm sure it could do even better in future editions.

Red Wines

Alto Plano Chilean Red Wine NV

£10.99 (3-litre bag-in-box)

(S) The gently rich, ultra-smooth, chocolaty fruit in this medium-bodied red puts it into a totally different class from the white Alto Plano bag-in-box wine. [*Chile*]

☞ ASDA'S BEST VALUE RED WINE

Don Darias Tinto NV Vino de Mesa, Bodegas Vitorianas £2.75

(B) As reliable as ever for its totally unpretentious, but immensely drinkable, chunky-coconutty fruit. [*Spain*]

Romanian Pinot Noir 1993 River Route Selection

£2.89

(B) Real Pinot Noir flavour with sweet-ripe fruit on the finish. [*Romania*]

Leon 1992 Castilla-Leon, Asda £2.99

(B) I would have thought this more 'elegant firm' than the 'elegant smooth' suggested on the label, although there is no disputing the elegance at this price. [*Spain*]

Saint-Laurent 1995 Vin de Pays de l'Hérault £2.99

Firm and dry, but richly flavoured for a medium-bodied red, and a nice tannic edge that would suit a good roast, particularly lamb. [*Languedoc-Roussillon, France*]

Remonte 1995 Navarra £2.99

(B) A good mouthful of unpretentious fruit. [*Spain*]

Côtes du Rhône 1995 Le Cellier des Trois Couronnes, Asda £2.99

Plenty of flavour for a basic Rhône at this price, with supple tannins supporting the fruit. [*France*]

Stowells of Chelsea Tempranillo NV
£12.49 (3-litre bag-in-box)

So soft and easy to drink it's hard to imagine that even three litres will last very long. The equivalent of £3.12 a bottle, but there is a great jump in quality between this wine and decent Tempranillo or Rioja at £3.99. [*Spain*]

Claret NV Paul Barbe, Asda £3.29

A surprisingly substantial aftertaste for such a soft and easy-drinking claret. [*Bordeaux, France*]

Terra Alta Old Vines Garnacha 1995 Pedro Rovira S.A.
£3.79

Australian winemakers Nick Butler and Mark Nairn make a very soft and genteel, much less jammy version of this grape than the Land of Oz normally turns out. [*Spain*]

Peter Lehmann Vine Vale Shiraz 1994 Barossa £3.99

Dry-coconutty oak aroma followed by very rich, creamy coconutty fruit. Well-balanced, well-proportioned wine – good with food. [*Australia*]

Mount Hurtle Grenache Shiraz 1994 Geoff Merrill
£4.49

Touch of strawberry jam cut by fine acidity to give a lovely long, crisp finish. [*Australia*]

Domaine de Grangeneuve Cuvée Tradition 1994 Coteaux-du-Tricastin £4.49

A good food wine that builds and builds in the mouth. [*France*]

Saint Emilion NV Paul Barbe, Asda £4.99

This wine has a really lovely, elegant aftertaste and just enough firm, dry tannin to tackle food. [*Bordeaux, France*]

James Herrick Cuvée Simone 1995 Vin de Pays d'Oc £4.99

Where can you buy such a lovely rich mouthful of lip-smacking fruit and tannins for the same price bearing an AOC? [*Languedoc-Roussillon, France*]

Campillo Rioja 1991 £4.99

Smooth and oaky with rich fruit on the finish and a nice dry, oaky edge to go with food. [*Spain*]

Baron de Ley Reserva 1991 Rioja £6.79

A smooth, classy wine of exceptional finesse with an elegantly rich flavour that builds and builds in the mouth, Baron de Ley comes from a single estate and a relatively new bodega that exclusively uses French, not American, oak. [*Spain*]

Châteauneuf-du-Pape 1993 Château des Fines Roches £8.99

The classic structure of true Châteauneuf-du-Pape supporting the most seductive array of fresh fruit flavours, mellow spicy complexity and rich, creamy finish. [*Rhône Valley, France*]

White Wines

Windmill Hill Bulgarian Dry White Wine NV The Lyaskovets Region £2.49

Citrussy-grapefruit thirst-quencher. [*Bulgaria*]

Hungarian Chardonnay Private Reserve 1995 Neszmély Winery £2.49

Real richness at this price level, lifted by a good spritz to make an ideal aperitif wine that also has enough substance to be quite flexible with food. [*Hungary*]

ASDA'S BEST VALUE WHITE WINE

Coltiva il Bianco NV Vino da Tavola Bianco £2.69

Soft, supple, easy-drinking Italian white wine made by a Chilean. [*Italy*]

Bela Fonte NV Vinho de Mesa Branco £2.69

Fresh and tangy with lemony fruit. [*Portugal*]

Cape White NV Simonsvlei Winery, Asda £10.99 (3-litre bag-in-box)

For its price (the equivalent of less than £2.75 a bottle) and style, this very fresh, clean, fruity medium-dry wine has to be a medal-winner. [*South Africa*]

Hungarian Muscat 1994 Aszár-Neszmély Region, Asda £2.79

A nicely balanced medium-dry Muscat that is more spicy than flowery. Try it with asparagus. [*Hungary*]

Bordeaux Blanc NV Paul Barbe £2.99

A lovely rich, fresh, tasty wine that is not so much medium-dry (as the bottle claims) as off-dry, which might be splitting hairs, but unless I mention it there could be many people who would not buy this because they do not like medium-anything. In fact, it just tastes as if it's made from riper fruit than usual, and there is a slight spritz to give even this a welcome lift on the finish. [*France*]

Dry Vinho Verde NV Aveleda £2.99

One of only two Vinhos Verdes that just scraped in, this won some admiration for its genuinely dry, barely perceptible spritzy style, which is a blessed relief from the sugared-up, fizzed-up concoctions this country has been fed for twenty years. The difference between the two recommended is that this wine has an exotic lavender fruit, while the other (*see* Tesco) is in a fresher, albeit somewhat soapy, style (the soapiness wears off). [*Portugal*]

Semillon Chardonnay 1995 South Eastern Australia, Yaldara, Asda £3.45

Fresh, lime-cream richness. [*Australia*]

South Australia Chardonnay 1995 Asda £3.99

Very rich fruit at this price point. [*Australia*]

Montagne Noire Chardonnay 1995 Vin de Pays d'Oc £3.99

In a sea of oaky £3.99 Chardonnay, the class and finesse of this wine floated well above the rest. [*Languedoc-Roussillon, France*]

Cono Sur Chardonnay 1995 Rapel Region £3.99

Pears and vanilla, but with a slow-building richness and a good food-wine structure. Should be *à point* at Christmas. [*Chile*]

Carden Vale 1995 Three Choirs £3·99

Fresh and spritzy, with more of a dry than an off-dry (as per label) finish. [*Gloucestershire, England*]

Orlando Jacob's Creek Semillon Chardonnay 1995 South Eastern Australia £4·39

This ubiquitous wine is a consistently good recommendation for its soft lime and melon fruit, but the 1995 vintage is so much fresher, with delicious sherbetty fruit, that it well deserves its gong and was, frankly, a borderline silver. [*Australia*]

Hungarian Chardonnay 1995 Mór Region, Asda £4·99

Oodles of fresh, crisp Chardonnay flavour, as clean as a whistle and emphasized by a nice spritz. [*Hungary*]

Hardys Nottage Hill Chardonnay 1995 South Eastern Australia £4·99

Fresh, breezy, rich-lemon fruit with a tangy finish. [*Australia*]

Penfolds Koonunga Hill Chardonnay 1995 South Australia £4·99

Very fresh, lemony-lime aroma with zippy-zingy lemony fruit and a rich-but-crisp, tangy finish. Koonunga Hill Chardonnay is very consistent, but this is drinking exceptionally well. [*Australia*]

Peter Lehmann Semillon 1994 Barossa £4·99

The lime-infused fruit and aroma of this wine is classic Australian Semillon. Firm, structured food wine. [*Australia*]

Ruppertsberger Nussbien Riesling Auslese 1991
£3·99 (half-litre bottle)

A decent Auslese for the equivalent of less than £5·99 a bottle must be worth a silver medal. With an intense liquorice aroma and rich, honeyed-liquorice fruit, this is more of an overripe style than a botrytised wine, but gorgeous all the same, with lovely ripe acidity. [*Pfälz, Germany*]

Rosemount Estate Chardonnay 1995 Hunter Valley
£6.49

Very fresh and sherbetty in an elegant, understated, easy-to-drink Chardonnay style. A bit like an Australian Mâcon! [*Australia*]

Saint-Véran 1994 Domaine des Deux Roches £6.49

Quite an intense flavour for Saint-Véran, but with just the right Mâcon-like, lightish structure. [*Burgundy, France*]

Saint Clair Sauvignon Blanc 1995 Marlborough £6.49

The clean, rich, lemony fruit in this wine makes it very different from other New Zealand Sauvignon. [*New Zealand*]

Chablis 1994 Guy Mothe, Asda £6.89

The authentic crisp Chablis style definitely makes this a food wine. [*Burgundy, France*]

Sancerre La Vigne des Rocs 1995 Duc Etienne de Loury
£7·69

Ultra-fresh and deliciously ripe. [*Loire, France*]

Sparkling Wines

Scharffenberger Brut NV Mendocino £8.99

This particular cuvée appears to have had quite a bit of landed-age, which is something I am particularly partial to in slowly evolving Champagnes, but I always prefer Scharffenberger to be as fresh and as elegant as possible, so I will be buying mine closer to Christmas when the latest shipment should be in. [*California, USA*]

Fortified Wines

Stanton & Killeen Liqueur Muscat NV Rutherglen, Victoria £5.49 (half-bottle)

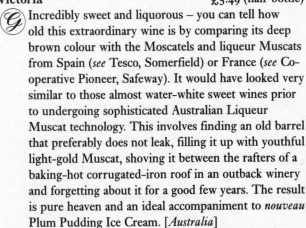

Incredibly sweet and liquorous – you can tell how old this extraordinary wine is by comparing its deep brown colour with the Moscatels and liqueur Muscats from Spain (*see* Tesco, Somerfield) or France (*see* Co-operative Pioneer, Safeway). It would have looked very similar to those almost water-white sweet wines prior to undergoing sophisticated Australian Liqueur Muscat technology. This involves finding an old barrel that preferably does not leak, filling it up with youthful light-gold Muscat, shoving it between the rafters of a baking-hot corrugated-iron roof in an outback winery and forgetting about it for a good few years. The result is pure heaven and an ideal accompaniment to *nouveau* Plum Pudding Ice Cream. [*Australia*]

Beers

Farm Stores Best Bitter Asda Per pint: £0.32

This is the only product featured in *SuperBooze* which is NOT recommended, but it should be mandatory for all football hooligans to drink Farm Stores Best Bitter. You could drink it all day and still not get pissed. If Farm Stores sponsored the UK for the World Cup in 2006 it would give British football fans a good reputation. £0.98 per 4 x 440ml cans. [*2.2%, UK*]

Strasbourg Lager Bière d'Alsace Per pint: £0.68

No more than a light-bodied, light-flavoured telly beer but clean and crisp, whereas most lager-style brews up to this price and well beyond are not. £2.99 per 10 x 25cl bottles. [*2.7%, France*]

Portland Draught Ale Traditional Style Asda Per pint: £0.85

The second-cheapest widgetized bitter, although this is probably because it is not technically widgetized but nitrogen-flushed (*q.v.*). This is, of course, no great brew, but it is eminently more drinkable than other, costlier brews – which alone merits a medal – and although not hugely flavoursome, it has a clean taste with a slight bitterness which makes it stand out from the sea of widgetized dross surrounding it. £2.99 per 4 x 500ml widgetized cans. [*4.5%, UK*]

Asda German Pilsener Premium Strength Export Lager Per pint: £0.85

Fresh, peppery-hop aroma; crisp, dry and really quite tasty (as far as lager goes) at this price. £2.99 per

4 x 500ml cans. [*5.0%, Germany*]

Asda Chesters Draught Ale Samlesbury Brewery
Per pint: £0.96

From a very short distance, the typeface used for the name 'Chesters' looks uncannily like that used in *Cheers* of TV fame. Not a coincidence, I suspect, but at least there is a tiny bitter-bite to this creamy widget beer that gives it an edge over most of the rest of the competition. £2.99 per 4 x 440ml widgetized cans. [*3.8%, UK*]

Asda French Bière de Luxe Premium Strength Export Lager, Meteor Brewery Per pint: £1.04

B Good flavour (for a lager) at this price, refreshingly crisp and sharp, with more of a *pétillance* than a fizz. £4.59 per 10 x 25cl bottles. [*5.0%, France*]

Gillespie's Draught Malt Stout Per pint: £1.08

S This may be the cheapest of the widgetized stouts, but it is also one of the most distinctive. Gillespie's is more malty-mellow than its Irish counterparts, and under blind tasting conditions has a smoky 'Camp Coffee' creaminess that I must admit I had not noticed when simply drinking it (and I often have a few tins in the fridge). £3.35 per 4 x 440ml widgetized cans. [*4.0%, Edinburgh, UK*]

Theakston Draught Best Bitter Per pint: £1.09

When this brew was first widgetized, it lacked the yeasty freshness of the original draught brew, but now if anything it is too pungently ripe-yeast on the nose (when it should be fresh-yeasty), but it does have more flavour than any of the cheaper widgetized brews and a number of the more expensive ones. Ironically, the non-widgetized version failed to survive the tastings. £3.39 per 4 x 440ml widgetized cans. [*3.8%, Yorkshire, UK*]

Pilsner Urquell Per pint: £1.27

G Smooth, flowery and fragrant, with the classic Urquell taste, crisp-fragrant finish and a nice slightly bitter touch. £2.95 per 4 x 330ml bottles. [*4.4%, Pilsen, Czech Republic*]

☞ THE BEST VALUE LIGHT BEER OF THE YEAR

Asda Italian Birra Premium Strength Export Lager Per pint: £1.29

Sharp and crisp, but definitely in a citric style that separates this from most other lager-style beers. £2.99 per 4 x 330ml bottles. [*5.0%, Italy*]

Asda German Pilsener Premium Strength Export Lager Per pint: £1.29

S Is this assertively hopped brew a bitter-drinker's Pilsner, or simply the best own-label Pilsner on the market? £2.99 per 4 x 330ml bottles. [*5.0%, Germany*]

Carling Premier Draught Lager Per pint: £1.29

Not a medal-winner, but none of the other Carlings was within a mile of surviving the tastings. Thankfully the widget has smothered the flavour. Smoother than other Carlings, although it's hardly a lager to die for. £3.99 per 4 x 440ml widgetized cans. [*4.7%, UK*]

Bishops Finger Kentish Strong Ale Shepherd Neame Per pint: £1.48

B An inferior version of the Bishops Finger bottled ale, yet superior for a canned beer, if you catch my drift. £4.59 per 4 x 440ml cans. [*5.4%, Kent, UK*]

Carlsberg Ice Beer Per pint: £1.54

The sharpest, crispest and best of the so-called Ice Beers. £3.59 per 4 x 330ml cans. [*5.6%, Denmark*]

Bitburger Premium Pils Klassisch Herb

Per pint: £1.72

Very perfumed hop aroma followed by a light, stylish, well-hopped taste with a crisp finish. Elegantly pristine Pilsner style. £3.99 per 4 x 330ml bottles. [*4.6%, Germany*]

Budweiser Anheuser-Busch Per pint: £1.72

The bottle is better than the can, being less sweet-watery, but there are many more light-styled Pilsner-type beers that are much cheaper and much better. £3.99 per 4 x 330ml bottles. [*5.0%, EU*]

Boddingtons Export Per pint: £1.91

A distinctive, well-hopped bitter that is enhanced, rather than masked, by the minimal effect of a bottled widget. £4.45 per 4 x 330ml widgetized bottles. [*4.8%, Manchester, UK*]

BOOTHS

STOCK ME AND BUY ONE

Regional Supermarket of the Year
Number of stores *23*
Opening hours *Vary from store to store, but the majority open Monday–Tuesday and Saturday 8.30a.m.–6p.m., Wednesday and Thursday 8.30a.m.–7p.m., Friday 8.30a.m.–8p.m. and (16 stores only) Sunday 10a.m.–4p.m.*
Maximum range *600 wines, 200 beers, 300 spirits*
Alternative methods of payment *Cheque with card, Switch and Delta debit cards, Access, Visa*
Delivery *Not provided*
Discounts *10% off a mixed case*
Other services *Sale or return on party purchases, free loan of glasses, free tasting every weekend (10 stores)*

Comment Well, well, what a surprise! I heard on my travels that this northern group was one to watch, but who would have thought any supermarket could notch up 13 gold medals? It's one of the most fascinating aspects of doing so many blind tastings. You know there are some gold medal wines and remember how exciting they were, but you have no idea which supermarket they are sold by until you throw all the data into the word processor and everything starts to come together.

Booths is certainly a very together supermarket as far as wines and beers are concerned, and the person responsible is Chris Dee, who was able to recite all the Port vintages at the age of 15. He read about wines for an entire year before tasting one, and was head-hunted by Booths after setting up his own wine retailing business in Yorkshire and establishing something of a reputation for cutting deals.

Red Wines

Alta Mesa Tinto 1994 Estremadura £2.79

Not as outstanding as it was a year ago, but it still stands out as an elegantly fruity wine at this price. Look out for the 1995. [*Portugal*]

BOOTHS' BEST VALUE RED WINE

Kumala Cinsault Pinotage 1995 Western Cape £3.39

It's a funny old world, but you cross Pinot Noir with Cinsault to get Pinotage, which honestly bears little resemblance to either variety. It is somewhat lacking unless you fiddle with the vinification process or, as in this case, blend it with one of its parents – Cinsault – which lends Pinotage the much-needed structure on which to hang its fruit. A very clever, inexpensive blend. [*South Africa*]

Côtes du Brulhois 1990 Cave de Donzac £3.99

Soft, easy-drinking red with white chocolate fruit and a pleasant dry tannin finish. [*South-west France*]

Terrasses de Landoc Carignan 1995 Vin de Pays de l'Hérault £3.99

A proper food wine, its character evolves in the glass and comes out as you drink – rather than taste – the wine. Well balanced. [*Languedoc-Roussillon, France*]

David Wynn Red 1993 South Eastern Australia £4.25

This is not as full-bodied as the writers of the back label copy would have you believe. It is merely medium-bodied, but is full in flavour with creamy-rich and supple tannin structure. [*Australia*]

Peter Lehmann Vine Vale Shiraz 1994 Barossa £4·49

(B) Dry-coconutty oak aroma followed by very rich, creamy coconutty fruit. Well-balanced, well-proportioned wine – good with food. [*Australia*]

Guelbenzu Jardin 1995 Navarra £4·99

This big, thick, unruly Garnacha from thirty to forty-year-old vines is more instructive than hedonistic, but there's much to be gained from the experience. [*Spain*]

Castel Pujol Tannat 1992 Las Violetas £4·99

(B) Confused by how a wine can taste 'meaty' and 'gamy' yet still be all fruit? Then taste this rich, meaty, gamy red and discover how winespeak is not always double Dutch, even if it sounds like it is. This wine also has a big spicy finish that is soft and long. [*Uruguay*]

Booths Oak Aged Vintage Claret 1990 £5·49

No-nonsense claret propped up by a good wedge of four-by-two. [*Bordeaux, France*]

Domaine La Réméjeanne Les Arbousiers 1994 Côtes du Rhône £5·49

Very smooth, easy-drinking fruity red from a top Côtes du Rhône property. [*France*]

Domaine de l'Hortus Classique 1994 Coteaux du Languedoc £5·99

(G) Soft, rich and smooth with an elegant tannin balance and fat, ripe, sweet fruit on the finish. [*Languedoc-Roussillon, France*]

Mas Champart 1994 Saint-Chinian £5·99

(S) The elegance and restrained richness of this wine really comes out with food. [*Languedoc-Roussillon, France*]

Château de Canterrane 1980 Côtes du Roussillon £6.25

(B) A sixteen-year-old Roussillon! I would never have guessed when tasting this blind. Perhaps it should get a gold for pure survival, but that would be cheating after having seen the crib sheet. My notes read, 'Put this up against a red Bordeaux of the same price and the claret would be obliterated by this wine's sweet, ripe creamy fruit. Some complexity.' [*Languedoc-Roussillon, France*]

Miranda Rovalley Ridge Cabernets 1992 Barossa Valley £6.99

(S) Luscious oaky fruit with a long, creamy-oaky finish. Complete on its own – food can add very little to this wine. [*Australia*]

Leasingham Domaine Shiraz 1993 Clare Valley £6.99

(S) A big wine with a rich, penetrating, cedary-oaky aroma, followed by a sweet-menthol-cedary concentration of fruit on the palate. [*Australia*]

Coriole Sangiovese 1993 McLaren Vale £8.25

(G) Intense fruit acidity underpinning lush, New World Sangiovese of a quality I have seldom encountered. Serious stuff! [*Australia*]

Penfolds Old Vine Shiraz Grenache Mourvèdre 1993 Barossa Valley £8.99

(S) Without doubt the biggest wine in the tasting, its black colour, thick-rich, inky-dense concentration of fruit and high acidity comes from a typically Châteauneuf-du-Pape troika of grapes, but this could not be mistaken for a Rhône wine and is far more expressive of Australia in general and Penfolds in particular. This will simply be too massive for some, yet it will be exactly what the doctor ordered for those who seek the magnified flavours of such mega-sized wines. [*Australia*]

Marqués de Murrieta Ygay 1989 Rioja £9.99

A potentially great Rioja that needs a further five years in bottle to mellow its great acidity, which is vital to keep the wine's tangy damson fruit fresh and vital in the meantime. [*Spain*]

Frog's Leap Zinfandel 1993 Napa Valley £11.99

Impeccably integrated oak brings a beautiful smoothness to the fruit, opening up into delightful aftertaste. Great finesse for Zinfandel, but you're paying a fair price for the privilege, thus it gets a silver rather than gold. [*California, USA*]

White Wines

Santa Carolina 1995 White Wine £2.99

Rich and ripe with peach-flesh and peach-stone fruit of a depth no one could reasonably expect at this price. [*Chile*]

☞ BOOTHS' BEST VALUE WHITE WINE

Gaillac 1995 Cave de Labastide de Lévis £3.89

A soft, rich, elegantly full style with fresh, crisp fruity finish made by Aussie technology. [*France*]

Sant'Antonio Frascati Superiore 1994 Colli di Catone £3.99

Most unusual to find such a full-flavoured Frascati as this. [*Italy*]

David Wynn Dry White 1994 South Eastern Australia £4.25

Lemony-rich fruit. [*Australia*]

Château Pierrail 1995 Bordeaux £4.99

With delicately rich, crisp, elegant, racy fruit, this wine includes 30 per cent Sauvignon Gris, which was very highly regarded in the last century but is seldom seen today (although Cousino Macul in Chile has a small plot dating back to pre-phylloxera times). [*France*]

Saint-Véran Les Terres Noires 1994 Domaine des Deux Roches £6.95

Gold medal Burgundy at supermarket prices is very difficult to find (there were none last year), but this Saint-Véran has a purity and succulence of fruit that is rare in Burgundy at any price. The only qualification I make to its well-deserved gold medal status is that I would not advise keeping it beyond spring 1997, as it is made for drinking, not cellaring – but in a supermarket wine such a qualification can hardly be a negative point. [*Burgundy, France*]

Mader Riesling Muhlforst 1994 Alsace £6.99

By far the richest true Riesling of the tasting – a big full flavour, yet crisp and racy. [*France*]

Ca' del Solo Malvasia Bianca NV Monterey White Table Wine £7.99

Lemony-limey fruit that is round and gentle yet zippy at the same time, with an invigoratingly fresh finish. Made by the part-crazy, part-genius Randall Graham, although there is no mention of his legendary Bonny Doon Winery on the bottle, which is mad considering the cult following it attracts. [*California, USA*]

Mader Gewurztraminer Cuvée Théophile 1994 Alsace £9·49

When logging the wines on to the computer, it did strike me as odd that Mader's Gewurztraminer happened to be 50 per cent more expensive than its Riesling. The Riesling did very well indeed, notching up a well-earned silver, but as soon as I tasted this wine I understood why there was such a price difference (it was blind, but there were no other Gewurztraminers at this price, so I have to admit that I knew what I was tasting): this exquisitely rich wine is a *Vendange Tardive* in all but name. [*France*]

Pazo de Barrantes Albariño 1994 Rias Baixas £9·75

I'm not sure that this wine is worth almost £10, but I am certain that it is as good as Rias Baixas gets, and thus deserves its recommendation on pure quality alone. Made from the Albariño grape, which is the finest variety used in the very best *vinhos verdes*, but grown in Spain, albeit in Galicia, the far north-western corner of the country – just north of Portugal's own *vinho verde* region, in fact. This is a truly beautiful example of Albariño, with electrifying acidity and a real depth of fruit. You could say it's more *vinho verde* than *vinho verde,* and certainly better than any *vinho verde* I've tasted – and I've tasted the best. But for the price, this would get a gold medal. [*Spain*]

Sparkling Wines

Champagne Booths Brut NV CM-835 £12.69

Lovely biscuity-rich, creamy fruit. Soft mousse of

very small bubbles. [*France*]

Champagne Jeeper Brut Grande Réserve NV £15.99

B Jeeper used to be a damn good grower of Champagne before changing to the ubiquitous peardrop style, but this is back to its former form and developing a lovely biscuity richness. [*France*]

Fortified Wines

Muscat Petits Grains 1993 Vin de Pays des Collines de la Moure £2.99 (half-bottle)

G This is ridiculously cheap! Under blind conditions this £2.99 half-bottle knocked the spots off Château Suduiraut 1989 at £17.29 for a half-bottle (also from Booths but overpriced), albeit this super-seductive Muscat is made for quick and easy drinking while the Suduiraut needs another ten or twelve years. When the Suduiraut is at its peak, this wine will be long dead and gone. At this moment, however, the exotic, succulently sweet, peachy-rich fruit in this wine gives immeasurably more pleasure. I'm not sure that this is a fortified wine, as it seems more like late-harvest to me, but I wanted to give it a top award and the only possibility was fortified, so I decided to treat it like a Muscat Rivesaltes and moved it into the fortified section. If I cannot bend the rules in my own book for the best of motives, where's the fun in life? [*Languedoc-Roussillon, France*]

☞ The Best Value Fortified Wine of the Year

Lustau Old East India Sherry NV Emilio Lustau £9.89

G A fabulously rich, rare and succulently sweet

style of Sherry that has been put through a similar process to that of Madeira. If you ever wondered what a Bual or Malmsey might taste like if made in Spain's Jerez district, rather than on Portugal's island of Madeira, then buy this extraordinary, voluptuous wine. [*Spain*]

☞ THE BEST QUALITY FORTIFIED WINE OF THE YEAR

Booths Crusted Port 1989 Martinez Gassiot £9.95

(G) The elegant, Bordeaux-like character dominating the spirit that fortified this wine is the first clue to its quality. Its gorgeously rich, plump fruit is the second clue, and the fire and spice on the finish is the confirmation. Extraordinary quality for the money. [*Portugal*]

Quarles Harris Vintage Port 1977 £18.99

(S) Although far superior to the gold medal-winning Booths Crusted Port, this is twice the price. For a wine of almost £20 to pick up a silver is remarkable, but this is from the awe-inspiring 1977 vintage, one of the two greatest vintages of the last fifty years (the other being 1963). Its ultra-smooth, impeccably integrated fruit on nose and palate reveal just how long great Ports take to harmonize. There is also a lovely oakiness that suggests this is more late-bottled than most vintage Ports. [*Portugal*]

Beers

Double Maxim Premium Quality Ale Vaux

Per pint: £1.29

(B) Taste this side by side with the canned version

and it's chalk and cheese. This is so much fresher, crisper and cleaner that it gets a medal (whereas Double Maxim in a can is a straightforward recommendation) despite being 35 per cent more expensive. £1.25 per 550ml bottle. [*4.7%, Sunderland, UK*]

Banks's Bitter Per pint: £1.31

Ⓑ Distinctive flowery-hopped aromas follow through on to the palate. Very smooth. £1.15 per 500ml bottle. [*3.8%, Wolverhampton, UK*]

Black Sheep Ale Paul Theakston Per pint: £1.31

Ⓖ Made by Paul Theakston, whose family brewery is now part of Scottish and Newcastle. He alone was determined to maintain an independent status, hence the name Black Sheep. This is classy, distinctive, soft and yet completely dry, with a delicious nutty-hoppy complexity. Although there was a time when M&S's own-label version was better than the original (smokier, with a more mellow bitterness), they are almost identical this year – but why doesn't Paul Theakston market a bottle-conditioned version? £1.15 per 500ml bottle. [*4.4%, Yorkshire, UK*]

☞ THE BEST VALUE BITTER OF THE YEAR

Masterbrew Premium Bitter Shepherd Neame

Per pint: £1.35

Ⓑ A good bronze for the dry, true-bitter character that stands out at this price point, although this particular brew is not quite as distinctive as Masterbrew normally is. £1.19 per 500ml bottle. [*4.0%, Kent, UK*]

Marston's Pedigree Bitter Per pint: £1.39

Classic coppery colour with a smooth, dry, complex taste highlighted by perfumed hoppy aromas. £1.39 per 568ml bottle. [*4.5%, Burton-on-Trent, UK*]

Jennings Sneck Lifter Per pint: £1.42

If you are intrigued by the name of this beer, you will find an explanation on the back label. A bronze medal beer for those who like the sweet caramel-malty taste. £1.25 per 500ml bottle. [*5.1%, Cumbria, UK*]

Fuller's London Pride Premium Ale Per pint: £1.44

This will hit home for those who prefer genuinely dry, authentically bitter beers. The fresh, intense, hoppy-maltiness of this brew is particularly well-suited to the bottling process. £1.39 per 550ml bottle. [*4.7%, London, UK*]

Waggle Dance Traditional Honey Beer Vaux Per pint: £1.44

Soft, full, luscious ale with perfumed-hop aromas, clean, off-dry malty taste and a crisp finish. Apparently named after the dance honey bees execute when they have located nectar, and if you drink enough Waggle Dance, you'll believe it. £1.39 per 550ml bottle. [*5.0%, Sunderland, UK*]

Bombardier Premium Bitter Charles Wells Per pint: £1.47

Has a good bitter finish, but many will find its strangely liquorous texture somewhat incongruous. £1.29 per 500ml bottle. [*4.3%, Bedford, UK*]

Greenmantle Ale Broughton Ales Per pint: £1.47

As someone who lives in a house with thirty-nine steps

in the staircase, I just wish there was a bit more to this nut-brown-coloured ale, inspired by the Buchan novel, than the extraordinarily smoky aromas that dominate the brew. £1.29 per 500ml bottle. [*3.9%, Peeblesshire, UK*]

Merlin's Ale Broughton Ales Per pint: £1.47

A medal-winning brew for those who like their beers light, fresh and tasting of pears, with a distinctive peppery-hop aroma. £1.29 per 500ml bottle. [*4.2%, Peeblesshire, UK*]

Scottish Oatmeal Stout Broughton Ales
Per pint: £1.47

Distinctive smoky-coffee brew. £1.29 per 500ml bottle. [*4.2%, Peeblesshire, UK*]

Samuel Smith's Old Brewery Strong Pale Ale
Per pint: £1.47

Firm and distinctive, with good malty bitterness. Only own-label pale ales were cheaper than this fine brew! £1.42 per 550ml bottle. [*5.0%, Yorkshire, UK*]

Batemans Victory Ale Per pint: £1.51

For me, this brew is spoiled by its amylic (peardrop) fermentation odours, but Batemans Victory Ale has a strong following for its strong, spicy-malty taste. £1.33 per 500ml bottle. [*6.0%, Lincolnshire, UK*]

Jennings Cocker Hoop Golden Bitter Per pint: £1.53

A sweet-creamy flavour with a fine crisp finish and a hoppy aftertaste. £1.35 per 500ml bottle. [*4.8%, Cumbria, UK*]

Bishops Finger Kentish Strong Ale Shepherd Neame

Per pint: £1.53

(S) Taste this side by side with the canned version and you will realize why the premium charged for bottled beers is well worth paying. Beautifully fresh and crisp, with a powerful true-bitter flavour and long, hoppy aftertaste. £1.35 per 500ml bottle. [*5.4%, Kent, UK*]

India Pale Ale Original Export Shepherd Neame

Per pint: £1.53

(B) A good, assertive pale ale bitterness. £1.35 per 500ml bottle. [*4.5%, Kent, UK*]

Original Porter Strong Dark Ale Shepherd Neame

Per pint: £1.53

Smoky malt and heady hops dominate this dry, assertive porter. £1.35 per 500ml bottle. [*5.2%, Kent, UK*]

Spitfire Bottle Conditioned Bitter Shepherd Neame

Per pint: £1.53

(G) A great bitter with an elegant fruity-yeasty fullness, delicate bitter-hop flavours and a beautifully dry, understated finish. One bottle of Spitfire tasted was unbelievably fizzy and aggressively tasteless as a result. The sediment looked to be twice the norm, so I can only imagine that it was a faulty batch, as can sometimes happen with a live beer. If you have ever had a similar experience, be advised that Spitfire should not be like that – but buy another bottle to satisfy yourself. £1.35 per 500ml bottle. [*4.7%, Kent, UK*]

☞ THE BEST QUALITY BITTER OF THE YEAR

Cain's Formidable Ale Per pint: £1.58

(B) A crisp, malty taste with delicate hoppy finish. £1.39 per 500ml bottle. [*5.0%, Liverpool, UK*]

Robert Cain's Superior Stout Per pint: £1.58

(G) Strong roasted-barley aromas lead on to coffee and liquorice on the palate and by far the best balance between bitter and mellowness in its category. £1.39 per 500ml bottle. [*4.8%, Liverpool, UK*]

Marston's Albion Porter Head Brewers Choice Per pint: £1.65

The sweetest and probably therefore the most authentic of the porters tasted. £1.45 per 500ml bottle. [*4.8%, Burton-on-Trent, UK*]

Marston's India Export Pale Ale Head Brewers Choice Per pint: £1.65

(S) Interesting to match this with Tesco's own-label IPA from the same brewery – the CO_2 content must be very similar, as they feel identical in the mouth, but this brew has more citrussy richness. £1.45 per 500ml bottle. [*5.5%, Burton-on-Trent, UK*]

Marston's Oyster Stout Bottle Conditioned Head Brewers Choice Per pint: £1.65

Very smooth and easy-drinking, but lacks the intensity, bitterness and complexity of a great stout. As it's bottle-conditioned, I'm going to try ageing it until next year to see if that makes any significant difference. Until then, however, this brew deserves recommending but not a medal. £1.45 per 500ml bottle. [*4.5%, Burton-on-Trent, UK*]

Directors Live Ale Courage Per pint: £1.69

This very smooth, aromatically perfumed beer has a nice bitter-hop finish and proves that big breweries can still produce good bottle-conditioned beers if they want to. £1.49 per 500ml bottle. [*4.8%, UK*]

6X Export Wadworth Per pint: £1.69

I cannot believe that anyone can seriously enjoy the almost salty richness of sour, sultana-malt taste in this beer, but 6X is so popular that I include it for those who obviously do. £1.49 per 500ml bottle. [*5.0%, Devizes, UK*]

Rutland Independence Very Strong Ale Ruddles Brewery Per pint: £1.70

If someone asked me whether I would like a beer that smells and tastes of celery, I'd probably say no thank you, yet this is absolutely compelling drinking, with a smooth, peppery-hop and – of course – celery finish. £0.99 per 330ml bottle. [*6.5%, UK*]

Worthington's White Shield Fine Strong Ale Per pint: £1.96

This bottle-conditioned beer still has a delicate, elegant hoppiness and truly deserves a silver medal – but is it my imagination, or does it lack the plump, ripe, yeastiness of old? £0.95 per 275ml bottle. [*5.6%, UK*]

BUDGENS

STOCK ME AND BUY ONE

Number of stores *92*
Opening hours *Vary too widely to generalize*
Maximum range *300 wines, 125 beers, 100 spirits*
Alternative methods of payment *Cheque with card, Switch and Delta debit cards, Access, Visa*
Local delivery *Not provided, but will help carry goods to car if requested*
Discounts *5 per cent on mixed cases of wine*
Other services *No free loan of glasses, no sale-or-return terms, but ice can be purchased from fifty of the larger stores*

Comment A supermarket chain pure and simple, with no outlets that could in any way be described as a superstore, although Budgens' aggressive pricing policy is certainly competitive with those of the big chains and the range of wines and beers submitted by Tony Finnerty, the group's one-man buying team, has beaten some of the more famous supermarkets this year.

Red Wines

Cabernet Sauvignon 1995 François Dulac, Vin de Pays d'Oc £2.99

The sweet-ripe chewy fruit in this wine makes a refreshing change from all the Bulgarian Cabernets, good and not so good, available at this price point. [*Languedoc-Roussillon, France*]

Dornfelder Qualitätsrotwein 1994 Rheinhessen, Gustav Adolf Schmitt £3.79

Not for red wine drinkers, but anyone who is finding it difficult to move from German white wines to any sort of red can drink this, close their eyes and dream of Nierstein! [*Germany*]

Vin de Crete 1995 Kourtaki £3·79

(B) A smooth red that is well made, with clean, nicely focused flavour and beautifully presented with a nicely understated label, Vin de Crete will probably bring home happier memories than most of the wines tasted while on holiday in Crete itself. [*Greece*]

Pepperwood Grove Cabernet Franc 1994 California £3·99

(G) Amazing quality and satisfaction for the price! An elegant wine with deliciously soft, succulent, violet-perfumed berry fruit. [*California, USA*]

☞ BUDGENS' BEST VALUE RED WINE

Pepperwood Grove Zinfandel 1994 California £3·99

(B) A soft, elegant, violety style of Zinfandel made to be drunk young. [*California, USA*]

Château Malijay 'Fontanilles' 1994 Côtes du Rhône £4·35

(B) Although this wine is seemingly light-flavoured, the fruit is actually very elegant and smoothly builds in the mouth as you go through a glass. This wine is at its best if you can linger over it with a meal, although the food should be quite mild-flavoured. These are exactly the qualities I worry that I might miss while my palate is in tasting mode, which is why I lock myself away from distractions and take my time, but I still feel really good when I pick up wines like this. [*France*]

Waimanu Premium Dry Red Wine NV Corbans £4·39

(B) Light garnet colour indicating some maturity,

confirmed by ripe, mature, blackcurranty fruit on nose and palate. [*New Zealand*]

Casablanca Cabernet Sauvignon 1991 Miraflores Estate £4.69

Ⓢ Appealing aroma of sweet peppers and blackcurrants, very rich fruit on the palate, excellent acidity and a long, penetrating finish, all wrapped up in a firm tannin structure, making it an ideal food wine that is capable of improving several years in bottle. [*Chile*]

Gallo Sonoma Cabernet Sauvignon 1992 £7.99

Ⓑ Lush and smooth with supple fruit tannins building slowly on the finish, making this a flexible partner with food and easy to drink on its own. From Gallo's own prestigious vineyard, it proves that the world's largest winery can make fine, individually crafted wines when it has a mind to. [*California, USA*]

White Wines

Waimanu Premium Dry White Wine NV Corbans £3.99

Very ripe, round and easy. Presumably this is predominantly Müller-Thurgau, a grape that Kiwis are far more successful at making generic wines with than the Germans are. [*New Zealand*]

Glen Ellen Chardonnay 1994 Proprietor's Reserve, Sonoma £3.99

Ⓑ This wine is just beginning to go toasty with a smooth oakiness on the finish, and should be really toasty-oaky by Christmas. [*California, USA*]

Casablanca Sauvignon Blanc 1994 Lontue Valley, Curico £4·69

Ⓖ Beautifully rich, yet absolutely crisp fruit of excellent varietal character. Really stands out. [*Chile*]

☞ BUDGENS' BEST VALUE WHITE WINE

Rosemount Estate Semillon Chardonnay 1995 £5·29

Although it is well worth its recommendation and will fill out over the next twelve months, Rosemount's Semillon Chardonnay is not as immediately attractive as the same winery's Semillon Sauvignon. [*South-eastern Australia*]

Gallo Sonoma Chardonnay 1993 £7·99

Ⓢ The elegant, sweet-ripe fruit in this single-vineyard wine does prove that Gallo can compete at the finer end of the market. [*California, USA*]

Rosé Wines

High Ridge Pink 1994 Lamberhurst Vineyards £4·49

Ⓑ It's the spritz that heightens the depth of floral fruit in this wine and pushes it into a different class. [*Kent, England*]

Sparkling Wines

Flinders Creek Brut Cuvée NV Savage £4·99

Softer and easier than any of the Cavas, which is a style that may be preferred by some. [*Australia*]

Flinders Creek Rosé Cuvée NV Savage £4.99

Delightful fizzy concoction full of strawberry, raspberry and cherry fruits. [*Australia*]

Champagne Germain Brut Réserve NV £14.99

A bronze for those who like fresh, easy-drinking, fruity Champagne. [*France*]

Beers

John Smith's Bitter Per pint: £1.13

Nothing to get excited about, but this is refreshing and dry with a clean bitter-hop finish and the cheapest bitter or ale to deserve a medal. £3.49 per 4 x 440ml cans. [*4.0%, Yorkshire, UK*]

DAB Original German Pilsener Lager Dortmunder Actien-Brauerei Per pint: £1.18

Pale, attractive, flowery-hopped aroma, fragrant on the palate, with a long, smooth, gently rich flavour, just a hint of bitterness, and lifted by a correctly crisp finish. £4.15 per 4 x 500ml cans. [*5.0%, Germany*]

John Smith's Extra Smooth Bitter Per pint: £1.29

Unless you're into creamy-sweet, ultra-soft brews, the nicely perfumed hops and a decent bitter taste will make this one of the two best widgetized beers at this price point. £3.99 per 4 x 440ml widgetized cans. [*4.0%, Yorkshire, UK*]

Draught Guinness Per pint: £1.29

The king of stouts is also the inventor of the widget, which most beer writers abhor and most draught stout drinkers adore. Guinness stands out from the rest by the intensity of its smoky-toasty-malty aroma. It is every bit as smoky as Beamish, but has a greater depth of other top-quality ingredients so that smokiness is not perceived as its main characteristic. Lovely roasted-barley tones echo through malty-rich, smoky-toasty aromas on the mid-palate to give a satisfying edge other stouts lack. £3.99 per 4 x 440ml widgetized cans. [*4.1%, Dublin/London, Ireland/UK*]

☞ THE BEST VALUE DARK BEER OF THE YEAR

Masterbrew Premium Bitter Shepherd Neame
Per pint: £1.35

(B) A good bronze for the dry, true-bitter character that stands out at this price point, although this particular brew is not quite as distinctive as Masterbrew normally is. £1.19 per 500ml bottle. [*4.0%, Kent, UK*]

Budweiser Budvar Per pint: £1.47

(S) Genuine Czech Budweiser has been made since the thirteenth century and the only remaining example is instantly recognizable by the Budvar part of its name. It is a classic beer: whereas American Budweiser is just bland-tasting, perfumed water made primarily from rice, Budvar is made from pure, top-quality malt. Compare the two beers for yourself and you'll be pleasantly surprised, not the least because the superior, authentic product also happens to be cheaper. £1.29 per 50cl bottle. [*5.0%, Czech Republic*]

Marston's Pedigree Bitter Per pint: £1.55

(B) Classic coppery colour with a smooth, dry, complex taste highlighted by perfumed hoppy aromas. £1.55 per 568ml bottle. [*4.5%, Burton-on-Trent, UK*]

Fuller's London Pride Premium Ale Per pint: £1.64

This will hit home for those who prefer genuinely dry, authentically bitter beers. The fresh, intense, hoppy-maltiness is particularly well-suited to the bottling process. £1.59 per 550ml bottle. [*4.7%, London, UK*]

Stella Artois Premium Lager Beer Per pint: £1.66

Really quite a decent lunchtime lager considering the brand's naff reputation amongst serious beer drinkers and the fact that it is brewed in the UK by Whitbread, rather than in Belgium by Stella Artois itself. £5.79 per 6 x 330ml bottles. [*5.2%, UK*]

Caffrey's Draught Irish Ale Per pint: £1.67

This light, fresh, creamy-sweet brew is brilliantly marketed. It is not as good as from the tap, even if that is connected to a pressurized keg, but the same could be said for Guinness Draught, and those who like this soft, easy beer will simply be thankful they can keep a reasonable replica ready-chilled in the fridge. Any Caffrey's drinker who has not tasted Wethered's Draught from M&S should do so. It's in a similar style, some will actually prefer it, and it costs 49p per pint less. £5.19 per 4 x 440ml widgetized cans. [*4.8%, County Antrim, UK*]

Bishops Finger Kentish Strong Ale Shepherd Neame Per pint: £1.69

Taste this against the canned version and you will realize why the premium charged for bottled beers is well worth paying. Beautifully fresh and crisp with a powerful true-bitter flavour and long, hoppy aftertaste. £1.49 per 500ml bottle. [*5.4%, Kent, UK*]

Spitfire Bottle Conditioned Bitter Shepherd Neame
Per pint: £1.69

(G) A great bitter with an elegant fruity-yeasty fullness, delicate bitter-hop flavours and a beautifully dry, understated finish. One bottle of Spitfire tasted was unbelievably fizzy and aggressively tasteless as a result. The sediment looked to be twice the norm, so I can only imagine that it was a faulty batch, as can sometimes happen with a live beer. If you have ever had a similar experience, be advised that Spitfire should not be like that – but buy another bottle to satisfy yourself. £1.49 per 500ml bottle. [*4.7%, Kent, UK*]

☞ THE BEST QUALITY BITTER OF THE YEAR

San Miguel Export Premium Lager Per pint: £1.70

(B) Has the same flowery-hoppy Pilsner aroma as the can (which is remarkable in a canned beer), but a slightly more hoppy flavour, with a longer, crisper finish. Better, yet a lower medal because the can is so exceptional and this is almost twice the price. £0.99 per 33cl bottle. [*5.4%, Spain*]

Beck's Per pint: £1.72

This beer is too popular for its own good. Its clean, fresh taste deserves a recommendation, not a medal, at this price point. If you're in a pub and want to be seen drinking a premium beer, why not go for a Bitburger or Budweiser Budvar and show your Beck's-swilling friends you know something they don't? £4.99 per 6 x 275ml bottles. [*5.0%, Germany*]

Fuller's ESB Export Extra Special Bitter
Per pint: £1.75

B Not my sort of beer, but its powerful, malty-rich flavour is adored by many. £1.69 per 550ml bottle. [*5.9%, London, UK*]

Murphy's Draught Irish Stout Per pint: £1.81

S The lightest of the three Irish stouts, it would not be unfair to describe it as the nearest to Caffrey's, although its smoky-malty aroma gives a far more distinctive edge to its creamy-smoky flavour. Not as dry or as bitter as the other two stouts, it does however fall into the dry, bitter category when tasted in isolation. The bottles used to be less creamy than the cans until Murphy's introduced floating widgets into the latter; now they are both very lightly widgetized. £1.59 per 500ml widgetized bottle. [*4.0%, Ireland/UK*]

Fuller's 1845 Bottle Conditioned Celebration Strong Ale
Per pint: £1.85

B Give me Fuller's London Pride any day, but others much prefer this bottle-conditioned beer and even I cannot help admiring its rich, liquorous malty taste and complex coffee-caramel-burnt-toffee aromas. £1.79 per 550ml bottle. [*6.3%, London, UK*]

'Old Speckled Hen' Strong Pale Ale Morland
Per pint: £2.03

B Fresh and tasty with a characterful maltiness in both the aroma and on the palate, which finishes with the barest hint of smoke. Not as good as the cask-conditioned draught, but what bottled beer is? £1.79 per 500ml bottle. [*5.2%, Oxfordshire, UK*]

CO-OP

STOCK ME AND BUY ONE

Number of stores *2,446*
Opening hours *Vary too widely to generalize*
Maximum range *550 wines, 250 beers, 260 spirits*
Alternative methods of payment *Cheque with card, but which credit cards are acceptable varies so much according to store and region that generalization is not possible*
Local delivery *Not provided, but 'selective stores' will help carry goods to car if requested*
Discounts *None*
Other services *Ice can be purchased*

Comment The biggest problem any drinks guide faces when contemplating coverage of the Co-op is the very nature of the beast, for its 2,446 outlets are owned by 30 totally independent societies. In the last few years, however, Co-op trading has polarized into a handful of buying groups. The Manchester-based CWS (Co-operative Wholesale Society) now controls about 70 per cent of all Co-op turnover and sources all Co-op own labels. The wine department has been run since 1986 by Arabella Woodrow, a Master of Wine and Doctor of Microbiology, who has done so much to improve the image, choice and value of Co-op wines. About 1,300 of the Co-op's 2,446 shops stock all the following products, but the remaining outlets will sell some.

Red Wines

Sliven Merlot & Pinot Noir NV The Bulgarian Vintners' £2.69

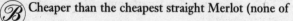

Cheaper than the cheapest straight Merlot (none of

which survived the tastings), this wine represents a good tasty mouthful at this price and just proves it is better to blend a wine which turns out to be superior to its constituent parts than to make a pure varietal wine because Merlot is *à la mode*. The Pinot Noir in this wine could not stand up on its own, but with the Merlot makes for a very gluggy blend indeed. [*Bulgaria*]

Ramada NV Vinho de Mesa Tinto £2.89

(G) Put this in a classy-looking bottle and you could sell it for twice the price. This wine does not merely possess the peppery typicity of a Portuguese red, but more complex and exotic spices, which underlay its very fruity flavour. Only the not-quite-dry finish would expose the fact that this is not really an expensive, particularly fine wine, but at this price such ultra-ripe fruitiness is more than welcome. [*Portugal*]

☞ CO-OP'S BEST VALUE RED WINE

Mission Peak Red NV £2.99

(B) Rich and tasty, with plenty of well-focused flavour. More contrived than an artisanal wine of great typicity. [*Argentina*]

Marqués de la Sierra 1994 Garnacha Puro £2.99

(B) A medium-bodied, assertive red that is unmistakably Spanish and absolutely Garnacha. Comparing this with Tesco's French Grenache is fascinating – both the same price, from the same grape and well worth the money in their own very different styles. [*Spain*]

Vino da Tavola Rosso NV Co-op £2.99

Fresh, fruity and very jammy, but without being cloying. [*Italy*]

Montepulciano d'Abruzzo 1994 Co-op £3·49

Very soft, creamy fruit. [*Italy*]

Villa Mantinera Montepulciano NV Vino da Tavola del Molise Rosso £3·59

S Creamy-jammy aroma followed by succulent strawberry fruit. Unusually for an Italian wine, this is just too yummy and gluggy to be consumed with food. [*Italy*]

Chilean Cabernet Sauvignon NV Curicó, Co-op £3·69

Fresh, sappy fruit hinting of blackcurrants, with a smooth finish. [*Chile*]

Kingston Shiraz Mataro 1995 Murray Valley £3·79

G Very smooth, creamy-rich fruit which is so complete and satisfying on its own that this wine does not need or benefit from food, even though it has a huge dry-tannin finish. [*Australia*]

South Australia Cabernet Sauvignon 1994 Angove's, Co-op £4·29

This lush, creamy-cedary Aussie Cabernet would have got a bronze medal if 50 pence cheaper, yet still deserves a strong recommendation at this price. The 1993 was still available at the time of writing and with an extra year in bottle had built up considerable sweetness on the finish. [*Australia*]

New Zealand Cabernet-Merlot NV Co-op £4·29

B The firm, warm, cedary-creamy fruit in this wine could easily stand up to spicy barbecued food. [*New Zealand*]

Berberana Tempranillo 1993 Rioja £4·29

B Nice oaky stuff. [*Spain*]

L.A. Cetto Petite Sirah 1993 £4·49

This rich, peppery-spicy Mexican wine is not my idea of Syrah, but it is the best vintage yet from Cetto. [*Mexico*]

Duque de Viseu Dão 1991 Vinhos Sogrape £5·49

A very elegant red that deserves its recommendation, although it lacks the weight of fruit and sheer finesse that was so evident last year, when the same vintage won a Silver Medal. [*Portugal*]

Fetzer 1993 Valley Oaks Cabernet Sauvignon £5·99

It is easy to make soft, luscious Cabernet in California, but they are all too often everyday drinking wines and it is difficult to make a wine as soft and ripe as this with such elegance and class. [*California, USA*]

Enate Tempranillo-Cabernet Sauvignon 1993 Somontano £5·99

It is the firm Cabernet that dominates this wine, despite there being more Tempranillo than Cabernet in the blend. An elegant, firm-structured food wine. [*Spain*]

Leasingham Cabernet Sauvignon Malbec 1992 Clare Valley £6.99

Very classy wine showing rich, minty, creamy fruit, with an intense finish and fine, menthol complexity. [*Australia*]

Châteauneuf-du-Pape 1992 Cellier des Princes £8.49

This wine thoroughly deserves a bronze medal in the £8 plus category, despite its curiously closed nose, because it has such concentration of rich spicy-fruit on the palate. Quite where the bouquet has gone is a mystery, especially after five years, when the aromatics should be building to a peak. It must be a temporary phase. Wine is a natural product and not always as predictable as we like to think. When the bouquet returns, this Châteauneuf-du-Pape should be worth a silver or even a gold. [*Rhône Valley, France*]

White Wines

Début Fumé Sauvignon Blanc 1995 Russe Region, The Bulgarian Vintners' £2.89

B The cheapest Sauvignon Blanc in the tasting and with so much rubbish Sauvignon up to a pound a bottle more expensive, the fresh, crisp, absolutely clean aroma and flavour of this wine made a very apt start to the tasting, even if it was very difficult to find anything worth recommending afterwards. In fact, just one wine out of almost twenty survived the tastings between Début Fumé and a Gaillac at £3.89. [*Bulgaria*]

☞ CO-OP'S BEST VALUE WHITE WINE

Vin de Pays des Côtes de Gascogne NV Dry White, Co-op £2.99

More rich-fruity than Côtes de Gascogne's typically tangy-fruity style. [*South-west France*]

Murrumbidgee Estate NV Fruity Australian White Wine £3.49

B I was tempted to give this a silver medal, but I was brought up on Rose's Lime Juice and others might not be equally appreciative. [*Australia*]

Chilean Long Slim White 1994 Chardonnay Semillon £3·49

Although this fresh, easy-drinking wine beat a number of more expensive Chardonnays, it still did not earn a medal after my super-selection process. [*Curico, Chile*]

Hungaroo Pinot Gris 1995 Neszmély Winery £3·49

B Hungaroo stands for Australian methodology from Hungarian winemakers, but it is not always a successful marriage, as some of the Hungaroo tasted did not even rate as drinkable, let alone capable of surviving the *SuperBooze* tastings and super-selection process. This wine has little in common with Pinot Gris, although it could surprise over the next twelve months, but it is a good-value dry white wine in its own right, with rich, very fresh, succulent fruit and nice balancing acidity. [*Hungary*]

Fair Martina Vermentino NV Vin de Pays d'Oc, Co-op £3·79

B Made by Australian winemaker Nick Butler, who obviously has an eye for the girls, as he fashioned this rich, racy, well-proportioned white wine for Fair Martina whereas it does not look as if he tried to come up with anything other than an ordinary southern French red for her opposite number, Bad Tempered Cyril (despite the promising sound of blending Syrah with Gallic-grown Spanish Tempranillo). Based solely on name alone, Cyril is the wine I would love to recommend, but for quality, content and value, Fair Martina wins hands down. [*Languedoc-Roussillon, France*]

Oak Village Chardonnay 1994 Stellenbosch, Cape Selection £3·99
Rich lemony oak. [*South Africa*]

Devil's Rock Riesling 1994 St. Ursula £3·99
Clean, dry, lemony Riesling fruit. [*Pfälz, Germany*]

Cape Afrika Rhine Riesling 1995 Co-op £3·99
(B) Crisp, fresh, genuine Riesling from South Africa's 'first black controlled wine négociant', who has achieved a far better, more natural Riesling in Robertson's less than ideal *terroir* (as far as Riesling is concerned) than the producers of some fifteen German Rieslings at up to 50 pence more expensive, most of which had unclean aromas. [*Robertson, South Africa*]

New Zealand Semillon-Sauvignon NV Co-op £4·29
(G) More Sauvignon than Semillon, although Semillon in New Zealand is so grassy that it is often used to boost the Sauvignon character of a wine. This one has lovely suck-a-stone freshness and finesse and deliciously ripe, racy fruit. [*New Zealand*]

Nobilo White Cloud NV Gisborne £4·39
(B) Fresh, ripe, tropical fruits. [*New Zealand*]

Philippe de Baudin Chardonnay 1994 La Baume, Vin de Pays d'Oc £4·69
(B) Elegantly rich, smooth flavoured Chardonnay fruit. [*Languedoc-Roussillon, France*]

Alasia 1994 Chardonnay del Piemonte £4·99
(S) I love it when under blind conditions I find something as cheap and as sensationally good as this wine, only to discover afterwards that it is from Italy,

one of my love-hate wine-producing countries, although I was less surprised to see that it was produced by Australian winemaker Martin Shaw. [*Italy*]

Rosemount Estate Chardonnay 1995 Hunter Valley £6.49

Very fresh and sherbetty in an elegant, understated, easy-to-drink Chardonnay style. A bit like an Australian Mâcon! [*Australia*]

Rosé Wines

Vin de Pays de l'Hérault Blush NV Co-op £3·69

Don't over-chill this wine and you will be surprised by how rich and tasty it is for the price. [*Languedoc-Roussillon, France*]

Sparkling Wines

Australian Barramundi Sparkling Wine Brut NV £5·49

A really jammy fizz. If you like bubbles in your raspberry jam, this is the wine for you! [*Australia*]

Seaview Brut NV McLaren Vale £5·79

What makes Seaview so successful is not just its cheap price and ultra-reliable fresh, zesty style, but the tiny size of the bubbles. [*Australia*]

Deinhard Yello NV £5·99

Superior for its category, but for diehard Sekt-lovers only. [*Germany*]

Beers

Ceres Royal Export Per pint: £0.85

Clean and fresh with some malty richness. £2.99 per 4 x 500ml cans. [*5.8%, Denmark*]

Co-op Super Strength Lager Per pint: £1.22

£3.79 per 4 x 440ml cans. [*8.5%, UK*]

St. Andrews Ale Belhaven Brewery Per pint: £1.42

A sweet, fruity beer with perfumed-hop aroma. £1.25 per 500ml bottle. [*4.6%, Dunbar, Scotland*]

Deakin's Red Admiral Mansfield Brewery Per pint: £1.58

A cross between Pilsner and a mellow, honeyed ale with a firm spritz. £1.39 per 500ml bottle. [*4.4%, Nottinghamshire, England*]

Boddingtons Manchester Gold Per pint: £1.59

By far the most distinctive of all the widgetized canned beers tasted this year, but it deserves to be sold in a bottle like the straight Boddingtons Draught, so that it can appeal to those who would not be seen dead with a tinned beer. One batch submitted had been canned without pressurized nitrogen and although it was not off, it looked and tasted mighty strange. It should not be flat, so if you happened to purchase some of the same batch, get a refund and give Boddingtons Gold a second try. £4.99 per 4 x 440ml widgetized cans. [*4.8%, England*]

Samuel Adams Boston Lager Per pint: £2.05

Very peppery-hoppy with a rich, bitter taste. £1.19 per 330ml bottle. [*4.8%, USA*]

CO-OPERATIVE PIONEER

STOCK ME AND BUY ONE

Number of stores 289
Opening hours *Vary too widely to generalize*
Maximum range *383 wines, 150 beers, 160 spirits*
Alternative methods of payment *Cheque with card, Access, Visa*
Local delivery *Not provided*
Discounts *None*
Other services *Ice can be purchased*

Comment Run by CRS (Co-operative Retail Service), the Leo's, Lo-Cost and Pioneer superstores are currently being amalgamated under one fascia, Co-operative Pioneer. CRS operates 535 stores, making it the largest society in the Co-operative movement, although not comparable to CWS, which services some 70 per cent of all the stores in the various regional societies (*see* the **Co-op** entry). CRS achieved its super-society status by virtue of its primary function, which is to rescue ailing societies; this is why CRS is not regionalized, but has stores located all over the country. Although CRS stocks a number of Co-op own-label and other CWS lines, it has its own range of products purchased by a dynamic buying team under the efficient control of Buying Manager Christine Sandys. Last year I promised to review these separately and they did very well, with a weighted position of 7th in the book.

Red Wines

Oriachovitza Cabernet Sauvignon Reserve 1991 Stara Zagora Region £3.19

B Rich, coconutty-oaky fruit on a firm tannin

structure makes this an ideal red to wash down hearty, unpretentious home-made cooking, such as a tasty steak and mushroom pie. [*Bulgaria*]

Cabernet Sauvignon Special Reserve 1986 Rovit £3.39

Rich, ripe, ultra-fruity Ribena-like flavour in a ten-year-old Romanian wine must be worth a medal. [*Romania*]

☞ CO-OPERATIVE PIONEER'S BEST VALUE RED WINE

Gandia Merlot 1993 Hoya Valley £3.39

Fresh, sappy berry-fruit with a creamy finish. This was the cheapest Merlot to qualify. [*Spain*]

Domaine de Borios 1994 Saint-Chinian £3.49

Quite easy to go streaming past this one in a line-up, but when it was given due consideration in an unrushed and undisturbed environment, I was pleasantly surprised by its aftertaste (more accurately an after-perfume in this case) – and this was enhanced by food when I tried it and several other borderline bottles with pasta. [*Languedoc-Roussillon, France*]

South African Pinotage 1995 Coastal Region, Teltscher Brothers £3.49

Rich and gutsy with a sweetish finish. [*South Africa*]

La Baume Cuvée Australe 1994 Vin de Pays d'Oc £3.99

The dry tannin structure belies the richness and depth of this wine. Classic French food-wine structure with a touch of Oz wizardry. [*Languedoc-Roussillon, France*]

Sutter Home Zinfandel 1993 Napa £4.29

More oomph but less elegance than the

Pepperwood Zinfandel (*see* **Budgens**), although it is just as smooth and easy to drink. [*California, USA*]

Miguel Torres Cabernet Sauvignon 1993 Santa Digna, Curico £4·49

This lovely, fresh, elegant Cabernet seems much younger than it is, and will slowly evolve into a much finer wine over the next two or three years. [*Chile*]

Caliterra Cabernet Sauvignon 1993 Maipo Valley £4·49

The menthol-herbal background hints in this smooth, classy, blackcurranty wine give it a degree of finesse that is lacking in most sub-£5 Cabernets. [*Chile*]

Sutter Home Cabernet Sauvignon 1993 Napa £4·49

Long, deep, fruit-bush Cabernet flavour, nice tannin grip, very good with food. [*California, USA*]

Peter Lehmann Vine Vale Shiraz 1994 Barossa £4·49

Dry-coconutty oak aroma followed by very rich, creamy coconutty fruit. Well-balanced, well-proportioned wine – good with food. [*Australia*]

Torres Sangre de Toro 1993 £4·59

A mini-classic produced in mega-quantities, Torres Sangre de Toro is an underrated wine that always gives excellent value, but this particular bottling is exceptional. If you want a Spanish red from indigenous grape varieties and heaps of traditional, coconutty American oak at an affordable price, then this rich-flavoured, full-bodied red is the wine for you. [*Penedés, Spain*]

Hardys Nottage Hill Cabernet Sauvignon Shiraz 1993 South Eastern Australia £4·79

There's no mistaking the Australian provenance of any wine with this much eucalyptus on the nose. Keep two years for full potential. [*Australia*]

Lindemans Bin 50 Shiraz 1993 South Eastern Australia £4·99

Spicy-cedary oak overlaying creamy-rich, spicy fruit. [*Australia*]

Rosemount Estate Shiraz Cabernet 1995 £4·99

An easy to drink red with oodles of fresh, uncomplicated, delightful jammy-fruit. [*Australia*]

Orlando RF Cabernet Sauvignon 1992 £5·39

Nicely concentrated fruit with cedary-herbal undertones and a hint of mint. [*Australia*]

Mitchelton Cabernet Shiraz 1992 South Eastern Australia £5·69

Soft, smooth, elegantly perfumed blackcurranty fruit. [*Australia*]

Penfolds Koonunga Hill Shiraz-Cabernet Sauvignon 1994 South Australia £5·99

I have to confess that this is a borderline silver, and it only won the gong because it's such a big, black and hugely concentrated wine. Although I spend much of my time looking for nuances of elegance and finesse because I do not want to fall into the trap of 'big is best', I cannot ignore the fact that for some people the bigger the wine the better it is. So if you want a monster to drink now or forget about for ten years, at £5·99 this must be a great bargain. [*Australia*]

White Wines

Posta Romana Classic Gewurztraminer 1993 Tarnave Region, Transylvania, Blaj Winery £2.79

Gewurztraminer is the spiciest grape variety in the world, but it is difficult to find a truly pungent example outside of Alsace, no matter how much you pay – yet this cheap Romanian wine has an amazing pungency of spice. Even Alsace freaks hooked on Gewurztraminer would be more than satisfied with this ridiculously inexpensive alternative. Truly inspired sourcing. [*Romania*]

☞ CO-OPERATIVE PIONEER'S BEST VALUE WHITE WINE

☞ THE BEST VALUE WHITE WINE OF THE YEAR

Retsina NV Boutari £3.19

The difference between good and bad Retsina is that the good stuff smells like a cheap aftershave while the bad stuff reeks of pine disinfectant. This smells of cheap aftershave, so it must get a recommendation, even if I personally would not even use it to disinfect a toilet! [*Greece*]

Kretikos Vin de Pays de Crete 1994 Boutari £3.69

An excellent example of what modern technology can do, this extremely fresh, elegant dry white wine has an appealing touch of sweetness on the finish. [*Greece*]

August Sebastiani White 1995 California £3.89

Crisp, perfumed fruit with a zingy spritz and a not entirely dry finish make this a very commercial wine indeed. [*USA*]

Etchart Cafayate Torrontes 1994 Vino Fino Blanco £3·99

(B) Very fresh and crisp, subtle muscat-like aromas. Very elegant dry white wine. [*Argentina*]

Cuckoo Hill Chardonnay 1995 Vin de Pays d'Oc £3·99

(B) Elegant richness of fruit highlighted by aromas of apple blossom and lime. [*Languedoc-Roussillon, France*]

Penfolds Bin 202 Riesling 1994 £3·99

(B) Pure lime juice; very fresh and zesty. [*Australia*]

Sutter Home Chardonnay 1994 Napa £4·49

(B) Very smooth, creamy-fruit concoction. [*California, USA*]

Caliterra Chardonnay 1995 Curico £4·49

(B) Deliciously fresh International style and quality of Chardonnay. [*Chile*]

Penfolds Rawson's Retreat Bin 21 1995 Semillon Chardonnay Colombard £4·49

(B) The fruit is so deliciously fresh and ripe, it's almost too easy to drink. [*Australia*]

Miguel Torres Chardonnay de la Cordillera 1995 £4·99

(B) Gentle toasty aromas mingling with very fresh, very elegant fruit. Capable of further development over the next twelve to eighteen months. [*Curico, Chile*]

Cooks Sauvignon Blanc 1995 Gisborne £4·99

(B) Very fresh gooseberry fruits with suck-a-stone finesse. [*New Zealand*]

Peter Lehmann Semillon 1994 Barossa £4·99

(S) The lime-infused fruit and aroma of this wine is

classic Australian Semillon. Firm-structured food wine. [*Australia*]

Rosemount Estate Semillon Sauvignon Blanc 1995 South Eastern £4·99

Very tangy, elegantly rich and easy drinking. [*Australia*]

Cuckoo Hill Viognier 1995 Vin de Pays d'Oc £4·99

Very juicy fruit, extremely fresh and long. [*Languedoc-Roussillon, France*]

Orlando RF Chardonnay 1994 £5·39

A fresh, rich and easy-drinking wine of crisp, clean fruit. [*Australia*]

Chateau Tahbilk Marsanne 1994 Victoria £5·99

The fresh, elegant and sherbetty fruit in this wine lifted it above the heaviness and oily richness of other Australian Marsanne and Roussanne. [*Australia*]

Rosé Wines

August Sebastiani White Zinfandel 1994 £3·79

Very fresh, zingy and spritzy with sweet, delicately perfumed fruit. In pure quality terms this might only be a bronze, but for medium rosé drinkers it more than deserves its silver medal. [*California, USA*]

Sparkling Wines

Seaview Brut NV McLaren Vale £5·99

What makes Seaview so successful is not just its

low price and ultra-reliable fresh, zesty style, but the tiny size of the bubbles. [*Australia*]

Codorníu Première Cuvée NV Brut Chardonnay £6.49

Richer than most current Cava cuvées, but less zesty and with slightly lower acidity. [*Spain*]

Lindauer Brut NV Montana Wine £6.95

Tangy-sherbetty, juicy-lime fruit with a fresh, zesty finish that develops a little honey in bottle. [*New Zealand*]

Bouvet Brut NV Saumur £7·79

Although I do not care for the ubiquitous peardrop aroma on this wine, I was impressed by the pristine fruit and finely balanced acidity, which enabled this to be the only Loire bubbly to survive the tastings. [*Loire Valley, France*]

Pongrácz Brut NV £8.99

Well-balanced richness and oxidative complexity, which should become a creamy-biscuity complexity by Christmas. [*South Africa*]

Cuvée Napa by Mumm Brut NV £8.99

Fresh, soft fruit on the palate, with a nicely sharp finish. [*California, USA*]

Fortified Wines

Castillo de Liria Moscatel NV Vicente Gandia £3·39

Very fresh, raisiny-muscat fruit aroma, very clean, rich, sweet fruit. This probably has the edge in freshness over the two other Spanish Moscatels recommended, but they are all extremely similar in style and quality. [*Spain*]

Beers

Boddingtons Draught Per pint: £1.26

A nicely hopped beer, this is much fruitier than John Smith's, the other best-performing widgetized bitter at this price point, and has a correctly crisp finish with some real bitterness on the aftertaste. £3.89 per 4 x 440ml widgetized cans. [*3.8%, Manchester, UK*]

Guinness Original Per pint: £1.29

Dense, dark, bitter chocolate, coffee and liquorice. Quite stern, but great with a Stilton ploughman. £2.99 per 4 x 330ml bottles. [*4.3%, Ireland/UK*]

Beamish Draught Per pint: £1.29

I always used to think that Beamish was the sweetest of Ireland's three stouts, but it is not – Murphy's is. Beamish is noticeably the smokiest and least creamy of the three, even with the creamy effect of the widget, and has a very distinctive smoky-bitter taste that is as dry as Guinness, although it lacks the toasty, roasted barley substance that gives Guinness such a satisfying mid-palate fill. I like it, however, as a really smoky change. £3.99 per 4 x 440ml widgetized cans. [*4.2%, Cork, Ireland*]

Kronenbourg 1664 Courage Per pint: £1.29

Its deep gold colour belies the fresh, hoppy aroma and crisp flavour beneath. Considering that this is canned, not bottled, and brewed in the UK by Courage rather than by Kronenbourg in Strasbourg, it is surprisingly good, with a very authentic character. £3.99 per 4 x 440ml cans. [*5.0%, UK*]

'33' Export Per pint: £1.47

There's no pretence about this easy-drinking, down-to-earth lager-style beer. Ideal telly beer for every couch potato. £6.49 per 10 x 25cl bottles. [*4.8%, France*]

Draught Guinness Per pint: £1.48

G The king of stouts is also the inventor of the widget, which most beer writers abhor and most draught stout drinkers adore. Guinness stands out from the rest by the intensity of its smoky-toasty-malty aroma. It is every bit as smoky as Beamish, but has a greater depth of other top-quality ingredients so that smokiness is not perceived as its main characteristic. Lovely roasted-barley tones echo through malty-rich, smoky-toasty aromas on the mid-palate to give a satisfying edge other stouts lack. £4.59 per 4 x 440ml widgetized cans. [*4.1%, Ireland/UK*]

☞ THE BEST VALUE DARK BEER OF THE YEAR

Marston's Pedigree Bitter Per pint: £1.49

B Classic coppery colour with a smooth, dry complex taste highlighted by perfumed hoppy aromas. £1.49 per 568ml bottle. [*4.5%, Burton-on-Trent, UK*]

Samuel Smith's Old Brewery Pale Ale Per pint: £1.52

S Firm and distinctive, with good malty bitterness. Only own-label pale ales were cheaper than this fine brew! £1.47 per 550ml bottle. [*5.0%, Yorkshire, UK*]

Fuller's London Pride Premium Ale Per pint: £1.54

(G) This will hit home for those who prefer genuinely dry, authentically bitter beers. The fresh, intense, hoppy-maltiness of this brew is particularly well-suited to the bottling process. £1.49 per 550ml bottle. [*4.7%, London, UK*]

Budweiser Budvar Per pint: £1.58

(S) Genuine Czech Budweiser has been made since the thirteenth century and the only remaining example is instantly recognizable by the Budvar part of its name. It is a classic beer: whereas American Budweiser is just bland-tasting, perfumed water made primarily from rice, Budvar is made from pure, top-quality malt. Compare the two beers for yourself and you'll be pleasantly surprised, not the least because the superior, authentic product also happens to be cheaper. £1.39 per 50cl bottle. [*5.0%, Ceske Budejovice, Czech Republic*]

Amstel Bier Lager Per pint: £1.59

Cleverly brewed to balance crispness and richness, Amstel has wide appeal and this is as good as it gets. £3.69 per 4 x 33cl bottles. [*5.0%, Netherlands*]

Caffrey's Draught Irish Ale Per pint: £1.61

(B) This light, fresh, creamy-sweet brew is brilliantly marketed. It is not as good as from the tap, even if that is connected to a pressurized keg, but the same could be said for Guinness Draught, and those who like this soft, easy beer will simply be thankful they can keep a reasonable replica ready-chilled in the fridge. Any Caffrey's drinker who has not tasted Wethered's Draught from M&S should do so. It's in a similar style, some will actually prefer it, and it costs 49 pence per pint less. £4.99 per 4 x 440ml widgetized cans. [*4.8%, County Antrim, UK*]

Samuel Smith's The Celebrated Oatmeal Stout Old Brewery Tadcaster Per pint: £1.61

Whereas The Famous Taddy (see below) is dry for a porter (as so many are these days, thank goodness), Samuel Smith's Celebrated is somewhat sweet for a stout, with a more malty, porter-like flavour. £1.56 per 550ml bottle. [*5.0%, Yorkshire, UK*]

Samuel Smith's The Famous Taddy Porter Old Brewery Tadcaster Per pint: £1.61

The darkest of all the porters tasted, with an attractive Ovaltine-coloured head. Very dry and very bitter, this beer cries out for a widget (which does not mean that Samuel Smith's should not continue with this pure bottled version – just that if offered in a widgetized bottle, it would open up sales to typical draught stout drinkers and it would be interesting to see how a widgetized Famous Taddy rated blind against the three Irish stouts). Not that Samuel Smith's would ever dare! £1.56 per 550ml bottle. [*5.0%, Yorkshire, UK*]

Stella Artois Premium Lager Beer Per pint: £1.63

Really quite a decent lunchtime lager considering the brand's naff reputation amongst serious beer drinkers and the fact that it is brewed in the UK by Whitbread, rather than in Belgium by Stella Artois itself. Light, flowery-Pilsner style. £5.69 per 6 x 33cl bottles. [*5.2%, UK*]

Fuller's ESB Export Extra Special Bitter Per pint: £1.64

Not my sort of beer, but its powerful, malty-rich

flavour is adored by many. £1.59 per 550ml bottle. [*5.9%, London, UK*]

Murphy's Draught Irish Stout Per pint: £1.69

Murphy's is the lightest of the three Irish stouts, and it would not be unfair to describe it as the nearest to Caffrey's, although its smoky-malty aroma gives a far more distinctive edge to its creamy-smoky flavour. Not as dry or as bitter as the other two stouts, it does however fall into the dry, bitter category when tasted in isolation. The bottles used to be less creamy than the cans until Murphy's introduced floating widgets into the latter; now they are both very lightly widgetized. £1.49 per 500ml widgetized bottle. [*4.0%, Ireland/ UK*]

Directors Live Ale Courage Per pint: £1.69

This very smooth, aromatically perfumed beer has a nice bitter-hop finish and proves that big breweries can still produce good bottle-conditioned beers if they want to. £1.49 per 500ml bottle. [*4.8%, UK*]

6X Export Wadworth Per pint: £1.69

I cannot believe that anyone can seriously enjoy the almost salty richness of sour, sultana-malt taste in this beer, but 6X is so popular that I include it for those who obviously do. £1.49 per 500ml bottle. [*5.0%, Devizes, UK*]

San Miguel Export Premium Lager Per pint: £1.70

Has the same flowery-hoppy Pilsner aroma as the can (which is remarkable in a canned beer), but a slightly more hoppy flavour, with a longer, crisper finish. Better, yet a lower medal because the can is so exceptional and this is almost twice the price. £3.95 per

4 x 33cl bottles. [5.4%, *Spain*]

Foster's Export Australia's Famous Beer Courage

Per pint: £1.70

Buy the bottled, export version of 'Australia's Famous Beer' and you'll find that it was brewed in the UK! It also happens – shock, horror – to have some flavour compared to Down Under's infamously bland golden nectar. £0.99 per 330ml bottle. [5.5%, *UK*]

'Old Speckled Hen' Strong Pale Ale Morland

Per pint: £1.92

Fresh and tasty with a characterful maltiness in both the aroma and on the palate, which finishes with the barest hint of smoke. Not as good as the cask-conditioned draught, but what bottled beer is? £1.69 per 500ml bottle. [5.2%, *Oxfordshire, UK*]

Beck's Per pint: £1.92

This beer is too popular for its own good. Its clean, fresh taste deserves a recommendation, not a medal, at this price point. If you're in a pub and want to be seen drinking a premium beer, why not go for a Bitburger or Budweiser Budvar and show your Beck's-swilling friends you know something they don't? £5.59 per 6 x 275ml bottles. [5.0%, *Bremen, Germany*]

Stella Artois Dry Premium Beer Export Strength

Per pint: £1.96

Not as dry as its name suggests, this has a richer malty taste than the British-brewed Stella Artois Premium Lager, with more aromatic hops on the finish, but still does not deserve a medal at this price. £5.69 per 6 x 275ml bottles. [5.5%, *Leuven, Belgium*]

Staropramen Beer Per pint: £1.98

Very elegant, with perfumed hops, this is a truly dry Pilsner style that is soft and so delicately aromatic that it can easily be consumed by those who do not usually like their beers so dry. £1.15 per 330ml bottle. [5.0%, *Prague, Czech Republic*]

Guinness Foreign Extra Stout Per pint: £2.01

Extra Stout is a very apt name for this exceptionally extracted brew, the complex flavours of which start remarkably concentrated yet build and build on the palate to a rousing crescendo of bitter-coffee, burnt-toffee, black treacle and liquorice intensity. £1.17 per 330ml bottle. [7.5%, *Dublin, Ireland*]

Prices

Prices were correct at the time of tasting. You should expect some changes due to exchange-rate fluctuations, prices rising at source, possible increases in VAT and other variables, but these should be within reason, and the historical price in this book will help you to spot any excessive increases.

Please note that prices were not updated prior to publication because all the wines and beers were tasted within their own price category and to change that would be to make a mockery of the blind tasting, the notes made and the medals awarded.

FOOD FAIR

A chain of eighty off-licensed supermarkets run by Yorkshire Co-operatives, Food Fair stores are similar in format to the Good Neighbour local supermarkets also operated by Yorkshire Co-operatives. Although the range varies according to the size of store (only one is a superstore), Food Fairs stock most of the wines recommended in the main Co-op entry although, curiously, not the Co-op's own-label Yorkshire Bitter. Does the Yorkshire Co-operatives buyer know something we don't? In addition to a selection of Co-op own-label wines and beers, Food Fair supermarkets stock a significant range of independently purchased wines. The chain expressed a desire to participate in the second edition, but failed to do so. In the meantime, please use the recommendations under the main **Co-op** entry (page 38).

FOOD GIANT

A northern-based group of twenty-seven superstores in which service has been reduced to a minimum in order to churn out the cheapest prices possible. You even have to buy the carrier bags at Food Giant, and its management is proud of the fact. After all, there is no such thing as a free anything in a supermarket, as the cost of any giveaway will be built into the prices you pay. By making customers fork out for things like carrier bags, Food Giant manages to sell the very same wines and beers as its sister chain Somerfield for 5–15 per cent cheaper. So why shop at Somerfield? According to Food Giant's Pat Lees, anyone who does shop at Somerfield must be mad if it's a straight choice between the two stores, although there are very few instances where they are in direct competition. Or for the moment, anyway. Although most Food Giant stores are north of Birmingham, including five in Scotland, there is one in Exeter, and rumours are rife about further branches due to open up in the south. Use the recommendations under the main **Somerfield** entry (page 155), but expect to pay 5–15 per cent less.

GATEWAY

Part of the Somerfield group, which also includes Food Giant and SoLo. The number of Gateway stores has dropped from 313 last year to just 132, although whether they will all disappear by the end of 1996, as planned, is yet to be seen. Most stores are being refurbished in the brighter, fresher Somerfield look. For the range of wines and beers recommended, use the main **Somerfield** entry (page 155).

GOOD NEIGHBOUR

Another small chain of supermarkets run by Yorkshire Co-operatives. Good Neighbour stores are similar in format to Food Fair supermarkets, but are only twenty-five in number. Although the range varies according to the size of store, Good Neighbour stocks most of the wines recommended in the main Co-op entry. In addition to a selection of Co-op own-label wines and beers, Good Neighbour supermarkets stock a significant range of other drink products. As indicated under the Food Fair entry, these independently purchased wines and beers were supposed to be covered in this edition, but the chain failed to respond. In the meantime, please use the recommendations under the main **Co-op** entry (page 38).

Different Vintages

Wines recommended in this book are specific to the vintages indicated. Follow-on vintages might be of a similar quality and character, but are likely to be either better or worse. Wines of real interest are seldom exactly the same from one year to the next. Cheap fruity wines, whether white or red, are often better the younger they are, and the difference between vintages is generally less important for bulk wines produced in hotter countries, but even these will vary in some vintages. The difference in vintage is usually most noticeable in individually crafted wines produced the world over. Don't be put off a wine because it is a different vintage, as you could be missing an even greater treat, but do try a bottle before laying out on a case or two.

KWIK SAVE

STOCK ME AND BUY ONE

Number of stores *950*
Opening hours *Monday–Wednesday and Saturday 9a.m.–5.30p.m., Thursday–Friday 9a.m.–8p.m., Sunday (selected stores only) 12 noon–4p.m.*
Maximum range *105 wines, 160 beers, 80 spirits*
Alternative methods of payment *Cheque with card, Switch and Delta debit cards*
Local delivery *None*
Discounts *None*
Other services *None*

Comment Kwik Save operates a typical discount store's 'no frills' service in order to minimize costs, which with a significantly lower than average profit margin helps to keep prices as low as possible. With such a low percentage profit, turnover has to be the priority, which is why Kwik Save's strategy has always been to target volume-selling products. Until relatively recently this meant a small range of cheap and rather dire wines, with Liebfraumilch and Lambrusco about as exciting as it got. Four years ago, however, Kwik Save realized that wine is different from baked beans, and hired Angela Muir, a hard-headed Master of Wine, to reorganize things. When she was satisfied with a product, Richard Graves the wine buyer would go in without any personal attachment to it but with the full purchasing power of Kwik Save to screw down the price – and a very successful strategy it has proved too. Observant readers will have noticed the use of the past tense. That's because Justin Addison has now taken over as the wine buyer.

If the number and level of medal-winners seems disappointingly low, think again. Apart from the Champagne, the most expensive white wine submitted was £3.99 (for a half-bottle) and the most expensive red was even less at £3.69. This is forced on them by Kwik Save's pile 'em high policy, and I wonder how many medals other supermarkets would have earned had they restricted their submissions to wines under £4? That Kwik Save has performed exceptionally well within these constraints is illustrated by the fact that for the second year running, it has walked off with the Best Value Red Wine of the Year award.

Red Wines

Macedonian Country Red NV £2.39

Fresh, clean, chunky fruit of real flavour. Capable of accompanying a good winter stew. [*Republic of Macedonia*]

Marino El Vino Tinto del Mediterráneo NV Bodegas Berberana £2.79

A real contradiction this one, providing lots of oomph and a gutsy mouthful of flavour, yet with a succulent fruity finish. [*Spain*]

Bulgarian Merlot & Cabernet Sauvignon 1995 Domaine Boyar £2.79

Very fresh fruit and nice dry tannins make a very inexpensive food wine that is capable of taking on a piping hot winter stew. [*Bulgaria*]

Promesa Tinto NV Cosecheros y Criadores £2.89

Another example of how modern technology is producing Portuguese reds that combine good typicity with real fruit, which always used to be the missing ingredient in these wines. The tannin is still there, but merely provides grip and makes the fruit nice and chewy. [*Spain*]

Montepulciano d'Abruzzo 1995 Venier £2.99

A serious wine, even if the price does not suggest it. Real varietal character and good, firm – almost assertively firm – fruit. [*Italy*]

Alta Mesa Tinto 1994 Estremadura £2.99

Not as outstanding as it was a year ago, but it still stands out as an elegantly fruity wine at this price. Look out for the 1995. [*Portugal*]

Bulgarian Cabernet Sauvignon 1992 Elhovo Winery £2.99

The rich fruit and big, coconutty oak aromas in this wine used to typify Bulgarian Cabernet, but sadly there are far too many wishy-washy examples around these days. [*Bulgaria*]

Gamza Reserve 1992 Lovico Suhindol £3.09

Nothing to do with Gamay, Gamza is in fact a native grape of Hungary, where it is called Kardaka and is the country's most widely planted red wine variety. This is a very soft and easy version, and, in typical Bulgarian style, the varietal flavour is smoothed out with more than a hint of oak. [*Bulgaria*]

Claret Cuvée VE Bordeaux 1995 Calvet/Guy Anderson £3.19

Not the cheapest claret submitted, but the best cheapest tasted. Made in a modern style with fresh, easy-drinking, youthful fruit and a nice creamy finish. [*Bordeaux, France*]

Côtes du Rhône 1995 F. Dubessy £3.29

(B) Plenty of soft, easy-drinking fruit for the price. [*France*]

Domaine des Bruyère 1994 Côtes de Malepère £3.49

(G) Rich coconutty fruit wrapped up in supple tannins with a hint of mint on the finish and just enough edge to make a fine food wine. [*Languedoc-Roussillon, France*]

☞ KWIK SAVE'S BEST VALUE RED WINE

☞ THE BEST VALUE RED WINE OF THE YEAR

Angove's Shiraz Classic Reserve 1994 £3.69

(B) A splendid creamy-coconutty concoction with jammy fruit on the finish. [*Australia*]

Angove's Butterfly Ridge Shiraz/Cabernet NV South Australia £3.69

(S) Almost a hint of Old World Syrah on the nose, but 100 per cent Oz on the palate. Very creamy-rich fruit with excellent acidity. [*Australia*]

White Wines

Khan Krum Riesling & Dimiat NV Bulgarian Country White Wine £2.59

(S) Fresh and tangy with enough depth to accompany a light starter, rather than the fruits and dessert recommended on the back label. [*Bulgaria*]

Vintage Blend Chardonnay Sauvignon Blanc 1995 Domaine Boyar £2.79

(S) Lovely oaky Chardonnay with heaps of flavour and definite hints of Australian wine wizardry. [*Bulgaria*]

☞ KWIK SAVE'S BEST VALUE WHITE WINE

Jun Carillo White 1995 Navarra £2.89

Clean and fresh, with more depth than I normally expect from a modern vinified Spanish white wine. [*Spain*]

Hungarian Chardonnay 1995 Mór Region, Neszmély Winery £2.89

(B) Oodles of fresh, crisp Chardonnay flavour, as clean as a whistle and emphasized by a nice spritz. [*Hungary*]

Skylark Hill Very Special White NV Vin de Pays d'Oc, Kwik Save £2.99

(B) Apart from a one-off substandard shipment in mid-1996, you can rely on this to be a lovely, rich, easy-drinking white with crisp, clean fruit. [*Languedoc-Roussillon, France*]

Stony Ridge Riesling Pfälz 1995 St. Ursula £2.99

A definite touch of sweetness makes this very clean, fresh Riesling all the more commercial. [*Germany*]

Hungarian Pinot Gris 1995 Neszmély Region £2.99

Hints of spice, which should develop over the next six to nine months. [*Hungary*]

Angove's Chardonnay Classic Reserve 1995

£3.99 (half-bottle)

(S) The provenance of this wine surprised me when the wraps came off. Although Angove is always a good bet for medal-winning wines at the lower-priced, value for money end of the market, I was surprised to see one of its wines do so well at £3.99 for a half-bottle – but the fruit is so deliciously fresh and sherbetty it really stands out in its price bracket. [*Australia*]

Sparkling Wines

Champagne Louis Raymond Brut NV £9.45

The sample submitted had a pepperiness that will develop into a creamy-biscuity complexity over the next six to twelve months, whereas the sample tasted at Kwik Save's annual tasting already had a lovely creamy-biscuity character, indicating two different shipments on the shelf, which happens to every non-vintage product on sale. For absolute fairness, I insist on basing my assessment on the blind tastings. If I did not, the more mature sample might well have been a bronze medal winner. [*France*]

Beers

Special Northern Bitter Mansfield Brewery
Per pint: £0.49

This is soft, with perfumed hops, and is one of the more palatable dirt-cheap brews, but it has no bitter character and you don't have to be macho to drink it! £2.59 per 3–litre party-size plastic bottle. [*3.5%, Nottinghamshire, UK*]

Cains Dark Mild Per pint: £0.65

B A smoky mild with a dry-coffee and burnt-toffee flavour that is more like porter than a true mild and, for me, all the much better. All it needs is a widget, and damn the beer snobs! £2.29 per 4 x 500ml cans. [*3.2%, Liverpool, UK*]

Brady's Traditional Stout Kwik Save Per pint: £0.84

Even without the aid of a widget this is so easy to drink, with a nice mellow-smoky finish. And it's the cheapest stout! £2.59 per 4 x 440ml cans. [*4.0%, UK*]

Pilsor Premiere Bière de Luxe Brasserie Jeanne d'Arc Per pint: £0.84

Really quite perfumed, a bit of a girl's blouse lager, but clean aroma and flavour sets it apart from the sea of smelly dross selling at a similar price. £3.69 per 10 x 25cl bottles. [*4.0%, France*]

San Miguel Export Premium Lager Per pint: £0.93

Soft, delicately perfumed, clean and crisp with, refreshingly, not too much fizz. Astonishingly good for a canned beer. It's ironic that the Spaniards know how to can a beer so well when they do not have a tinny culture, yet we Brits, who are second only to Australians in our perverse taste for canned brews, invariably mess up a beer when we put it in a tin. I have to hand it to them, this is not just good, it's the nearest to Pilsner purity I have ever found in a can. £3.29 per 4 x 500ml cans. [*5.4%, Spain*]

John Smith's Bitter Per pint: £0.95

Nothing to get excited about, but this is refreshing and dry with a clean bitter-hop finish, and is the cheapest bitter or ale to deserve a medal. £2.95 per 4 x 440ml cans. [*4.0%, Yorkshire, UK*]

Double Maxim Premium Quality Ale Vaux Per pint: £0.96

Strong and malty. £3.39 per 4 x 500ml cans. [*4.7%, Sunderland, UK*]

Tetley's Draught Yorkshire Bitter Per pint: £1.16

The least widget-affected: the widget delivers a creamy head, but has little effect on the overall taste, which is less creamy than any other widgetized beer. For some, this might be a godsend. £3.59 per 4 x 440ml widgetized cans. [*3.6%, Leeds, UK*]

John Smith's Extra Smooth Bitter Per pint: £1.24

Unless you're into creamy-sweet, ultra-soft brews, the nicely perfumed hops and a decent bitter taste will make this one of the two best widgetized beers at this price point. £3.85 per 4 x 440ml widgetized cans. [*4.0%, Yorkshire, UK*]

Amstel Bier Lager Per pint: £1.27

Cleverly brewed to balance crispness and richness, Amstel has wide appeal and this is as good as it gets. £2.95 per 4 x 33cl bottles. [*5.0%, Netherlands*]

Bavaria 8.6 Holland Beer Per pint: £1.29

There was a cheaper super-strength 8.5 per cent lager, but it was like drinking pure alcohol and burned not just the back of my throat, but my entire mouth (funny how an 8.5 per cent wine would be perceived as under strength and you would not even notice the alcohol – in fact, you'd probably notice its absence!), but this proved to be much better balanced, with a sweet, fragrant, flowery aroma and flavour. Despite its name, Bavaria is brewed in the Netherlands, not Germany. £2.99 per 4 x 33cl bottles. [*8.6%, Netherlands*]

Waggle Dance Traditional Honey Beer Vaux
Per pint: £1.44

Soft, full, luscious ale with perfumed-hop aromas,

clean, off-dry malty taste and a crisp finish. Apparently named after the dance honey bees execute when they have located nectar, and if you drink enough Waggle Dance, you'll believe it. £1.39 per 550ml bottle. [*5.0%, Sunderland, UK*]

Beck's Per pint: £1.91

This beer is too popular for its own good. Its clean, fresh taste deserves a recommendation, not a medal, at this price point. If you're in a pub and want to be seen drinking a premium beer, why not go for a Bitburger or Budweiser Budvar and show your Beck's-swilling friends you know something they don't? £5.55 per 6 x 275ml bottles. [*5.0%, Bremen, Germany*]

Is a £3 Gold medal as good as a £6 Gold medal?

It *is* possible, and no doubt there are some in this edition – but remember that a medal is awarded for style and price category, thus the higher the price the harder it is to earn one and the probability of a significantly cheaper product being just as good is a slim one.

LEO'S

STOCK ME AND BUY ONE

This chain of eighty-nine off-licensed supermarkets and superstores is operated by CRS (Co-operative Retail Service), which is currently rebadging them under the Co-operative Pioneer banner. Both facias will exist during the shelf-life of this book (*see* **Co-operative Pioneer** entry, page 47).

Prices

Prices were correct at the time of tasting. You should expect some changes due to exchange-rate fluctuations, prices rising at source, possible increases in VAT and other variables, but these should be within reason, and the historical price in this book will help you to spot any excessive increases.

Please note that prices were not updated prior to publication because all the wines and beers were tasted within their own price category and to change that would be to make a mockery of the blind tasting, the notes made and the medals awarded.

LITTLEWOODS

Number of stores 96
Opening hours *Mostly Monday–Saturday 9a.m.–5.30pm.*
Maximum range *N/A*
Alternative methods of payment *Cheque with card, Access, Visa*
Local delivery *None*
Discounts *None*
Other services *None*

Comment Only Spar performed worse, but whereas that symbol group could and should do better, there is little indication that Littlewoods can. It's a far cry from the days when Littlewoods had Bill Riley in charge and Littlewoods' own-label Mosel Auslese was in fact Lieserer Sussenberg 1979 Von Schorlemer selling at £2.99. That said, the wines and beers recommended here do include some real bargains and there are probably more than enough goodies here to keep most Littlewoods customers happy.

Red Wines

Pieters Drift Cinsaut Ruby Cabernet NV Western Cape £2.99

ℬ Deceptively light and jammy when it first hits the palate, this wine builds considerably in flavour in the mouth. [*South Africa*]

Posta Romana Classic Pinot Noir 1991 Dealul Mare Region, Valea Calugareasca £2.99

ℬ Very rich, sweet-ripe strawberry fruit. [*Romania*]

☞ LITTLEWOODS' BEST VALUE RED WINE

Australian Dry Red Wine NV Darlington
£11.99 (3-litre bag-in-box)

Fresh, light, easy-drinking Oz red in a box must be a bronze medal winner at this price. [*Australia*]

Misty Mooring Australian Dry Red Wine NV Angove's
£3.29

Do I detect a little strawberry Pinot Noir in this creamy-jammy Oz fruit? [*Australia*]

Wallaby Ridge Australian Dry Red Wine NV £3.49

At the equivalent of less than £3 a bottle, the bag-in-box Australian Dry Red is much better value, but if you cannot afford three litres at a time this wine can compete in the £3.50 price bracket. [*Australia*]

Eagle Ridge California Red NV The California Winery
£3.49

The least expensive California red wine to survive the tastings, Eagle Ridge showed a creamy richness and depth of fruit lacking in the other cheaper products. [*California, USA*]

Eagle Ridge Cabernet Sauvignon 1992 The California Winery £3.89

Sweet-ripe, violety perfumed fruit for red wine drinkers with a sweet tooth, but with some real richness, not just simple sweetness. [*California, USA*]

Hardys Shiraz Cabernet Sauvignon 1994 Stamps of Australia £3.99

Some will find the smokiness that wafts this smooth, creamy-rich fruit an added complexity, while others will not care for it at all, but one way or the other it is a distinctive wine, with creamy-cedary oak dominating the finish. [*Australia*]

Caliterra Cabernet Sauvignon 1993 Maipo Valley £4.49

(B) The menthol-herbal background hints in this smooth, classy blackcurranty wine give it a degree of finesse that is lacking in most sub-£5 Cabernets. [*Chile*]

Hardys Nottage Hill Cabernet Sauvignon 1992 South Eastern Australia £4.89

(B) There's no mistaking the Australian provenance of any wine with this much eucalyptus on the nose. Keep two years for full potential. [*Australia*]

Montana Cabernet Sauvignon 1994 £4.99

(B) Rich, herbaceous, plummy, blackcurranty fruit. [*New Zealand*]

Parrots Hill Shiraz 1992 Barossa Valley £4.99

(S) Very creamy-oaky fruit with big, cedary-spicy finish. [*Australia*]

McLarens Shiraz 1993 South Eastern Australia £4.99

(B) A very smooth, rich, fruit-driven Shiraz without too much oak. [*Australia*]

Andrew Garrett Black Shiraz 1993 McLaren Vale £6.29

(B) Distinctive eucalyptus nose with dry-spicy, minty-cedary, creamy fruit. The 1992 vintage of this wine was of a very similar style and still available at the time of tasting, but going past its best, so opt for the 1993 if there's a choice. [*Australia*]

Hardys Coonawarra Cabernet Sauvignon 1993 £6.49
Ⓢ Smoky complexity, firm structure and fine acidity help make this a food wine *par excellence.* [*Australia*]

White Wines

Hock NV Deutscher Tafelwein Rhein, Littlewoods
£2.49
Ⓑ The grapy-floral aromas and tangy fruit in this cheap Hock were fresher and more enjoyable than in most German wines up to £3.99 and medium-sweet French wines (mostly Vouvray) up to £4.99. [*Germany*]
☞ LITTLEWOODS' BEST VALUE WHITE WINE

Bereich Nierstein 1994 Schmitt Söhne, Littlewoods
£2.99
Not better than Littlewoods' basic Hock, and certainly not as fresh on the nose, but has more liveliness on the palate. [*Rheinhessen, Germany*]

Wallaby Ridge Australian Dry White Wine NV
£11.99 (3-litre bag-in-box)
This typical buttery-fruity Oz wine is just the ticket to keep on tap in the bag-in-box format, but the bottled version failed to survive the tastings at the equivalent of almost 50 pence per bottle more expensive. [*Australia*]

Eagle Ridge California Chardonnay 1993 The California Winery £3.49
Some people will adore this Chardonnay-flavoured coconut cream while others will hate it. Me? I'll just

add a dash of rum, some crushed pineapple and a little paper umbrella and pretend it's a Piña Colada. [*USA*]

Sparkling Wines

Riviera Moscato Spumante NV Littlewoods £3.69

When Moscato Spumante was £1.99 and sold much faster than £5.99 Asti, it was fresher, better and a bargain, but now that it has broken through the £3 barrier and Asti can be found as cheap as £4.49 (thanks to higher volumes under supermarket own-labels), the opposite is true. For those who simply do not have more than £4 to spend on a bottle of wine, this has the richest, most peachy fruit of the lot. [*Italy*]

Martini Asti NV £5.99

Very rich fruit, but not as sweet as it used to be. [*Italy*]

Champagne François Daumale Brut NV £10.99

Easy-drinking fruity style with nice acidity to keep it fresh. [*France*]

Champagne Cattier 1er Cru NV £14.99

This has refreshing, plump, juicy fruit on the palate, but needs another six months (Christmas?) to mellow the nose and another year to develop a creamy-biscuitiness. [*France*]

Beers

Boddingtons Draught Per pint: £1.47

A nicely hopped beer, this is much fruitier than

John Smith's, the other best-performing widgetized bitter at this price point, and has a correctly crisp finish with some real bitterness on the aftertaste. £1.14 per 440ml widgetized can. [*3.8%, Manchester, UK*]

Draught Guinness Per pint: £1.52

G The king of stouts is also the inventor of the widget, which most beer writers abhor and most draught stout drinkers adore. Guinness stands out from the rest by the intensity of its smoky-toasty-malty aroma. It is every bit as smoky as Beamish, but has a greater depth of other top-quality ingredients so that smokiness is not perceived as its main characteristic. Lovely roasted-barley tones echo through malty-rich, smoky-toasty aromas on the mid-palate to give a satisfying edge other stouts lack. £1.18 per 440ml widgetized can. [*4.1%, Ireland/ UK*]

☞ THE BEST VALUE DARK BEER OF THE YEAR

Caffrey's Draught Irish Ale Per pint: £1.61

B This light, fresh, creamy-sweet brew is brilliantly marketed. It is not as good as from the tap, even if that is connected to a pressurized keg, but the same could be said for Guinness Draught, and those who like this soft, easy beer will simply be thankful they can keep a reasonable replica ready-chilled in the fridge. Any Caffrey's drinker who has not tasted Wethered's Draught from M&S should do so. It's in a similar style, some will actually prefer it, and it costs 49 pence per pint less. £1.25 per 440ml widgetized can. [*4.8%, County Antrim, UK*]

Kilkenny Draught Irish Beer Guinness Per pint: £1.61

B This is much better than Guinness Draught

Bitter and it is quite different from Caffrey's, being deeper flavoured with a fruitier taste and ripe-yeastiness on the finish. £1.25 per 440ml widgetized can. [*5.0%, County Kilkenny, Ireland*]

Budweiser Anheuser-Busch Inc Per pint: £1.64

The bottle is better than the can, being less sweet-watery, but there are many more light-styled Pilsner-type beers that are much cheaper and much better. £0.95 per 330ml bottle. [*5.0%, EU*]

Beck's Per pint: £1.92

This beer is too popular for its own good. Its clean, fresh taste deserves a recommendation, not a medal, at this price point. If you're in a pub and want to be seen drinking a premium beer, why not go for a Bitburger or Budweiser Budvar and show your Beck's-swilling friends you know something they don't? £5.59 per 6 x 275ml bottles. [*5.0%, Germany*]

Different Vintages

Wines recommended in this book are specific to the vintages indicated. Follow-on vintages might be of a similar quality and character, but are likely to be either better or worse. Wines of real interest are seldom exactly the same from one year to the next. Cheap fruity wines, whether white or red, are often better the younger they are, and the difference between vintages is generally less important for bulk wines produced in hotter countries, but even these will vary in some vintages. The difference in vintage is usually most noticeable in individually crafted wines produced the world over. Don't be put off a wine because it is a different vintage, as you could be missing an even greater treat, but do try a bottle before laying out on a case or two.

LO-COST

STOCK ME AND BUY ONE

This chain of 100 off-licensed supermarkets and superstores is operated by CRS (Co-operative Retail Service), which is currently rebadging them under the Co-operative Pioneer banner. Both facias will exist during the shelf-life of this book (*see* **Co-operative Pioneer** entry, page 47).

LONDIS

STOCK ME AND BUY ONE

Number of stores *1,600*
Opening hours *At least half the shops open for a minimum of fourteen hours a day, seven days a week*
Maximum range *250 wines, 100 beers, 100 spirits*
Alternative methods of payment *Cheque with card*
Local delivery *Most shops do, especially those in villages or rural locations*
Discounts *Most shops offer a discount for quantity, but it's up to the individual retailers, so try haggling*
Other services *Some shops offer sale-or-return terms, and free loan of glasses*

Comment Londis is a symbol group, indeed an award-winning symbol group, receiving the Symbol Group Award in 1991 and the Independent Grocer of the Year award in 1994. The group is obviously doing something right, which probably explains why its total number of shops has increased by some 200 since last year and is due to expand by another 50 over the next twelve months, when other symbol groups are shrinking. It should be explained that no Londis retailer has to stock any Londis wines and spirits, but some 1,250 do.

There is, in fact, a listing agreement whereby each retailer is committed to stock a minimum number of products and, more importantly, to sell all Londis products at the recommended price.

Red Wines

Posta Romana Classic Pinot Noir 1991 Dealul Mare Region, Valea Calugareasca £3.29

(B) Very rich, sweet-ripe strawberry fruit. [*Romania*]

☞ LONDIS'S BEST VALUE RED WINE

Fitou 1994 Les Celliers de Champsbilloux £3.49

(B) Soft, sweet-spicy fruit. [*Languedoc-Roussillon, France*]

Blossom Hill Collection Red NV £3.89

(B) Raspberry fruit aromas followed by an aftertaste of violets make this California's answer to Anjou Rouge. [*California, USA*]

Sutter Home Zinfandel 1993 Napa £4.49

(B) More oomph but less elegance than the Pepperwood Zinfandel (*see* **Budgens**), although it is just as smooth and easy to drink. [*California, USA*]

Palacio De La Vega 1992 Navarra £4.99

(S) Like a smoother, even more coconutty version of Torres Sangre de Toro (*see* **Co-operative Pioneer**). [*Spain*]

Casa Porta Cabernet Sauvignon 1993 Valle del Chachapoal £4.99

Looks as smooth as it smells, but the fruit has an unexpectedly dry, grippy tannin structure, the quality of which is not immediately obvious if the palate is on automatic tasting pilot, but comes out very well with winter-warmer food. [*Chile*]

Orlando RF Cabernet Sauvignon 1992 £5·39
Nicely concentrated fruit with cedary-herbal undertones and a hint of mint. [*Australia*]

Montana Cabernet Sauvignon 1994 £5·49
B Rich, herbaceous, plummy, blackcurranty fruit. [*New Zealand*]

Lindemans Bin 45 Cabernet Sauvignon 1994 £5·99
B Rich, dense, purple-plummy fruit with firm, grippy tannins and fine acidity. [*Australia*]

Wolf Blass Shiraz/Cabernet Sauvignon 'Red Label' 1994 South Australia £6.29
B Fresh, medium-bodied red with a light, elegant, oaky balance and a long finish of very rich fruit. [*Australia*]

Châteauneuf-du-Pape 1995 Les Maîtres Goustiers, Jacques Mousset £7·99
B Sweet-ripe, upfront fruit with a touch of fat spice on the finish make this an unashamed guzzler rather than fully fledged food wine. [*Rhône Valley, France*]

White Wines

Nagyréde Estate Pinot Blanc 1995 Szoloskert Co-operative £3·29
B Fresh, creamy, very breezy fruit with a crisp finish. [*Hungary*]
☞ LONDIS'S BEST VALUE WHITE WINE

Waimanu Premium Dry White Wine NV Corbans **£3·99**

Very ripe, round and easy. Presumably this is predominantly Müller-Thurgau, a grape that Kiwis are far more successful at making generic wines with than the Germans are. [*New Zealand*]

Chapel Hill Chardonnay Barrique Aged 1993 Balatonboglár Estate Bottled **£3·99**

The toasty-oaky fruit is too rich for food, but very satisfying if this wine is consumed on its own. [*Hungary*]

Chardonnay Vin de Pays d'Oc NV Cellier du Grangeon, Londis **£3·99**

Fresh, pineapple fruit makes this wine satisfying to drink on its own, but it has a firm enough structure also to accompany food. [*Languedoc-Roussillon, France*]

Long Mountain Chenin Blanc 1995 Western Cape **£3·99**

B A sweetish dry Chenin that easily beats most Vouvray a pound a bottle more expensive. [*South Africa*]

Cooks Sauvignon Blanc 1995 Gisborne **£4·99**

B Very fresh gooseberry fruits with suck-a-stone finesse. [*New Zealand*]

Orlando RF Chardonnay 1994 **£5·39**

A fresh, rich and easy-drinking wine of crisp, clean fruit. [*Australia*]

Rosé Wines

Blossom Hill Collection White Zinfandel NV Sonoma £4.29

Citrussy aromas and off-dry floral fruit, with a crisp finish and perfumed after-aromas. [*California, USA*]

Sparkling Wines

Seaview Brut NV McLaren Vale £5.99

What makes Seaview so successful is not just its low price and ultra-reliable fresh, zesty style, but the tiny size of the bubbles. [*Australia*]

Lindauer Brut NV £6.99

Tangy-sherbetty, juicy-lime fruit with a fresh, zesty finish that develops a little honey in bottle. [*New Zealand*]

Cuvée Napa by Mumm Brut NV £8.99

Although exactly identical in price with the same wine submitted by Co-operative Pioneer and of a very similar style, this particular shipment definitely showed much fresher, with more intense flavour. When I later realized they were the same wine, I checked the back-up samples only to find they had different lot numbers. The variation is, however, within acceptable limits for bottles of supposedly the same *cuvée* from different shipments, and all bottles of Cuvée Napa benefit from six to nine months further ageing. [*California, USA*]

Champagne André Simon Brut NV NM-243 £10.29

Rich and gentle, easy-drinking fruit with a soft, cushiony mousse of tiny bubbles. [*France*]

Beers

Best Bitter Londis Per pint: £0.56

This nut-brown-coloured brew is the cheapest bitter with some true bitterness. Buy better if you can afford to, but this will do if you cannot. £0.49 per 500ml can. [*3.0%, UK*]

Bavaria Dutch Lager Per pint: £0.64

Bavaria Dutch might seem like a contradiction, but it is not an error, and this is the cleanest, crispest and most flavoured of the cheapest lagers. £5.99 per 12 x 440ml cans. [*3.0%, Lieshout, Holland*]

Bavaria Lager Beer Per pint: £0.68

More perfumed hops than the canned version, making this a softer, more elegant lager for just 3 pence per pint more. Despite its name, Bavaria is brewed in the Netherlands, not Germany. £2.99 per 10 x 25cl bottles. [*3.0%, Netherlands*]

Faxe Premium Danish Export Lager Per pint: £1.13

Like drinking sweet, slightly fizzy water; you have little idea that it contains 5 per cent alcohol, which no doubt explains the success of this litre-sized can at parties. Partygoers should be aware, however, that it has the original ring-pull, which sliced up many a foot in outdoor pools when it first appeared in the 1960s – which was why the current, integral opener was invented. So if you see Faxe at a party, don't dance bare-footed. £1.99 per one-litre can. [*5.0%, Denmark*]

Grolsch Premium Lager Per pint: £1.19

This UK-brewed, canned version has a fine, flowery-hopped aroma, but a softer, less distinctive flavour than the Dutch-brewed bottled version. £1.05 per 500ml can. [*5.0%, UK*]

Beamish Draught Per pint: £1.28

S I always used to think that Beamish was the sweetest of Ireland's three stouts, but it is not – Murphy's is. Beamish is noticeably the smokiest and least creamy of the three, even with the creamy effect of the widget, and has a very distinctive smoky-bitter taste that is as dry as Guinness, although it lacks the toasty, roasted barley substance that gives Guinness such a satisfying mid-palate fill. I like it, however, as a really smoky change. £0.99 per 440ml widgetized can. [*4.2%, Cork, Ireland*]

Brains S.A. Draught Best Bitter Per pint: £1.54

B The perfumed, hoppy aromas and clean, crisp taste (despite the widget) with a touch of bitterness put it on par with John Smith's, but at 15–28 pence per pint more expensive, Brains S.A. Draught only just retains its bronze medal. £1.19 per 440ml widgetized can. [*4.2%, Cardiff, UK*]

Murphy's Draught Irish Stout Per pint: £1.65

S Murphy's is the lightest of the three Irish stouts, and it would not be unfair to describe it as the nearest to Caffrey's, although its smoky-malty aroma gives a far more distinctive edge to its creamy-smoky flavour. Not as dry or as bitter as the other two stouts, it does however fall into the dry, bitter category when tasted in isolation. The bottles used to be less creamy than the cans until Murphy's introduced floating widgets into the latter; now they are both very lightly widgetized. £1.45 per 500ml widgetized bottle. [*4.0%, Ireland/ UK*]

Kilkenny Draught Irish Beer Guinness Per pint: £1.67

This is much better than Guinness Draught Bitter and it is quite different from Caffrey's, being deeper flavoured with a fruitier taste and ripe-yeastiness on the finish. £1.29 per 440ml widgetized can. [*5.0%, County Kilkenny, Ireland*]

Carlsberg Ice Beer Per pint: £1.70

The sharpest, crispest and best of the so-called Ice Beers. £0.99 per 330ml bottle. [*5.6%, Denmark*]

'Old Speckled Hen' Strong Pale Ale Morland Per pint: £1.81

Fresh and tasty, with a characterful maltiness in both the aroma and on the palate, which finishes with the barest hint of smoke. Not as good as the cask-conditioned draught, but what bottled beer is? £1.59 per 500ml bottle. [*5.2%, Oxfordshire, UK*]

Bishops Finger Kentish Strong Ale Shepherd Neame Per pint: £1.81

Taste this side by side with the canned version, and you will realize why the premium charged for bottled beers is well worth paying. Beautifully fresh and crisp with a powerful true-bitter flavour and long, hoppy aftertaste. £1.59 per 500ml bottle. [*5.4%, Kent, England*]

Spitfire Bottle Conditioned Bitter Shepherd Neame
Per pint: £1.81

Ⓖ A great bitter with an elegant fruity-yeasty fullness, delicate bitter-hop flavours and a beautifully dry, understated finish. One bottle of Spitfire tasted was unbelievably fizzy and aggressively tasteless as a result. The sediment looked to be twice the norm, so I can only imagine that it was a faulty batch, as can sometimes happen with a live beer. If you have ever had a similar experience, be advised that Spitfire should not be like that – but buy another bottle to satisfy yourself. £1.59 per 500ml bottle. [*4.7%, Kent, England*]

☞ THE BEST QUALITY BITTER OF THE YEAR

Beck's Per pint: £1.96

This beer is too popular for its own good. Its clean, fresh taste deserves a recommendation, not a medal, at this price point. If you're in a pub and want to be seen drinking a premium beer, why not go for a Bitburger or Budweiser Budvar and show your Beck's-swilling friends you know something they don't? £5.69 per 6 x 275ml bottles. [*5.0%, Germany*]

MARKS & SPENCER

Number of stores *283*
Opening hours *Vary too widely to generalize*
Maximum range *200 wines, 20 beers, 10 spirits*
Alternative methods of payment *Cheque with card, M&S Charge Card and Switch and Delta debit cards*
Delivery *Not provided, although M&S Mail Order will deliver any of its special purchase wines (ask your local store to send you the list, which is updated every three months), and staff will help carry goods to car if requested*
Discounts *12 bottles for the price of 11*
Other services *None*

Comment Not only is M&S prepared food considered *chic* by Parisians, but the branch that outsells every other when it comes to Champagne is the one in Reims. So it's official: even the Champenois appreciate M&S Champagne. Taste its top-of-the-range Cuvée Orpale and you'll see they are not wrong – it's the Best Quality Sparkling Wine of the Year. Chief wine buyer Chris Murphy will be pleased; it's his favourite tipple. For the second year running M&S has collected the Best Quality Red Wine of the Year award and, although 6th is a good position to be in the ranking, this does not accurately reflect M&S's true strength, as the group stocks only own-label beers and therefore cannot rake in anywhere near the amount of beer medals as most other retailers do.

Red Wines

Tempranillo La Mancha NV Wine Selection, St Michael £10.99 (3-litre bag-in-box)

B It might be cheap and it comes in a box, but this is not your average Spanish plonk. Very soft, pristine fruit that is all too easy to drink. [*Spain*]

☞ M&S's Best Value Red Wine

Bulgarian Cabernet Sauvignon 1991 Vinprom Svischtov, St Michael £2.99

Mature blackcurranty fruit on a firm food wine structure. [*Bulgaria*]

Cardillo Rosso di Sicilia 1995 Casa Vinicola Calatrasi, St Michael £3.49

Smooth, medium-bodied with crisp, clean spicy-cherry fruit. [*Italy*]

Domaine Saint-Germain Minervois 1994 St Michael £3.99

Spicy, plummy fruit with a dry tannin finish that demands a juicy loin of lamb. [*Languedoc-Roussillon, France*]

Casa Leona Cabernet Sauvignon 1994 Rapel, St Michael £3.99

B Truly elegant Cabernet with smooth, creamy fruit on the finish. [*Chile*]

Domaine Mandeville Merlot 1995 Vin de Pays d'Oc, St Michael £3.99

Lots of raspberry jam flavour. [*Languedoc-Roussillon, France*]

Merlot Tannat 1995 Juanico, St Michael £3·99

The succulently rich berry fruits stand out at this price point. [*Uruguay*]

Stellenbosch Merlot 1995 St Michael £3·99

Inky colour and rich blackberry flavour followed by an even richer strawberry preserve flavour. [*South Africa*]

Fitou 1994 Caves du Mont Tauch, St Michael £3·99

Sweet, ripe fruit: this may lack the spiciness of other bronze medal Fitou, but it is just as good and as substantial. [*Languedoc-Roussillon, France*]

Domaine Mandeville Syrah 1995 Vin de Pays d'Oc, St Michael £3·99

Big, rich, luscious, purple-plummy fruit. Lovely richness, fine supple tannin structure – so French amid a sea of Oz Shiraz under blind conditions. [*Languedoc-Roussillon, France*]

Peñascal Vino de Mesa Tinto NV Castilla y Leon, St Michael £3·99

If you like picking splinters from between your teeth, then this four-by-two of solid oak is just the wine for you. It's also very instructive for anyone who wants to know the difference between grape tannins and oak tannins. [*Spain*]

Carmen Cabernet Sauvignon 1994 Maipo, St Michael £4·49

It is the excellent acidity, a characteristic often overlooked in red wines, that makes this the ideal accompaniment to M&S beef sandwiches! [*Chile*]

Shiraz Cabernet Bin 505 1994 Southcorp Wines, St Michael £4·49

(B) Rich and tasty red made in a fresh, easy-drinking, fruit-driven style. [*South Australia*]

Kaituna Hills Cabernet Merlot 1994 Averill Estate, St Michael £4·99

(B) Typical Kiwi-herbaceous Cabernet aroma and very fresh, gluggy but elegant blackcurrant fruit. [*Marlborough, New Zealand*]

Trapiche Malbec Oak Cask Reserve 1992 St Michael £4·99

(S) No pretensions here: just a big mouthful of gloriously rich, creamy-oaky fruit and a long, smooth oaky finish. [*Argentina*]

Pinot Noir Vin de Pays d'Oc 1994 Domaine Virginie, St Michael £4·99

(B) This is a much firmer version of Pinot Noir than all the sub-£4 medal-winners in this book, and gets its bronze as a food wine: the others lose their succulence with a meal, whereas this gains in succulence. [*Languedoc-Roussillon, France*]

Shiraz South Eastern Australia 1993 Lindemans, St Michael £4·99

(S) More fruit-driven than most Australian Shiraz, this has lashings of fresh, tasty fruit with rich, creamy-fruit on the finish. [*Australia*]

Honey Tree Shiraz Cabernet 1995 Rosemount Estate, St Michael £4·99

(S) Although the bottle and label do not matter in terms of quality or value, it is nice to have something that looks classy on the table, and the extraordinarily minute and understated label on this wine does indeed look chic. In addition to this, the wine is very silky, with creamy-smooth fruit that hints of Old World Syrah as much as New World Shiraz, which should be irresistible for some. [*Australia*]

Gran Calesa Costers del Segre 1991 Raimat, St Michael £5.50

B Good typicity of fruit and provenance, showing some browning at the edge, accurately reflecting the mellow-matured, oaky style. Rich, soft, serious blackcurrant fruit. [*Spain*]

Carmen Cabernet Sauvignon Reserve 1994 Maipo, St Michael £5.99

B Not obvious, but builds into a very tasty red wine with food. [*Chile*]

Canyon Road Cabernet Sauvignon 1994 St Michael £5.99

S A California wine made by an Aussie – resident, not flying – this delicious Cabernet has ultra-smooth, elegantly rich, creamy fruit of some minty-oaky complexity and a beautifully smooth, long, oaky aftertaste. [*California, USA*]

Chianti Classico 1994 Basilica Cafaggio, St Michael £5.99

B Sweet, spicy fruit. [*Italy*]

Rosemount Estate Shiraz 1994 St Michael £5.99

G Lovely creamy-perfumed, sweet-spicy fruit with a touch of easy-drinking jamminess on the finish; a lot of elegance and finesse for the price. [*Australia*]

Primitivo di Manduria 1993 Giordano, St Michael £6.99

(G) This is the first great Primitivo I have ever tasted. Although this grape is in fact the Zinfandel, it has never produced a wine that can be compared, either in quality or character, with the best California Zinfandels. This big, rich, oaky wine certainly compares with the very best West Coast Zin, but with more of the weight, size, class and complexity of a great Barolo. Mega-delicious! [*Italy*]

Saints Cabernet Merlot 1994 Montana £6.99

(S) Lovely herbaceous aroma, silky-smooth fruit and dry-oak finish. Great food wine. [*Hawkes Bay, New Zealand*]

Fleurie Cru du Beaujolais 1995 Cellier des Samsons, St Michael £7.99

(B) Fresh, elegant, flowery fruit of some substance. [*Burgundy, France*]

Capel Vale Shiraz 1993 Western Australia, St Michael £9.99

(G) So big, fat, ripe and mellow, with a complete and wonderfully satisfying flavour of blackcurranty and blackberry fruit, an impressively smooth but nicely dry finish, and a touch of French pepperiness on the finish. This wine is not unlike an Australian's attempt at a Cornas. It definitely has an Antipodean feel, but is more fruit-driven than the creamy-cedary-spicy oak-driven style that typifies so much Australian Shiraz, wonderful though they are. [*Australia*]

Rosemount McLaren Vale Shiraz 1993 St Michael
£9.99

𝒮 So very soft that it slips down the back of the throat before you realize what's happening. A luscious, incredibly succulent Shiraz with a beautiful jammy richness that is much better consumed on its own than with food. [*Australia*]

James Halliday Coonawarra Cabernet Sauvignon 1992 St Michael £11.99

𝒢 Very rich, yet so elegant; and if I saw the label, that is exactly what I would expect from James Halliday. Readers can be confident that his name on a label is synonymous with elegance. The lovely, long, gentle, dry-oak finish makes this superb with food. [*Australia*]

☞ THE BEST QUALITY RED WINE OF THE YEAR

Brunello di Montalcino 1990 Val di Suga, St Michael
£12.99

𝒮 Extraordinary finesse for such huge, fat, spicy-plummy fruit. [*Italy*]

White Wines

Vin de Pays du Gers 1995 Patrick Azcué, St Michael
£2.99

A very fresh and thirst-quenching crisp dry white. [*South-west France*]

Vin de Pays du Gers NV Wine Selection, St Michael
£11.99 (3-litre bag-in-box)

Just as attractive and thirst-quenching, this box wine is

softer and more perfumed than its bottled version. [*South-west France*]

Conca de Barbera 1995 Bodegas Concavins, St Michael £3·29

Ⓑ Coconutty nose with crisp, tight-packed fruit on the palate and a hint of peaches. [*Spain*]

Vin de Pays des Côtes de Gascogne 1995 Patrick Azcué, St Michael £3·49

Ⓢ A good spritz gives this fresh, zippy, zingy crisp white wine an electrifying lift on the finish. [*South-west France*]

☞ M&S's Best Value White Wine

Casa Leona Chardonnay 1995 Rapel, St Michael £3·99

Very rich fruit. Too rich, in fact, to go with food, which will only detract, but makes a satisfying mouthful on its own. [*Chile*]

McGregor Chenin Blanc 1996 KWV, St Michael £3·99

Ⓑ Definitely dry, but the sherbetty freshness of its fruit makes it very easy to quaff. [*South Africa*]

Australian Medium Dry NV Lindemans, St Michael £3·99

Ⓑ Typical Oz buttery fruit, but with a spicy edge. [*Australia*]

Roussanne Vin de Pays d'Oc 1995 Domaine Virginie, St Michael £3·99

Delicious clean, ripe fruit with a nice hint of pineapple and good acidity. Only spoiled by the ubiquitous cool-fermentation aroma of peardrops. [*Languedoc-Roussillon, France*]

Frascati Superiore 1995 Azienda Vinicola, St Michael £4.49

Fresh, sherbetty fruit of some real depth, which is surprising for Frascati, and a truly dry finish that does not end like a damp squid. [*Italy*]

Kaituna Hills Chardonnay Semillon 1995 Averill Estate, St Michael £4.49

B The Sauvignon-like character of fruit in this wine is probably due to its Semillon content, as the Kiwis often use this variety to turbocharge their own Sauvignon Blanc. [*Gisborne, New Zealand*]

Gold Label Chardonnay Vin de Pays d'Oc 1995 Domaine Virginie, St Michael £4.49

An Aussie had a hand in making this wine, and from the wealth of coconutty aromas he probably used a fair bit of American oak in the process. [*Languedoc-Roussillon, France*]

Semillon Chardonnay Bin 501 1995 Southcorp Wines, St Michael £4.49

Fresh and tangy with a hint of lime on the finish. [*Australia*]

Carmen Chardonnay Semillon Oak Aged 1995 St Michael £4.99

B Full and flavoursome, yet fresh, crisp fruit. [*Maipo, Chile*]

Kaituna Hills Chardonnay 1995 Averill Estate, St Michael £4.99

B Very fresh, fruity Chardonnay with a fine zesty finish. [*Gisborne, New Zealand*]

Johannisberg Riesling 1995 Klosterhof, St Michael £4·99

Classic, if basic, Rheingau Riesling with a touch of yeasty fullness. [*Germany*]

Zell Castle Riesling Spätlese 1995 Klosterhof, St Michael £4·99

Very fresh, clean, youthful apricot fruit. [*Germany*]

Kaituna Hills Sauvignon Blanc 1995 Averill Estate, Marlborough, St Michael £4·99

S Very expressive gooseberry fruit full of suck-a-stone freshness. Try this rich, clean, pristine wine with fresh asparagus. [*New Zealand*]

Honey Tree Semillon Chardonnay 1995 Rosemount Estate, St Michael £4·99

B Luscious, crisp, lemony-pineapple fruit with a very fresh, smooth finish. [*Australia*]

Domaine Mandeville Viognier 1995 Vin de Pays d'Oc, St Michael £4·99

B More of a food-wine style than the other Viogniers tasted, yet still very fresh and a delight to drink on its own. [*Languedoc-Roussillon, France*]

Canyon Road Chardonnay 1994 St Michael £5·99

Nicely fat, fresh, rich Chardonnay that well deserves its recommendation, but not in the same class as Canyon Road's Cabernet. [*California, USA*]

Petit Chablis 1995 CVC, St Michael £6·99

Good basic Chardonnay, but it is difficult get a medal at Chablis prices. [*Burgundy, France*]

Saints Chardonnay 1995 Montana, St Michael £6.99

(B) Upfront coconutty aroma dominates this wine, but it has lovely ripe fruit underneath, and thus deserves a bronze as far as American oak freaks will be concerned. [*Gisborne, New Zealand*]

Rosemount Estate Chardonnay 1995 Hunter Valley, St Michael £6.99

(B) Although this M&S own-label version is indeed in the same elegant, understated, easy-to-drink Oz-Mâcon-type style as the regular Rosemount label, I got the impression that it was just a tad fresher and more sherbetty, although this might just be because they were eight wines apart under blind conditions. [*Australia*]

Pouilly Fumé 1995 Domaine Mathilde de Favray, St Michael £7.99

(B) Another Pouilly Fumé with the intensity of a Sancerre. [*Loire, France*]

Rosemount Orange Vineyard Chardonnay 1994 St Michael £9.99

(S) Not in the same class as the 1993 – it has neither the concentration nor the acidity – and yet it is £3 a bottle more expensive. At £9.99 this cannot be a gold medal winner, but its much softer, more succulent fruit might be appreciated by a wider audience and certainly deserves a silver. [*Australia*]

Rosé Wines

Rosé de Valencia 1995 Vicente Gandia, St Michael £3.49

Fresh and clean, with more flavour than most cheap rosés. [*Spain*]

Sparkling Wines

Cava Brut NV Sevisa, St Michael £4.99

Fresh, zesty, with citrus aromas and excellent acidity. [*Spain*]

Bluff Hill Brut NV Averill Estate, Marlborough, St Michael £6.99

The crisp, elegant, lemony-lime fruit in this wine will get richer and more exotic in bottle. [*New Zealand*]

Australian Chardonnay Blanc de Blancs Brut 1993 Seppelt Great Western Winery, St Michael £7.99

Very elegant Aussie fizz of serious quality. [*South-east Australia*]

Champagne Veuve de Medts Brut NV St Michael £13.99

Firm mousse, good richness of fruit for the price, and will improve with an extra nine to twelve months' bottle-age. [*France*]

Champagne Oudinot Brut 1989 St Michael £14.99

This is so fresh and easy-going that it is difficult to believe it is already almost seven years old. Not truly *brut*, this will be ideal for those who do not like their

Champagne too dry, and the generous *dosage* will slow down the wine's maturation even further, so you can confidently keep it another three or four years in the knowledge that it will only get better, eventually becoming a silver medal contender. [*France*]

Champagne Cuvée Orpale Blanc de Blancs Brut 1985 Union Champagne £22.50

(G) Heavenly! I cannot think of another Champagne of a similar style (elegance, pristine fruit, great finesse) and price that comes anywhere near the quality of this *cuvée*. [*France*]

☞ THE BEST QUALITY SPARKLING WINE OF THE YEAR

Fortified Wines

10 Years Old Port NV Morgan Brothers, St Michael £9.99

(S) Lovely deep, penetrating flavour of spiced-liquorice fruit, which fans out into a beautiful peacock's tail finish. [*Portugal*]

20 Years Old Port NV Morgan Brothers, St Michael £14.99

(S) Almost the liqueur-like texture of a 30 Years Old tawny. The fact that this deserves a silver medal at one-and-a-half times the price of M&S's 10 Years Old tawny demonstrates the great depth, richness and finesse of this wine. If you want to spoil yourself this Christmas, settle down to an inexhaustible supply of freshly roasted chestnuts, a bottle of this exquisite tawny and a sensibly sized, normal wine glass from which to drink it. [*Portugal*]

Beers

Schonbrau Pilsner Lager St Michael Per pint: £0.76

Very clean telly beer. £2.69 per 4 x 500ml cans. [*3.5%, UK*]

Wethered's Draught Bitter St Michael Per pint: £1.13

Not a bitter-drinker's brew, but definitely a winner for those who like sweet, creamy, ultra-soft beers. This is rather like a lighter, sweeter, creamier version of Caffrey's. Indeed, put the two together and Caffrey's actually tastes dry in comparison – now that's what I call real Celtic magic. £3.49 per 4 x 440ml widgetized cans. [*3.8%, UK*]

Original Premium Pilsener Lager St. Pauli, St Michael Per pint: £1.13

Soft, easy and mellow, yet fresh. £3.99 per 4 x 500ml cans. [*4.9%, Germany*]

Bière d'Alsace Brasserie Fischer, M&S Per pint: £1.13

Last year this was mellow, this year it's citric, but clean and sharp enough both years to deserve recommending above the dross that exists in very similar-looking 25cl bottles. £4.99 per 10 x 25cl bottles. [*5.0%, France*]

Premium German Pilsener Lager St Michael Per pint: £1.13

An unpretentious lager that's fuller and richer than most at this price point. £4.99 per 10 x 25cl bottles. [*4.9%, Germany*]

Traditional Yorkshire Bitter St Michael Per pint: £1.47

Not as smoky as last year's brew, but still a

distinctive bottled beer with a truly dry, satisfying taste and crisp, bitter finish. Made by Paul Theakston's star-performing Black Sheep Brewery. £1.29 per 500ml bottle. [*4.4%, UK*]

Caledonian 80/- Export Ale St Michael Per pint: £1.47

A classic as far as sweet-toothed beer lovers are concerned, Caledonian 80/- is marked by the perfumed-hop aromas that drift lazily through its clean, sweet-ripe, floral taste. £1.29 per 500ml bottle. [*4.4%, Edinburgh, UK*]

Alsace Gold Fischer, St Michael Per pint: £1.72

Perfumed hop aromas, smooth tasting with citric undertones, in a traditional flip-top bottle that can be resealed if you cannot manage the entire contents (sad, considering the capacity!). £3.99 per 4 x 33cl bottles. [*6.5%, France*]

Australian Sparkling Ale Coopers Brewery, South Australia, St Michael Per pint: £1.74

You're not supposed to take the 'Sparkling' attribute too seriously, although like any bottle-conditioned beer, this has a noticeable fizz. A real, yeasty-fruitiness and a ripe, round, yeasty-hoppy flavour. This improves so much with bottle-age that you would not go wrong if you treated the 'sell by' date as a 'do not open before' date. £1.15 per 375ml bottle. [*5.9%, Australia*]

MORRISONS

Number of stores *81*
Opening hours *Mondays–Saturdays 8a.m.–8p.m., Sundays 10a.m.–5p.m.*
Maximum range *450 wines, 350 beers, 250 spirits*
Alternative methods of payment *Cheque with card, Access, Switch*
Local delivery *None*
Discounts *None*
Other services *Free loan of glasses*

Comment I welcome Morrisons to *SuperBooze* for the first time. Not only am I impressed by many of the wines that this group stocks, but I also enjoy its stores, which have wide carriageways and different departments dressed up to look like shop fronts. Stuart Purdie is a one-man buying department, just as Tony Finnerty is at Budgens and, like him, pretty damn good at it too. This group has a strong following of very loyal customers, as I found out touting a Morrisonsless *SuperBooze* last year.

Red Wines

Soveral Tinto NV Vinho de Mesa £2.49

I know this is a cheap wine, but does the label really have to be so shoddy? I wonder how many shoppers have not purchased Soveral Tinto because they would not be seen dead with such an obviously cheap wine on their table? It's a pity, because it contains some really good fruit, yet still retains the peppery typicity that regular consumers of Portuguese red appreciate.

Another good red to accompany a piping-hot bowl of winter-warming stew. [*Portugal*]

Cellier La Chouf NV Minervois £2.75

More fruit than most at this price, but still has authentic French food-wine structure. [*Languedoc-Roussillon, France*]

Winter Hill 1995 Vin de Pays de l'Aude £2.99

If you've wondered why and how so many wines are developing anglicized names such as Winter Hill, the why is very logical: to attract English-speaking customers who might not know what a *vin de pays* is, let alone anything about the *vin de pays* in question. As to how they acquire their particular anglicized name, each has a different story and this just happens to be where the importer lives. It's a sturdy red made by modern technology without being Ozzified. [*Languedoc-Roussillon, France*]

Vin de Crete 1995 Kourtaki £3.15

B A smooth, full-bodied red that is well made with clean, nicely focused flavour and beautifully presented with a nicely understated label, Vin de Crete will probably bring home happier memories than most of the wines tasted while on holiday in Crete itself. [*Greece*]

Cabernet Sauvignon Special Reserve 1986 Rovit £3.15

B Rich, ripe, ultra-fruity Ribena-like flavour in a ten-year-old Romanian wine must be worth a medal. [*Romania*]

Eclisse NV Vino da Tavola di Puglia £3.29

B Soft and succulent with oodles of pure fruit flavour. [*Italy*]

La Source Cabernet Sauvignon 1993 Vin de Pays d'Oc £3.35

Smooth Cabernet fruit in the firm grip of enough supple tannins to accompany a wide range of savoury dishes. [*Languedoc-Roussillon, France*]

Pinot Noir Special Reserve 1990 Valea Mieilor Vineyards, Dealul Mare £3.39

(S) Succulent, creamy-ripe fruit with more than a hint of real Pinot Noir and a very creamy-sweet finish. [*Romania*]

☞ MORRISONS' BEST VALUE RED WINE

Stambolovo Merlot 1990 The Bulgarian Vintners' Reserve £3.55

(B) Although there's no chance of recognizing any Merlot character beneath all the spicy-dry coconutty oak on this wine, cheap Merlots are so lacking in richness that this is certainly a bronze medal winner as far as four-by-two lovers are concerned. [*Bulgaria*]

Château Jougrand Saint Chinian 1994 Cuvée Réservée à la Gastronomie £3.59

(B) Long, warm and spicy with good grip on the finish, this wine has substantially more body and flavour than any other Saint Chinian at this price or cheaper. [*Languedoc-Roussillon, France*]

Blossom Hill Collection Red NV £3.69

(B) Raspberry fruit aromas followed by an aftertaste of violets make this California's answer to Anjou Rouge. [*California, USA*]

Sutter Home Zinfandel 1993 Napa £4.05

(B) More oomph but less elegance than the

Pepperwood Zinfandel (*see* **Budgens**), although it is just as smooth and easy to drink. [*California, USA*]

Glen Ellen Merlot 1993 Proprietor's Reserve, Sonoma £4.29

B Cream-oaky richness of fruit. [*California, USA*]

Uggiano Chianti Classico 1992 £4.39

G A Chianti of unbelievable quality for its price, this wine is currently dominated by its dry, creamy-oak finish, but the intensity of fruit that comes back on the aftertaste indicates the even greater heights it will reach if cellared for another two or three years. [*Italy*]

Château Saint Galier 1993 Graves £4.85

B Not an obvious, upfront wine, but one that builds slowly in the glass, making it interesting on its own, but with enough supple tannin structure to accompany food. [*Bordeaux, France*]

Lindemans Bin 45 Cabernet Sauvignon 1994 £4.99

B Rich, dense, purple-plummy fruit with firm grippy tannins and fine acidity. [*Australia*]

Uggiano Chianti Riserva 1990 £6.15

G Utterly delicious! How many times can you say that about a Chianti? Well, this one truly is, with its lush, mellow fruit and dry, creamy-oak finish – and it's a food wine too. [*Italy*]

Willamette Valley Vineyards 1994 Oregon Pinot Noir £7.49

G An outstanding balance between huge richness of flavour, elegant style and purity of varietal fruit. [*USA*]

Jamiesons Run 1992 Coonawarra £7.65

(B) Very smooth, long and oaky. [*Australia*]

White Wines

Entre Rios NV Chilean White Wine £2.99

(B) Fuller and richer than most of its French namesake, Entre Deux Mers. [*Chile*]

Chapel Hill Chardonnay Oaked NV Balatonboglár Estate Bottled £3.05

(B) Ozzified oaky Chardonnay with fresh, buttery fruit. [*Hungary*]

Uggiano Orvieto Classico 1994 £3.19

(S) Very fresh, zippy-sherbetty fruit with a refreshing hint of spritz on the palate. If Morrisons' wine buyer is not careful, he's likely to give Italian wine a good name! [*Italy*]

☞ MORRISONS' BEST VALUE WHITE WINE

Eclisse NV Vino da Tavola di Puglia £3.29

(B) Rich, ripe and ultra-fruity. [*Italy*]

Entre Deux Mers Sec 1994 G.V.A. Ets Fleury £3.39

(B) Very fresh, breezy fruit with a crisp yet soft finish. [*Bordeaux, France*]

Devil's Rock Riesling 1994 St. Ursula £3.49

Clean, dry, lemony Riesling fruit. [*Pfälz, Germany*]

Domaine du Rey 1994 Vin de Pays des Côtes de Gascogne £3.69

(G) Côtes de Gascogne is a predictable, if refreshing,

tangy-dry white wine, but no one could have imagined the gentle ripeness of fruit in this wine. A tip-top Côtes de Gascogne if ever I've tasted one. [*South-west France*]

La Source Chardonnay 1995 Vin de Pays d'Oc £3.69
Fresh, elegant, well-made Chardonnay. [*Languedoc-Roussillon, France*]

Glen Ellen Chardonnay 1994 Proprietor's Reserve, Sonoma £4.29
The Chardonnay in this wine is just beginning to go toasty with a smooth oakiness on the finish, and should be really toasty-oaky by Christmas. [*California, USA*]

Preiss-Zimmer Gewurztraminer 1994 Vin d'Alsace Tradition £5.29
Classic lychee fruit laced with pungent spice. [*France*]

Rosé Wines

La Source Syrah Rosé 1995 Vin de Pays d'Oc £3.35
Very fresh, clean and easy to drink, which might not sound much, but it's darn near a miracle as far as inexpensive rosé is concerned. Hell, it's a miracle even for an expensive rosé! [*Languedoc-Roussillon, France*]

Sparkling Wines

Champagne Nicole d'Aurigny Réserve Brut NV £9.49
Fresh, elegant, easy-drinking Champagne at this price must be worth a medal. [*France*]

Beers

Ceres Royal Export Per pint: £0.85

Clean and fresh with some malty richness. £2.99 per 4 x 500ml cans. [*5.8%, Denmark*]

Bière d'Alsace Premium Strength French Lager, Morrisons Per pint: £0.91

Decent, sharp, 25cl lager-style beer. £3.99 per 10 x 25cl bottles. [*4.9%, France*]

Faxe Premium Danish Export Lager Per pint: £1.13

Like drinking sweet, slightly fizzy water; you have little idea that it contains 5 per cent alcohol, which no doubt explains the success of this litre-sized can at parties. Party-goers should be aware, however, that it has the original ring-pull, which sliced up many a foot in outdoor pools when it appeared in the 1960s – which was why the current, integral opener was invented. So if you see Faxe at a party, don't dance bare-footed. £1.99 per one-litre can. [*5.0%, Denmark*]

Caledonian 70/- Amber Ale Caledonian Brewery Per pint: £1.35

A definite bronze medal for those who like sweetish beers, this has a clean malty taste dominated by peppery-hop aromas and a touch of Mediterranean herbal-scrub. £1.19 per 500ml bottle. [*3.8%, Edinburgh, UK*]

Marston's Pedigree Bitter Per pint: £1.49

Classic coppery colour with a smooth, dry complex taste highlighted by perfumed hoppy aromas. £1.49 per 568ml bottle. [*4.5%, Burton-on-Trent, UK*]

Merrimans Old Fart Merrimans Brewery
Per pint: £1.53

A smart label for a not too gassy, peppery-hopped brew that should be bottle-conditioned. Making this a live beer would add a ripe, yeasty fullness and really get the Old Farts going. £1.35 per 500ml bottle. [*5.0%, Yorkshire, UK*]

Black Sheep Ale Paul Theakston Per pint: £1.53

G Made by Paul Theakston, whose family brewery is now part of Scottish & Newcastle. He alone was determined to maintain an independent status, hence the name Black Sheep. This is classy, distinctive, soft and yet completely dry, with a delicious nutty-hoppy complexity. Although there was a time when M&S's own-label version was better than the original (smokier, with a more mellow bitterness), they are almost identical this year – but why doesn't Paul Theakston market a bottle-conditioned version? £1.35 per 500ml bottle. [*4.4%, Yorkshire, UK*]

☞ THE BEST VALUE BITTER OF THE YEAR

Bombardier Premium Bitter Charles Wells
Per pint: £1.58

Has a good bitter finish, but many will find its strangely liquorous texture somewhat incongruous. £1.39 per 500ml bottle. [*4.3%, Bedford, UK*]

Kilkenny Draught Irish Beer Guinness Per pint: £1.61

B This is much better than Guinness Draught Bitter and it is quite different from Caffrey's, being deeper flavoured with a fruitier taste and ripe-yeastiness on the finish. £4.99 per 4 x 440ml widgetized cans. [*5.0%, County Kilkenny, Ireland*]

Deuchars Export Strength IPA India Pale Ale Caledonian Brewery Per pint: £1.65

(S) Saturated with malty-hoppy aromas with intriguing smoky-malt wisps drifting through. Arguably the best quality beer in the pale ale tasting, but is it pale ale, let alone IPA? £1.45 per 500ml bottle. [*4.4%, Edinburgh, UK*]

Marston's Oyster Stout Bottle Conditioned Head Brewers Choice Per pint: £1.65

Very smooth and easy drinking, but lacks the intensity, bitterness and complexity of a great stout. As it's bottle-conditioned, I'm going to try ageing it until next year to see if that makes any significant difference. Until then, however, this brew deserves recommending, but not a medal. £1.45 per 500ml bottle. [*4.5%, Burton-on-Trent, UK*]

Marston's India Export Pale Ale Head Brewers Choice Per pint: £1.69

(S) Interesting to match this with Tesco's own-label IPA from the same brewery: the CO_2 content must be very similar, as they feel identical in the mouth, but this brew has more citrussy richness. £1.49 per 500ml bottle. [*5.5%, Burton-on-Trent, UK*]

Waggle Dance Traditional Honey Beer Vaux Breweries Per pint: £1.69

(S) Soft, full, luscious ale with perfumed-hop aromas, clean, off-dry malty taste and a crisp finish. Apparently named after the dance honey bees execute when they have located nectar, and if you drink enough Waggle Dance, you'll believe it. £1.49 per 550ml bottle. [*5.0%, Sunderland, UK*]

6X Export Wadworth Per pint: £1.69

I do not believe anyone can enjoy the almost salty richness of sour, sultana-malt taste in this beer, but 6X is so popular that I include it for those who obviously do. £1.49 per 500ml bottle. [*5.0%, Devizes, UK*]

Bishops Finger Kentish Strong Ale Shepherd Neame Per pint: £1.76

S Taste this against the canned version and you will realize why the premium charged for bottled beers is well worth paying. Beautifully fresh and crisp with a powerful true-bitter flavour and long, hoppy aftertaste. £1.55 per 500ml bottle. [*5.4%, Kent, UK*]

'Old Speckled Hen' Strong Pale Ale Morland Per pint: £1.76

B Fresh and tasty with a characterful maltiness in both the aroma and on the palate, which finishes with the barest hint of smoke. Not as good as the cask-conditioned draught, but what bottled beer is? £1.55 per 500ml bottle. [*5.2%, Oxfordshire, UK*]

Spitfire Bottle Conditioned Bitter Shepherd Neame Per pint: £1.76

G A great bitter with an elegant fruity-yeasty fullness, delicate bitter-hop flavours and a beautifully dry, understated finish. One bottle of Spitfire tasted was unbelievably fizzy and aggressively tasteless as a result. The sediment looked to be twice the norm, so I can only imagine that it was a faulty batch, as can sometimes happen with a live beer. If you have ever had a similar experience, be advised that Spitfire should not be like that – but buy another bottle to satisfy yourself. £1.55 per 500ml bottle. [*4.7%, Kent, UK*]

☞ THE BEST QUALITY BITTER OF THE YEAR

PLYMCO

A group of forty superstores, supermarkets and late-night shops in the Torbay-Cornwall area that belong to the Plymouth & South Devon Co-operative Society. Plymco stores stock most of the Co-op wines and beers tasted, plus a significant range of independently purchased products. Please see the main **Co-op** entry (page 38) for recommendations.

PRESTO

Part of the Argyll group, Presto has 170 stores, all of which sell exactly the same wines as its big sister chain Safeway – although the range of what you can actually buy in each outlet is narrower owing to the smaller size of these typically local, supermarket-type stores. Please see the **Safeway** entry (page 120) for recommendations.

SAFEWAY

National Supermarket of the Year
Number of stores *370*
Opening hours *Monday-Saturday 8.30a.m.–8p.m. (some stores open until 10p.m.), Sunday 10a.m.–4p.m.*
Maximum range *380 wines, 149 beers, 150 spirits*
Alternative methods of payment *Cheque with card, Switch and Delta debit cards, Access, Visa*
Local delivery *Not provided, but will help carry goods to car if requested*
Discounts *A 5 per cent discount on a case of any wine*
Other services *A glass service in some stores, occasional in-store tastings*

Comment Put to the blind test, Safeway came out well ahead of the rest of the national pack. Only Booths challenged Safeway's supremacy, and darned if I could tell which one really came out on top. I was just happy to discover one of them to be a regional group, which enabled me to split the decision. It's the sheer number of qualifying wines and beers that makes Safeway's result so remarkable, and the *National Supermarket of the Year* award is a just tribute to the hard work and enthusiasm of this supermarket's indefatigable chief buyer, Liz Robertson MW.

Red Wines

Côtes du Lubéron 1995 Cellier de Marrenon, Safeway £3.29

If you're into Hooch, Two Dogs and all that stuff, but cannot find a red wine you like, then try this, because it tastes like spicy lemonade to me! [*Rhône Valley, France*]

Tocornal Chilean Cabernet-Malbec NV Central Valley £3·49

Smooth and fruity with silky-oak on the finish. [*Chile*]

☞ SAFEWAY'S BEST VALUE RED WINE

Romanian Pinot Noir Special Reserve 1993 Dealul Mare, Safeway £3·49

Elegant Pinot fruit. [*Romania*]

Landskroon Cinsaut Shiraz 1995 Paarl £3·59

Lots of raspberry jam richness with a clean, non-cloying finish. [*South Africa*]

Chilean Cabernet Sauvignon 1995 Lontue Region, Safeway £3·79

Creamy-fresh grippy Cabernet fruit. [*Chile*]

The Bulgarian Vintners' Merlot Aged in Oak 1995 Rousse Region £3·79

Far more fruit than Bulgarian Vintners' Stambolovo Merlot, yet just as much oak. To achieve this in a wine barely six months old illustrates how contrived it is, but it is *brilliantly* contrived, and with so much dross in the sub-£4 Merlot category it must be a medal winner. [*Bulgaria*]

Chianti 1994 Rocca Delle Macie Castellina, Safeway £3·79

Fresh, tasty, tangy fruit of very good typicity for the price. [*Italy*]

Zagara Nero d'Avola 1995 Vino da Tavola di Sicilia £3·99

Made by flying Aussie MW Kym Milne, who

made his name at Villa Maria in Auckland, New Zealand – so it seems natural he should team up with Rebecca Salmond, the winemaker at Pleasant Valley, another Auckland winery, to make a wine with electrifying acidity for a red, as fresh acidity is one of Kiwi wine's hallmarks. It would not work, however, if there were not enough flavour and substance to back up the acidity. Try ageing it for a year or two for a real treat. [*Italy*]

Domaine de Picheral Merlot 1995 Vin de Pays d'Oc £3·99

A deep colour with a very full and tasty flavour and good grippy tannins on the finish. An organic wine. [*Languedoc-Roussillon, France*]

La Baume Cuvée Australe 1994 Vin de Pays d'Oc £3·99

(B) The dry tannin structure belies the richness and depth of this wine. Classic French food-wine structure with a touch of Oz wizardry. [*Languedoc-Roussillon, France*]

Bin No. 60 Shiraz Ruby Cabernet 1995 H. G. Brown £3·99

(S) Just a hint of chewy, blood-orange fruit coming through from the Ruby Cabernet, but the creamy-sweet Shiraz eventually dominates. [*Australia*]

Valdepeñas Reserva Aged in Oak 1989 Bodegas Felix Solis, Safeway £3·99

(B) I thought this was a bit rustic at first, which is why it missed a silver medal by a whisker, but it has a lovely, smooth, coffee-oak finish and a creamy-fruity, coffee-oak aftertaste. [*Spain*]

Fiuza Merlot 1994 Vinho Regional Ribatejo £4·49

Persistent and tangy, berry fruit flavours, with ripe, creamy acidity on the finish. Made by Peter Bright, a resident (rather than flying) Australian winemaker who has long pioneered positive fruit in Portuguese wines. [*Portugal*]

Simonsvlei Wynkelder Pinotage Reserve 1995 Paarl £4·49

Ultra-modern Pinotage with smooth, well-focused fruit underpinned by exceptionally smooth, elegant oak. [*South Africa*]

Simonsvlei Wynkelder Shiraz Reserve 1994 Paarl £4·49

So distinctively spicy on the nose that some will positively dislike this wine, but others will love it, and it has nice dry tannins to balance the richness. [*South Africa*]

Stonybrook Cabernet Sauvignon 1993 California £4·99

Very elegant wine with ultra-smooth, creamy-oaky fruit. [*USA*]

Breakaway Grenache Shiraz 1994 South Australia £4·99

A lovely balance between succulent fruit, elegantly smooth texture and genuinely dry style. [*Australia*]

Claret Aged in Oak NV Etienne Lalande, Safeway £4·99

Well-oaked with a long, fruity finish and nice dry tannins giving grip on the finish. [*Bordeaux, France*]

Rosemount Estate Shiraz Cabernet 1995 £5·29

An easy-to-drink red with oodles of fresh, uncomplicated, delightful jammy-fruit. [*Australia*]

Tenuta San Vito Chianti 1994 £5·49

An uncomplicated fresh and fruity, organically made Chianti. [*Italy*]

Fetzer Vineyards Zinfandel 1993 Mendocino £5·49

A definite bronze for those who like their Zinfandel spread between two planks of oak. [*California, USA*]

La Cuvée Mythique 1993 Vin de Pays d'Oc £5·99

The oak has really intensified since last year, billowing out big coconutty aromas that under blind conditions are more reminiscent of American oak than the French Allier claimed on the back label. The extra year has also added a mellow richness to the fruit. Lovely tannin structure for food. [*Languedoc-Roussillon, France*]

Hardys Barossa Valley Cabernet Sauvignon Merlot 1993 £5·99

Gets its medal despite being so contrived, or because it is so *cleverly* contrived: very oaky nose, lots of very ripe fruit, with an almost Spanish mid-palate mellow-oakiness, followed by fresh coconut on the finish. [*Australia*]

Bankside Shiraz 1993 Hardys, Padthaway Clare Valley £5·99

Elegant, creamy-cedary fruit with a firmer finish than the 1992 (*see* **Somerfield**); however, both wines are very similar in pure quality terms, so it's a matter of which style you prefer. This will go better with food, and will soften over the next couple of years. [*Australia*]

Faustino V Reserva 1991 Rioja £6.89

B Classic Rioja. [*Spain*]

Hardys Coonawarra Cabernet Sauvignon 1993 £7.99

S Smoky complexity, firm structure and fine acidity help to make this a food wine *par excellence.* [*Australia*]

White Wines

Bordeaux Blanc Sec Aged in Oak 1995 Union Prodiffu Landerrouat, Safeway £3.19

B The 1994 will still be drinking well by Christmas 1996, and the 1995 is an even better wine. Buy a few bottles and drink it while it is still fresh and Sauvignon-driven, with just a delicate touch of oak lingering in the background, then follow the development of this wine as it trades crispness for a mellow-ripeness, as the Sauvignon gives way to Semillon and bottle-maturity brings out the oak, yet still retains the freshness. [*France*]

Viña Malea Viura Lightly Oak Aged 1995 Vino de la Tierra Manchuela £3.29

S Very fresh, zippy, zesty, zingy fruit with a touch of oak. [*Spain*]

Moscato d'Asti 1995 Le Monferrine £3.29

G Not a fully sparkling Asti, but one with a very prominent spritz; its aroma and lusciously sweet fruit are as fresh and clean as driven snow. It is very difficult to imagine anyone not being totally besotted by this wine. [*Italy*]

☞ SAFEWAY'S BEST VALUE WHITE WINE

La Coume de Peyre 1995 Vin de Pays des Côtes de Gascogne £3·49

Deliciously rich and fresh with thirst-quenching zippy-zingy fruit. [*South-west France*]

Kirkwood Chardonnay 1994 Vitis Hincesti £3·49

Hugh Ryman always manages to keep ahead of the Eastern Bloc Chardonnay pack with this wine, and the 1994 vintage is no exception, with its delicious balance of fruit and oak, which really stands out in the sub-£3.50 price group. [*Moldova*]

Mátra Mountain Chardonnay Oaked 1995 Nagyréde £3·49

Yet more east European Chardonnay with elegantly understated oak from flying MW Kym Milne. [*Hungary*]

Bright Brothers Fernao Pires/Chardonnay 1994 Vinho Regional Ribatejo £3·69

Anyone who tastes this blind and thinks it is anything other than Australian with a good dollop of Chardonnay knows nothing about wine – yet it is not Australian and does not contain a single Chardonnay grape. That it is made by the Bright Brothers, a couple of Aussies, is perhaps less surprising, although how the wine wizards of Oz can project their Antipodean identity on a wine wherever it comes from is truly remarkable. [*Portugal*]

Domaine du Rey 1995 Vin de Pays des Côtes de Gascogne £3·75

Not in the class of Domaine du Rey 1994 (*see* **Morrisons**), this vintage has a definite Sauvignon-like character. Customers may not be aware that Safeways persistently describes this wine on the price list sent out to all journalists as 'Vegetarian' in big bold lettering, which indeed it might be (that is, made without the animal products such as gelatin and egg whites often used to clarify a wine) – but if it is, it must be the only vegetarian wine that, acording to the back label, is recommended to accompany a 'wide range of meat dishes'. [*South-west France*]

Reserve Chardonnay Aged in Oak 1993 Rousse, The Bulgarian Vintners' £3·79

B Good Chardonnay fruit with an elegant use of understated oak. [*Bulgaria*]

Semillon Chardonnay 1995 South Eastern Australia, Barossa Winery, Safeway £3·99

B Sherbetty-fresh fruit aroma followed by very clean, elegantly rich fruit. [*Australia*]

Ruppertsberger Nussbien Riesling Kabinett 1992 Pfälz £4·15

B Lovely Spätlese-like nose, ripe lemony-apricot fruit with a dry-tangy finish. [*Germany*]

Côtes du Rhône Cuvée Spéciale 1995 Domaine Vieux Manoir de Maransan £4·49

B Plenty of fresh, clean, ripe fruit with a crisp, mouthwatering finish. A cheap white Rhône of this quality really surprised me. [*Rhône Valley, France*]

Philippe de Baudin Sauvignon Blanc 1994 La Baume, Vin de Pays d'Oc £4·49

B Really excellent racy richness, with very fresh fruit and a crisp finish. Good supping wine made with Aussie technolog [*Languedoc-Roussillon, France*]

Château Haut Bonfils Sémillon 1994 Bordeaux Blanc £4.49

This creamy-oaky pure Sémillon from Bordeaux is of much more serious quality than its price suggests. Another Hugh Ryman success, this will be drinking beautifully by Christmas. [*France*]

Penfolds Rawson's Retreat Bin 21 1995 Semillon Chardonnay Colombard £4.49

The fruit is so deliciously fresh and ripe, it's almost too easy to drink. [*Australia*]

Agramont Viura Chardonnay 1994 Navarra £4.79

Fat and oaky, yet very fresh and not at all heavy. [*Spain*]

Stonybrook Chardonnay 1994 California £4.99

Smooth, rich, coconutty-oaky fruit of some elegance. [*USA*]

Casillero del Diablo Chardonnay 1994 Casablanca Valley, Concha y Toro £4.99

So called because the wine was matured in the 'Devil's Cellar' where this winery has traditionally kept all its best wines. Concha y Toro deliberately started the rumour that the cellar was occupied by the devil in order to scare away potential pilferers. It would be pointless telling this little story if the Casillero del Diablo did not also happen to be a devil of a good Chardonnay, and this rich, fresh zingy wine is all of that. [*Chile*]

Breakaway Sauvignon Blanc Semillon 1995 South Eastern Australia £4.99

The Semillon might play a secondary role as far as its percentage of the blend is concerned, but on the nose and palate it is the primary variety, the Sauvignon being relegated to providing a zingy lift to the creamy-ripe finish. A very clever wine made by Geoff Merrill. [*Australia*]

Rosemount Estate Semillon Chardonnay 1995 £5·29

Although it is well worth its recommendation and will fill out over the next twelve months, Rosemount's Semillon Chardonnay is not as immediately attractive as the same winery's Semillon Sauvignon. [*Australia*]

Gewurztraminer Vin d'Alsace 1994 Cave des Vignerons Turckheim £5·79

Gentle, rounded spice on easy-drinking fruit. [*France*]

Hunter Valley Chardonnay 1994 Rosemount £5·99

Very rich and satisfying. [*Australia*]

Penfolds Organic Wine 1994 Chardonnay-Sauvignon Blanc, Clare Valley £5·99

Mouthwatering lemony-lime fruit on nose and palate with a refreshing crispness, rather than taste, of Sauvignon on the finish. [*Australia*]

Muscadet de Sèvre et Maine Sur Lie 1994 Domaine de l'Ecu £5·99

In pure quality terms this is really a bronze, but as far as Muscadet is concerned, this unquestionably rates a silver medal. Made by Guy Bossard, one of Muscadet's finest and an organic winemaker to boot, this is very clean, very fresh, very accessible, with real fruit, yet possesses the appellation's authentic, lean structure. What more could any sane person expect from Muscadet? [*Loire Valley, France*]

Rosé Wines

Breakaway Grenache 1996 Stratmer Vineyards £4.99
Ⓖ A lovely richness of fruit with a delicious medley of cherry, strawberry and raspberry jam flavours make this the most joyous rosé I have ever tasted. [*Australia*]
☞ THE BEST VALUE ROSÉ WINE OF THE YEAR
☞ THE BEST QUALITY ROSÉ WINE OF THE YEAR

Sparkling Wines

Cava Brut NV Safeway £4.99
Ⓑ Fresh, zesty, citrussy aromas. [*Spain*]

Australian Quality Sparkling Wine Brut NV Seppelt, Safeway £4.99
Typical fizzy Oz fruit. [*Australia*]

Champagne Albert Etienne Brut 1990 Safeway £14.99
Ⓢ The producer in small print at the base of the label is Massé, which is a second brand of Lanson, which in turn is owned by Marne et Champagne, whose better *cuvées* develop a biscuity-richness similar to this Champagne when given sufficient landed-age. [*France*]

Fortified Wines

Dom Brial Muscat de Rivesaltes 1995 £3.79 (half-bottle)
Ⓢ Two other supermarkets submitted the 1994

vintage of this wine, which did not even scrape in, never mind pick up a medal, whereas this super-fresh, sweeter, riper, far more elegant 1995 easily picked up a silver. [*Languedoc-Roussillon, France*]

Beers

Bavaria Lager Beer Per pint: £0.66

S More perfumed hops than the canned version, making this a softer, more elegant lager for just 3 pence per pint more. Despite its name, Bavaria is brewed in the Netherlands, not Germany. £6.99 per 24 x 25cl bottles. [*3.0%, Netherlands*]

Banks's Bitter Per pint: £0.89

B Distinctive flowery-hopped aromas follow through on to the palate. Very smooth. £3.15 per 4 x 500ml bottles. [*3.8%, Wolverhampton, UK*]

John Smith's Bitter Per pint: £0.96

B Nothing to get excited about, but this is refreshing and dry with a clean bitter-hop finish, and it is the cheapest bitter or ale to deserve a medal. £2.99 per 4 x 440ml cans. [*4.0%, Yorkshire, UK*]

Faxe Premium Danish Export Lager Per pint: £1.13

Like drinking sweet, slightly fizzy water; you have little idea that it contains 5 per cent alcohol, which no doubt explains the success of this litre-sized can at parties. Party-goers should be aware, however, that it has the original ring-pull, which sliced up many a foot in outdoor pools when it first appeared in the 1960s – which was why the current, integral opener was invented. So if you see Faxe at a party, don't dance bare-footed. £1.99 per one-litre can. [*5.0%, Denmark*]

Guinness Original Per pint: £1.29

Dense, dark, bitter chocolate, coffee and liquorice. Quite stern, but great with a Stilton ploughman. £2.99 per 4 x 330ml bottles. [*4.3%, Ireland/ UK*]

Kronenbourg 1664 Courage Per pint: £1.29

Its deep gold colour belies the fresh, hoppy aroma and crisp flavour beneath. Considering this is canned, not bottled, and brewed in the UK by Courage rather than Kronenbourg in Strasbourg, it is surprisingly good, with a very authentic character. £3.99 per 4 x 440ml cans. [*5.0%, UK*]

Adnams Suffolk Strong Ale Per pint: £1.33

I'm all for better quality beer, but if you have to pay the equivalent of £1.30 a pint, it does not make much sense buying it in two-litre plastic bottles. That said, this good strong ale does get my vote as the best quality party-sized beer on the market. £4.69 per 2-litre party-size plastic bottle. [*4.5%, UK*]

Caledonian 70/- Amber Ale Caledonian Brewery Per pint: £1.35

A definite bronze medal for those who like sweetish beers, this has a clean malty taste dominated by peppery-hop aromas and a touch of Mediterranean herbal-scrub. £1.19 per 500ml bottle. [*3.8%, Edinburgh, UK*]

John Smith's Extra Smooth Bitter Per pint: £1.38

Unless you're into creamy-sweet, ultra-soft

brews, the nicely perfumed hops and a decent bitter taste will make this one of the two best widgetized beers at this price point. £4.29 per 4 x 440ml widgetized cans. [*4.0%, Yorkshire, UK*]

Tetley's Draught Yorkshire Bitter Per pint: £1.40

The least widget-affected: the widget delivers a creamy head, but has little effect on the overall taste, which is less creamy than any other widgetized beer. For some, this might be a godsend. £4.35 per 4 x 440ml widgetized cans. [*3.6%, Leeds, UK*]

Brains S.A. Draught Best Bitter Per pint: £1.45

B The perfumed, hoppy aromas and clean, crisp taste (despite the widget) with a touch of bitterness put it on par with John Smith's, but at 15–28 pence per pint more expensive, Brains S.A. Draught only just retains its bronze medal. £4.49 per 4 x 440ml widgetized cans. [*4.2%, Cardiff, UK*]

Masterbrew Premium Bitter Shepherd Neame Per pint: £1.47

B A good bronze for the dry, true-bitter character that stands out at this price point, although this particular brew is not quite as distinctive as Masterbrew normally is. £1.29 per 500ml bottle. [*4.0%, Kent, UK*]

Boddingtons Draught Per pint: £1.47

B A nicely hopped beer, this is much fruitier than John Smith's, the other best-performing widgetized bitter at this price point, and has a correctly crisp finish with some real bitterness on the aftertaste. £4.55 per 4 x 440ml widgetized cans. [*3.8%, Manchester, UK*]

'33' Export Per pint: £1.47

There's no pretence about this easy-drinking, down-to-earth lager-style beer. Ideal telly beer for every couch potato. £6.49 per 10 x 25cl bottles. [*4.8%, France*]

Kronenbourg 1664 Premium Bière Per pint: £1.51

The bottled, Strasbourg-brewed version does have the edge over the British-brewed can, but they both represent the same value for money at their respective price points. £3.99 per 6 x 25cl bottles. [*5.0%, France*]

Bishops Finger Kentish Strong Ale Shepherd Neame Per pint: £1.53

An inferior version of the Bishops Finger bottled ale, yet superior for a canned beer, if you catch my drift. £4.75 per 4 x 440ml cans. [*5.4%, Kent, UK*]

Budweiser Budvar Per pint: £1.53

Genuine Czech Budweiser has been made since the thirteenth century and the only remaining example is instantly recognizable by the Budvar part of its name. It is a classic beer: whereas American Budweiser is just bland-tasting, perfumed water made primarily from rice, Budvar is made from pure, top-quality malt. Compare the two beers for yourself and you'll be pleasantly surprised, not the least because the superior, authentic product also happens to be cheaper. £1.35 per 50cl bottle. [*5.0%, Ceske Budejovice, Czech Republic*]

Caledonian 80/- Export Ale Caledonian Brewery Per pint: £1.53

A classic as far as sweet-toothed beer-lovers are

concerned, Caledonian 80/- is marked by the perfumed-hop aromas that drift lazily through its clean, sweet-ripe, floral taste. £1.35 per 500ml bottle. [*4.4%, Edinburgh, UK*]

Black Sheep Ale Paul Theakston Per pint: £1.58

Ⓖ Made by Paul Theakston, whose family brewery is now part of Scottish & Newcastle. He alone was determined to maintain an independent status, hence the name Black Sheep. This is classy, distinctive, soft and yet completely dry, with a delicious nutty-hoppy complexity. Although there was a time when M&S's own-label version was better than the original (smokier, with a more mellow bitterness), they are almost identical this year – but why doesn't Paul Theakston market a bottle-conditioned version? £1.39 per 500ml bottle. [*4.4%, Yorkshire, UK*]

☞ THE BEST VALUE BITTER OF THE YEAR

Bombardier Premium Bitter Charles Wells
Per pint: £1.58

Has a good bitter finish, but many will find its strangely liquorous texture somewhat incongruous. £1.39 per 500ml bottle. [*4.3%, Bedford, UK*]

Samuel Smith's The Famous Taddy Porter Old Brewery Tadcaster Per pint: £1.60

The darkest of all the porters tasted, with an attractive Ovaltine-coloured head. Very dry and very bitter, this beer cries out for a widget (which does not mean that Samuel Smith's should not continue with this pure bottled version – just that if offered in a widgetized bottle, it would open up sales to typical draught stout drinkers, and it would be interesting to see how a widgetized Famous Taddy rated blind against the three Irish stouts). Not that Samuel Smith's would ever dare! £1.55 per 550ml bottle. [*5.0%, Yorkshire, UK*]

Caffrey's Draught Irish Ale Per pint: £1.61

(B) This light, fresh, creamy-sweet brew is brilliantly marketed. It is not as good as from the tap, even if that is connected to a pressurized keg, but the same could be said for Guinness Draught, and those who like this soft, easy beer will simply be thankful they can keep a reasonable replica ready-chilled in the fridge. Any Caffrey's drinker who has not tasted Wethered's Draught from M&S should do so. It's in a similar style, some will actually prefer it, and it costs 49 pence per pint less. £4.99 per 4 x 440ml widgetized cans. [*4.8%, County Antrim, UK*]

Stella Artois Premium Lager Beer Per pint: £1.63

Really quite a decent lunchtime lager considering the brand's naff reputation amongst serious beer drinkers and the fact that it is brewed in the UK by Whitbread, rather than in Belgium by Stella Artois itself. Light, flowery-Pilsner style. £5.69 per 6 x 330ml bottles. [*5.2%, UK*]

Merlin's Ale Broughton Ales Per pint: £1.65

(B) A medal-winning brew for those who like their beers light, fresh and tasting of pears, with a distinctive peppery-hop aroma. £1.45 per 500ml bottle. [*4.2%, Peeblesshire, UK*]

Directors Live Ale Courage Per pint: £1.69

(S) This very smooth, aromatically perfumed beer has a nice bitter-hop finish and proves that big breweries can still produce good bottle-conditioned beers if they want to. £1.49 per 500ml bottle. [*4.8%, UK*]

Murphy's Draught Irish Stout Per pint: £1.69

(S) Murphy's is the lightest of the three Irish stouts, and it would not be unfair to describe it as the nearest to Caffrey's, although its smoky-malty aroma gives a far more distinctive edge to its creamy-smoky flavour. Not as dry or as bitter as the other two stouts, it does however fall into the dry, bitter category when tasted in isolation. The bottles used to be less creamy than the cans until Murphy's introduced floating widgets into the latter; now they are both very lightly widgetized. £1.49 per 500ml widgetized bottle. [*4.0%, Ireland/ UK*]

San Miguel Export Premium Lager Per pint: £1.70

(B) Has the same flowery-hoppy Pilsner aroma as the can (which is remarkable in a canned beer), but a slightly more hoppy flavour, with a longer, crisper finish. Better, yet a lower medal because the can is so exceptional and this is almost twice the price. £3.95 per 4 x 33cl bottles. [*5.4%, Spain*]

Carlsberg Ice Beer Per pint: £1.70

(S) The sharpest, crispest and best of the so-called Ice Beers. £0.99 per 330ml bottle. [*5.6%, Denmark*]

Hoegaarden White Beer Per pint: £1.70

(B) This has a classic, soapy-spicy aroma and stewed, spiced-apple flavour, but is it worth 23 pence a pint more than Tesco's extraordinarily good own-label? £0.99 per 330ml bottle. [*5.0%, Belgium*]

Bishops Finger Kentish Strong Ale Shepherd Neame
Per pint: £1.76

S Taste this side by side with the canned version and you will realize why the premium charged for bottled beers is well worth paying. Beautifully fresh and crisp, with a powerful true-bitter flavour and long, hoppy aftertaste. £1.55 per 500ml bottle. [*5.4%, Kent, England*]

'Old Speckled Hen' Strong Pale Ale Morland
Per pint: £1.76

B Fresh and tasty with a characterful maltiness in both the aroma and on the palate, which finishes with the barest hint of smoke. Not as good as the cask-conditioned draught, but what bottled beer is? £1.55 per 500ml bottle. [*5.2%, Oxfordshire, UK*]

Spitfire Bottle Conditioned Bitter Shepherd Neame
Per pint: £1.76

G A great bitter with an elegant fruity-yeasty fullness, delicate bitter-hop flavours and a beautifully dry, understated finish. One bottle of Spitfire tasted was unbelievably fizzy and aggressively tasteless as a result. The sediment looked to be twice the norm, so I can only imagine that it was a faulty batch, as can sometimes happen with a live beer. If you have ever had a similar experience, be advised that Spitfire should not be like that – but buy another bottle to satisfy yourself. £1.55 per 500ml bottle. [*4.7%, Kent, England*]

☞ THE BEST QUALITY BITTER OF THE YEAR

Boddingtons Export Per pint: £1.91

S A distinctive, well-hopped bitter that is enhanced,

rather than masked, by the minimal effect of a bottled widget. £4.45 per 4 x 330ml bottles. [*4.8%, Manchester, UK*]

Beck's Per pint: £1.92

This beer is too popular for its own good. Its clean, fresh taste deserves a recommendation, not a medal, at this price point. If you're in a pub and want to be seen drinking a premium beer, why not go for a Bitburger or Budweiser Budvar and show your Beck's-swilling friends you know something they don't? £5.59 per 6 x 275ml bottles. [*5.0%, Bremen, Germany*]

Stella Artois Dry Premium Beer Export Strength
Per pint: £1.96

Not as dry as its name suggests, this has a richer malty taste than the British-brewed Stella Artois Premium Lager, with more aromatic hops on the finish, but still does not deserve a medal at this price. £5.69 per 6 x 275ml bottles. [*5.5%, Belgium*]

Staropramen Beer Per pint: £1.98

Very elegant, with perfumed hops, this is a truly dry Pilsner style that is soft and so delicately aromatic that it can easily be consumed by those who do not usually like their beers so dry. £1.15 per 330ml bottle. [*5.0%, Prague, Czech Republic*]

Guinness Foreign Extra Stout Per pint: £2.01

Extra Stout is a very apt name for this exceptionally extracted brew, the complex flavours of which start remarkably concentrated yet build and build on the palate to a rousing crescendo of bitter-coffee, burnt-toffee, black treacle and liquorice intensity. £1.17 per 330ml bottle. [*7.5%, Dublin, Ireland*]

Grolsch Premium Lager Per pint: £2.13

(G) The perfect lager (in bottles anyway). £1.69 per 450ml bottle. [*5.0%, Netherlands*]

☞ THE BEST QUALITY LIGHT BEER OF THE YEAR

Is a £3 Gold medal as good as a £6 Gold medal?

It *is* possible, and no doubt there are some in this edition – but remember that a medal is awarded for style and price category, thus the higher the price the harder it is to earn one and the probability of a significantly cheaper product being just as good is a slim one.

SAINSBURY'S

Number of stores *365*
Opening hours *Vary too much from store to store to generalize*
Maximum range *500 wines, 300 beers, 200 spirits*
Alternative methods of payment *Cheque with card, Switch and Delta debit cards, Access, American Express, Visa, Eurocard*
Delivery *Not provided from any of the stores, but will help carry goods to car if requested, and wines can be delivered to your doorstep via* Wine Direct *(choose a minimum of one case, which can be mixed six bottles of one wine and six bottles of another, phone through your order – even on a Sunday – to 0800 716129, and the wine will be delivered for the same price as it is sold in the supermarket, plus £3.95 carriage charge or free delivery for two cases or more)*
Discounts *Various multi-buy offers*
Other services *Sale or return, ice*

Comment Sainsbury's 365 outlets include no fewer than 200 superstores, with another 16 due to open during the next year. It's been a dismal year for the country's premier supermarket group: having predicted pre-tax profits would jump from £808 million to £875 million, it only ended up with £712 million. As a consequence, belts were tightened all round, and all bulk samples to journalists suspended, although a dribble of new lines reached a few lucky souls. My only option was to buy the products off the shelf, which I did using my notes from the annual tasting as a guide, and it cost a small fortune. I do not mind admitting that, having been the first to review Sainsbury's wines in an annual guide as long ago as 1982, it hurt to be snubbed in this way, but at least the result (Sainsbury's came third in straight-gold terms) demonstrated the objectivity of blind tastings and a lack of pique on my part.

Red Wines

Côtes du Ventoux 1995 £3·35

Full and fruity, with good tannins for food. [*Rhône Valley, France*]

Sainsbury's Chilean Cabernet Sauvignon Merlot NV Curico £13·49 (3–litre bag-in-box)

Nice tannin grip and some real flavour make this the best cheapest Cabernet blend of the tastings, despite a number of cheaper offerings from Bulgaria. Chile is fast becoming the best source of cheap wines, as well as one of the most exciting sources for premium quality varietals. [*Chile*]

Bush Vine Grenache 1995 Coteaux du Languedoc £3·39

Fat and fresh. [*Languedoc-Roussillon, France*]

Sainsbury's Vin de Pays de l'Aude NV Rouge £3·39

A deep colour and a big mouthful of gluggy, plummy fruit. [*France*]

Sainsbury's Reserve Cabernet Sauvignon 1992 Iambol Region £3·69

This soft, smooth and fruity red wine slips down the back of the throat dangerously easily. [*Bulgaria*]

Sainsbury's Australian Cabernet Sauvignon 1994 £4·49

Lots and lots of creamy-ripe fruit, but not at all heavy. [*Australia*]

Sainsbury's Cuvée Prestige Bordeaux Rouge NV £4·49

A full red wine with real Bordeaux character and

attractive menthol complexity on the aftertaste. [*Bordeaux, France*]

South Bay Vineyards Pinot Noir NV Sainsbury's £4·99

Ⓢ Perfumed Pinot aroma, with very soft, elegant fruit on the palate and a gentle touch of strawberry on the finish. [*California, USA*]

Domaine de Sours 1993 Rouge £4·99

Ⓢ Elegant and stylish fruit with a touch of oak and nice tannic grip on the finish. [*Bordeaux, France*]

James Herrick Cuvée Simone 1995 Vin de Pays d'Oc £4·99

Ⓢ Where can you buy such a lovely, rich mouthful of lip-smacking fruit and tannins for the same price bearing an AOC? [*Languedoc-Roussillon, France*]

☞ SAINSBURY'S BEST VALUE RED WINE

Domaine Joseph de Bel Air 1994 Pinot Noir £5·45

Ⓑ Hardly textbook Pinot, but a deliciously oaky red wine in its own right at this price. [*Languedoc-Roussillon, France*]

Morgon 1994 Georges Duboeuf £5·95

Good sappy Gamay fruit, with nicely high acidity to make it more of a food wine than a guzzler. [*Beaujolais, France*]

Domaine de la Baume 1994 Estate Merlot £5·95

Ⓑ Smoky-oaky Merlot with a big, inky-tannic finish. [*Languedoc-Roussillon, France*]

Quinta da Bacalhôa Cabernet Sauvignon 1993 £6.25

Ⓑ Both 1992 and 1993 were available at the time of

tasting, and the difference between them illustrates how safe it is to hang on to this wine for a year or so. Both vintages deserve a bronze medal, but the 1992 is more ready to drink, showing an attractive violety perfume, whereas the 1993 seems more peppery and rustic, although this will smooth out to a perfumed elegance over the next year in bottle. If anything, the 1993 is longer and potentially better. [*Portugal*]

Tim Knappstein The Franc 1994 Clare Valley £6.95

Deep, dark colour, with cedary-oaky, raspberry-herbaceous fruit aromas that glide through the long, dry-raspberry varietal fruit flavour on to the dry, cedary-oaky finish. [*Australia*]

Wynns Coonawarra Cabernet Sauvignon 1991 South Australia £7.95

Big, rich, assertive flavour by the bucket-load. [*Australia*]

Crozes-Hermitage Les Jalets 1994 Paul Jaboulet Ainé £7.95

Intriguing wisp of coffee and smoke drifting through firm Syrah fruit. Excellent acidity. Great food wine. [*Rhône Valley, France*]

Sainsbury's Classic Selection Rioja 1990 £7.95

Lovely sweet-ripe fruit. [*Rioja, Spain*]

Penfolds Bin 389 Cabernet Shiraz 1993 South Australia £9.95

Classic Shiraz – big, rich and cedary. [*Australia*]

Château de Rully 1993 Rodet £9.95

An elegant Burgundy with a nice clarity of Pinot fruit. [*Burgundy, France*]

Château Marquis de Terme 1992 3ème Cru Classé Margaux £12.95

One of two outstandingly good Bordeaux wines for the vintage that Sainsbury's has managed to dig out from the otherwise diabolical 1992 vintage (the wettest in fifty years and the least sunny since 1980), this Margaux shows astonishing finesse and elegance, lovely ripe fruit (how?) and nice tannic structure with a nice touch of oak on the finish. Brilliantly sourced and very reasonably priced for the quality. [*Bordeaux, France*]

Cornas 1990 Les Serras £12.95

Wonderfully fresh, ripe and juicy-rich blackberry fruit make this an absolute delight to drink. If you have had trouble finding a Rhône Syrah you like, then try this. If this does not set you alight, nothing will, and you may as well forget the Rhône in future. This might be the price of a good value *cru classé* Bordeaux (Château Marquis de Terme 1992, for example, which Sainsbury's also sells at £12.95), but it is of the same quality. [*Rhône Valley, France*]

Château Lagrange 1992 3ème Cru Classé Margaux £13.95

Gorgeously rich and long with lush, succulent fruit; another incredible 1992 and at this quality, it represents even better value, despite being slightly more expensive. [*Bordeaux, France*]

Château Ferrière 1993 3ème Cru Classé Margaux £15.95

Full-bodied for Margaux, with heaps of oaky-rich, tasty fruit. A classy wine, but at a classy price. [*Bordeaux, France*]

Beaune 1er Cru Clos de la Féguine 1992 Domaine Jacques Prieur £16.95

B Fat and juicy Pinot fruit. So elegant and easy to drink, it would be a shame to complicate such hedonistic qualities with food. [*Burgundy, France*]

White Wines

Devil's Rock Riesling 1994 St. Ursula £2.99

Clean, dry, lemony Riesling fruit. [*Pfälz, Germany*]

Saltram Classic Semillon 1994 £4.99

G There's even a green tinge to this star-bright, lemon-coloured wine. A huge mouthful of luscious fruit flavour in the true Saltram tradition. I absent-mindedly gave this a silver, thinking that it must be £7–8 or thereabouts, but immediately upped this to a Gold-plus when I realized what price bracket I was tasting in. [*Australia*]

☞ SAINSBURY'S BEST VALUE WHITE WINE

Danie de Wet Chardonnay 1995 Robertson £5.45

Although the richness stands out, this vintage has never been in the same class as Danie de Wet's exquisite 1993 Grey Label Chardonnay. [*South Africa*]

Erdener Treppchen 1985 Riesling Spätlese £5.45

Very easy-going, clean as a whistle Mosel. So fresh, it's

hard to believe this is 11 years old! How come this is so beautifully clean while most inexpensive German wines go 'dirty' after just a couple of years in bottle? [*Mosel-Saar-Ruwer, Germany*]

Sainsbury's Classic Selection 1995 Muscadet de Sèvre et Maine Sur Lie £5·95

Excellent Muscadet with real length, fruit and flavour, yet not sacrificing the correct lean structure and all the attributes that make the best Muscadet such good food wine. Lifted by a slight spritz on the finish, this wine also makes good drinking on its own. [*Loire Valley, France*]

Wormser Liebfrauenmorgen 1994 Beerenauslese £5·95

How can you buy a Beerenauslese for under a tenner, let alone £5.95? Well, not for me to wonder why, just to taste and buy, and the intense aroma and very concentrated, tangy fruit in this wine is well worth a punt. Not available for the blind tasting, thus not a potential medal-winner. [*Rheinhessen, Germany*]

Piesporter Goldtröpfchen Riesling Spätlese 1990 Reichsgraf von Kesselstatt £7·75

Delicious, soft, peach-pie fruit. A lovely mature Riesling. Limited availability – just ten stores – which is ridiculous for a major national retailer. [*Mosel-Saar-Ruwer, Germany*]

Lindemans Padthaway Chardonnay 1994 South Australia £7·95

When tasting the Lindemans range, the step up to Padthaway for sourcing Chardonnay is always noticeable, and proved itself under blind conditions against other brands. It's the emphatic acidity that blasts its way through the creamy-oaky richness of fruit to such great effect that puts this on a different level from so many other Australian Chardonnays. [*Australia*]

☞ THE BEST QUALITY WHITE WINE OF THE YEAR

Château Carbonnieux 1993 Pessac-Léognan £16.95

This is a superb example of the lush, elegantly oaky, dry white Bordeaux this château is producing these days. [*Bordeaux, France*]

Sparkling Wines

Sainsbury's Australian Sparkling £4·99

This exotic, fizzy blend of tropical fruit flavours will appeal to most lovers of the upfront Aussie sparkling wine style, and nobody could complain about the price. [*Australia*]

Sainsbury's Asti NV £5·49

Very fresh, pears and peaches. [*Italy*]

Madeba Brut NV Robertson, Sainsbury's £5·79

Sweetish fruity fizz, very fresh and easy to drink. [*South Africa*]

Seaview Pinot Noir Chardonnay NV £7·95

Definitely a step up from Seaview Brut, but probably worth an extra £1 rather than £2 for its richer, lemony flavour, thus does not get the bronze awarded to its lesser quality sister *cuvée.* [*Australia*]

Yalumba Cuvée One Pinot Noir Chardonnay NV £8.49

A fresh, elegant balance of full yet restrained

flavour and good fruit acidity. Although I have tasted better examples of this *cuvée*, such is its quality that even a below-par example well deserves a bronze medal. [*Australia*]

Sainsbury's Blanc de Noirs Champagne NV £11.95

(B) Very fruity for Champagne from Producteurs Grands Terroirs, for which you can read Champagne Palmer, the co-operative that many famous houses respect the most. [*France*]

Sainsbury's Extra Dry Champagne NV £12.95

(S) A Champagne of some finesse for an own-label non-vintage and I suspect much of this is due to a good proportion of Côte des Blancs Chardonnay. Made by Duval Leroy, which is currently going from strength to strength. [*France*]

Sainsbury's Vintage Champagne 1990 £14.95

(S) Rich and creamy now, but keep it a year or two if you want the toasty-biscuity aromas to build. A vintage Champagne for less than £15 just has to be a bargain and one that is as loaded with Chardonnay as this is would normally cost a lot more, but it's made by UCVB, an efficient co-operative at Bethon in the Sézannais, an area that is chock-a-block full of the most reasonably priced Chardonnay in all of Champagne. [*France*]

Fortified Wines

Sainsbury's L.B.V. Port 1989 Temilobos £7.29

(B) Has good fire and spice, as well as lovely rich,

sweet fruit and a plump but nicely dry finish. [*Portugal*]

Sainsbury's 10 Year Old Tawny Port £9.99

Own-label 10 Year Old Tawny with the coffee complexity of a real 20 Year Old has to be worth a silver. [*Portugal*]

Pedro Ximenez NV Montilla £5.59 (half-bottle)

Known in the business as a 'Wow!' wine, this super-rich, cream-of-cream-of-cream Pedro Ximenez comes from my least favourite fortified wine appellation – Montilla – but under blind tasting conditions I would challenge anyone to guess correctly the provenance of this lusciously sweet, succulent, raisiny wonder wine. [*Spain*]

Fonseca 1982 £17.95

Has good fire in the belly for such fat, sweet, juicy fruit. [*Portugal*]

Beers

Sainsbury's German Pilsener Premium Lager

Per pint: £1.16

Elegant, flowery, Pilsner aroma and flavour, with a fresh, crisp finish. £2.69 per 4 x 33cl bottles. [*4.9%, Germany*]

Sainsbury's Nazdravi Per pint: £1.29

A lovely crisp, rich, malty taste. £2.99 per 4 x 33cl bottles. [*5.0%, Pilsen, Czech Republic*]

HB Original Hofbräuhaus München Premium Lager
Per pint: £1.58

A fruity brew with gentle hoppiness from the famous Bavarian Royal Court Brewery (HB is short for *Hofbräu*, which means 'court brew'), although it would be more accurate to call it the State Brewery these days. £1.39 per 500ml bottle. [*4.9%, Germany*]

Marston's Oyster Stout Bottle Conditioned Head Brewers Choice
Per pint: £1.65

Very smooth and easy-drinking, but lacks the intensity, bitterness and complexity of a great stout. As it's bottle-conditioned, I'm going to try ageing it until next year to see if that makes any significant difference. Until then, however, this brew deserves recommending, but not a medal. £1.45 per 500ml bottle. [*4.5%, Burton-on-Trent, UK*]

Sainsbury's Bière de Prestige Premium French Lager, Fischer
Per pint: £1.74

In the same-shaped flip-top bottle as Fischer's own Tradition brew (*see* **Tesco**), only green rather than brown; the difference in colour seems to reflect the contrast in style, this being fresher and crisper than the more mellow Tradition, with a very elegant hop-pillow aroma and an almost green tang to the finish. More Pilsner-like. £1.99 per 650ml bottle. [*6.5%, France*]

Sainsbury's Blackfriars Porter
Per pint: £1.76

A dry style porter with a great intensity of bitter-sweet chocolate, coffee-toffee and smoky-liquorice aromas and flavours. £1.55 per 500ml bottle. [*5.5%, UK*]

Staropramen Dark Lager Per pint: £1.98

(G) This particular dark lager is stunning stuff, looking not unlike bottled mild, but full of wonderful creamy-coffee and chicory richness. £1.15 per 330ml bottle. [*4.6%, Prague, Czech Republic*]

Staropramen Beer Per pint: £1.98

(S) Very elegant, with perfumed hops, this is a truly dry Pilsner style that is soft and so delicately aromatic that it can easily be consumed by those who do not usually like their beers so dry. £1.15 per 330ml bottle. [*5.0%, Prague, Czech Republic*]

Sainsbury's Bière de Garde Brewery Castelain

Per pint: £2.10

Not for me, but this huge, dark, almost sickly-malty beer is considered a classic by the sort of beer drinkers you never see supping a pint at your local. £1.85 per 500ml bottle. [*6.0%, France*]

Grolsch Premium Lager Per pint: £2.13

(G) The perfect lager (in bottles anyway). £1.69 per 450ml bottle. [*5.0%, Netherlands*]

☞ THE BEST QUALITY LIGHT BEER OF THE YEAR

SAVACENTRE

A group of twelve hypermarkets, Savacentre was originally a collaboration between Sainsbury's and British Home Stores, but has been totally owned by Sainsbury's for the last five years or so. Each Savacentre hypermarket carries the complete range of Sainsbury's wines, beers and spirits, thus for those recommended, please see the **Sainsbury's** entry (page 141).

SOLO

Having diminished to just twenty-six stores from forty-five last year, the SoLo trading name is gradually being phased out, as some outlets are converted to Somerfield or Food Giant and others are sold off. For the range of wines and beers recommended, please see the **Somerfield** entry (page 155).

SOMERFIELD

STOCK ME AND BUY ONE

Number of stores *232*
Opening hours *Vary widely, but can be summarized as Monday–Saturday 8.30a.m.–6.30p.m., Sunday 10a.m.–4p.m.*
Maximum range *410 wines, 163 beers, 122 spirits*
Alternative methods of payment *Cheque with card, Switch and Delta debit cards, Access, American Express, Visa*
Local delivery *Not provided, but will help carry goods to car if requested*
Discounts *None*
Other services *In-store tastings*
Parent company *Somerfield is the parent and owns Food Giant, Gateway and SoLo*

Comment Remember International? Well, Key Markets swallowed those supermarkets up. What happened to Key Markets? Gateways took them over. And Gateways? You've guessed – they became part of Somerfield's diet. International was good for bacon (I learned to bone a side of bacon at one branch when I had an after-school job), but pretty useless for wine. Key Markets and Gateway were not much better, although the buyers tried harder, but Somerfield is a whole different kettle of fish. There are still people who would not shop in one by choice, despite their brighter, refurbished look, and it was mostly people like that who have written to me saying what an eye-opener *SuperBooze* proved to be. Many had never set foot inside one of these stores, yet they were all impressed by the value of the wines recommended, especially when they found some to be on special offer at a pound a bottle cheaper. As I said last year, Somerfield's Angela Mount has quietly worked away at building up one of the country's best supermarket wine selections, and coming fourth by 'weighting' this year only serves to reinforce this judgement. Mount is probably Britain's most underrated wine buyer.

Red Wines

Bulgarian Country Wine Merlot & Pinot Noir NV Sliven Region, Vini Sliven, Somerfield £2.89

Heaps of blackberry and strawberry jam flavour, which is very welcome at this price point, plus dry tannic finish, making it a very reasonably priced food wine. [*Bulgaria*]

Bulgarian Cabernet Sauvignon 1989 Melnik Region, Vinprom Damianitza, Somerfield £2.95

Cheap Cabernets start at around £2.29, but this was the cheapest to have anything of an individual character worth recommending, with its soft, violety fruit and elegant aromatics, although for the same price the Chilean Cabernet is much the better buy. [*Bulgaria*]

Chilean Cabernet Sauvignon NV Viña Cornellana, Somerfield £2.95

B The soft, chocolaty fruit in this Chilean Cabernet excels at this price point. [*Rapel Region, Chile*]

☞ SOMERFIELD'S BEST VALUE RED WINE

Argentine Country Red NV Somerfield £2.99

Smooth and creamy at this price. [*San Juan, Argentina*]

Vin de Pays des Coteaux de l'Ardèche NV Vignerons Ardéchois, Somerfield £2.99

Plenty of gutsy fruit with a hint of sweetness on the finish makes this a very amenable cheap red. [*Rhône Valley, France*]

Sangiovese di Romagna NV Somerfield £3·49

B Ultra-modern style of pristine fruit and a very smooth finish. [*Italy*]

Fitou Cuvée Rocher d'Embrée NV Somerfield £3·65

B Full-bodied with rich, sweet-ripe-spicy fruit. [*Languedoc-Roussillon, France*]

I Grilli di Villa Thalia 1993 Calatrasi £3·65

S Elegant, violety-perfumed sweet-ripe fruit and firm, food-wine structure. [*Sicily, Italy*]

Montepulciano d'Abruzzo 1994 Umani Ronchi £3·79

Violety fruit aromas on nose and finish, with fine acidity-richness for food. [*Italy*]

South African Cabernet Sauvignon NV Somerfield £3·99

Very soft, easy-drinking fruit. [*South Africa*]

Kumala Cinsault Pinotage 1995 Western Cape £3·99

It's a funny old world, but you cross Pinot Noir with Cinsault to get Pinotage, which honestly bears little resemblance to either variety. It is somewhat lacking unless you fiddle with the vinification process or, as in this case, blend it with one of its parents – Cinsault – which lends Pinotage the much needed structure on which to hang its fruit. A very clever, inexpensive blend. [*South Africa*]

Château Valoussière 1993 Coteaux-du-Languedoc £4·49

B A big mouthful of smooth, spicy, oak-laden fruit, with a firm-tannin food-wine finish. [*France*]

Chianti Classico 1994 Montecchio £4.69

This wine needs another six to twelve months in bottle to develop its bouquet, but is already showing an excellent richness backed up by attractive, dry, oak-influenced fruit on the finish. [*Italy*]

Hardys Nottage Hill Cabernet Sauvignon Shiraz 1994 South Eastern Australia £4.99

Distinctive smoky aroma, very fresh, medium-bodied fruit with lots of juicy-ripe acidity. [*Australia*]

Penfolds Rawson's Retreat Bin 35 1994 Cabernet Sauvignon-Shiraz £4.99

Although this lacks elegance and finesse, it rates a mention for those who want as much big-rich-thick flavour per pound sterling as possible. [*South Australia*]

Redwood Trail Pinot Noir 1994 By Sterling Vineyards £4.99

Very elegant fruit with a delicate touch of oak. [*California, USA*]

Claret Oak Aged NV Peter A. Sichel, Somerfield £4.99

Good basic claret with nice richness of flavour, but oak-lovers might be disappointed not to find more obvious oak characteristics, although that is not necessarily a bad thing. [*Bordeaux, France*]

Vieux Clocher 1994 Vacqueyras £4.99

Sweet-spicy aroma and fruit, with good grip and acidity sustaining the finish. [*Rhône Valley, France*]

Taurino Salice Salentino Riserva 1990 Rosso £5·49

Ⓑ Rich, mellow, warm-spicy fruit. [*South-western Puglia, Italy*]

Red Burgundy Pinot Noir 1994 Somerfield £5·49

Ⓑ Fine redcurranty varietal fruit in a firm, food-wine structure. [*France*]

Chianti Classico Conti Serristori 1995 Villa Primavera, Somerfield £5·49

Ⓖ Beautifully elegant, plummy fruit of extraordinary finesse for this price. [*Italy*]

Bankside Shiraz 1992 Hardys £5·99

Ⓑ The creamy, jammy-spicy fruit in this wine is fatter and softer than the 1993 Bankside Shiraz (*see* Safeway), which makes it easier to drink on its own, but both are good bronze medal-winners, so take your pick. [*South Eastern Australia*]

Penfolds Koonunga Hill Shiraz-Cabernet Sauvignon 1994 South Australia £5·99

Ⓢ I have to confess that this is a borderline silver, and it only won the gong because it's such a big, black and hugely concentrated wine. Although I spend much of my time looking for nuances of elegance and finesse because I do not want to fall into the trap of 'big is best', I cannot ignore the fact that for some people the bigger the wine the better it is. So if you want a monster to drink now or to forget about for ten years, at £5·99 this must be a great bargain. [*Australia*]

Bourgogne Hautes-Côtes de Beaune 1994 Georges Désire £6·49

Ⓑ Very rich fruit, good Pinot character,

ample-bodied food wine. [*France*]

Chateau Musar 1988 Gaston Hochar £7·99

B Very rich, mellow, sweet baked-spicy fruit. [*Lebanon*]

Penfolds Bin 407 Cabernet Sauvignon 1992 South Australia £7·99

G Amazing finesse for such a huge, massively flavoured wine. I cannot imagine a wine of this size having a better balance – it's perfect. Those who love big, rich Oz wines should taste this side by side with Rawson's Retreat (also sold by Somerfield) to see why Penfolds sell this for more than twice the price. [*Australia*]

Saint-Joseph Cuvée Médaille d'Or 1991 Cave de Saint-Désirat £8.25

S A basketful of freshly picked blackberry, raspberry and blackcurrant fruit flavours. [*Rhône Valley, France*]

Domaine de la Solitude 1994 Châteauneuf-du-Pape £8.99

S Ultra-modern style of ultra-fresh, elegantly fruity Châteauneuf-du-Pape. [*Rhône Valley, France*]

White Wines

Vin de Pays des Côtes de Gascogne 1995 Somerfield £2.99

B All the tanginess expected from Côtes de Gascogne, but with fatter, riper fruit. [*South-west France*]

The Gyöngyös Estate Chardonnay 1995 Mátraalja **£2.99**

(B) A must for anyone who likes pineapple chunks. [*Hungary*]

Viognier Chais Cuxac 1995 Vin de Pays d'Oc **£3.49**

(B) Lovely fresh, lively fruit for the price. Not much Viognier character, but a nice inexpensive dry white wine in its own right, and a refreshing change from Chardonnay. [*Languedoc-Roussillon, France*]

Niersteiner Spiegelberg Kabinett 1995 Rheinhessen **£3.99**

(S) The freshness of this wine just leapt out of the glass, but then it is 1995 whereas most supermarket German wines are 1994. This will change by Christmas, but most supermarkets have long been uncharacteristically slow in giving most drinkers of German wines what they want: each year's vintage by the spring of the following year. The huge difference that this freshness makes to the easy-drinking, grapy-tangy fruit in this wine should be an object lesson to all supermarket wine buyers. [*Germany*]

☞ SOMERFIELD'S BEST VALUE WHITE WINE

Entre Deux Mers NV Yvon Mau, Somerfield **£3.99**

(B) Elegant, fresh, breezy fruitiness with a crisp, lively finish. [*Bordeaux, France*]

Caliterra Chardonnay 1995 Curico **£4.49**

(B) Deliciously fresh, International style and quality of Chardonnay. [*Curico, Chile*]

Berri Estates Unwooded Chardonnay 1995 South Australia £4·49

Typical bulk-produced Oz Chardonnay. Can't fault the taste or value for your money here. [*Australia*]

Pinot Blanc Vin d'Alsace 1995 Cave des Vignerons Turckheim £4·49

Very clean and precise, with sherbetty-fresh fruit and a genuinely dry finish. [*France*]

Sauvignon Blanc Vin de Pays d'Oc 1995 Le Vieux Mas £4·49

Crisp and fresh, yet as softly structured as the best Bordeaux Sauvignon can sometimes be. Delightful drinking now. Ideal with salads, starters and fish. Great with poached salmon and asparagus. [*Languedoc-Roussillon, France*]

James Herrick Chardonnay 1995 Vin de Pays d'Oc £4·99

Its pure, fresh, immaculate fruit stands out in a comparative tasting of £4.99 Chardonnays. [*Languedoc-Roussillon, France*]

Penfolds Koonunga Hill Chardonnay 1995 South Australia £4·99

Very fresh, lemony-lime aroma with zippy-zingy lemony fruit and a rich but crisp, tangy finish. Koonunga Hill Chardonnay is very consistent, but this is drinking exceptionally well. [*Australia*]

Hardys Nottage Hill Chardonnay 1995 South Eastern Australia £4·99

Fresh, breezy, rich-lemon fruit with a tangy finish. [*Australia*]

Vin d'Alsace Gewurztraminer 1995 Cave des Vignerons Turckheim, Somerfield £5.25

Genuinely dry, which is something of a rarity for Alsace Gewurztraminer these days. Will develop more pungency and greater depth over the next one or two years in bottle. [*France*]

Rosemount Estate Semillon 1995 Hunter Valley £6.49

A fresh, very crisp dry Oz white that demands food. [*Australia*]

Penfolds Padthaway Chardonnay 1992 £6.99

Rich limey fruit balanced by fine acidity make this very appealing and mouthwatering as soon as it hits the palate, and this is followed by very satisfying fruit on the finish, with a definite hint of coconut-oak. [*South Australia*]

Rosé Wines

Syrah Rosé Vin de Pays d'Oc 1995 Les Vignerons du Val d'Orbieu £3.25

Very fresh and clean, this is one of the two cheapest dry rosés I can recommend. [*Languedoc-Roussillon, France*]

Sparkling Wines

Cava Brut Blanc de Blancs NV Coniusa, Somerfield £4.99

Lovely lemony-rich fizz. [*Spain*]

Codorníu Première Cuvée NV Brut Chardonnay £5.99
Richer than most current Cava cuvées, but less zesty and with slightly lower acidity. [*Spain*]

Seaview Brut NV £5.99
What makes Seaview so successful is not just its low price and ultra-reliable fresh, zesty style, but the tiny size of the bubbles. [*McLaren Vale, Australia*]

Crémant de Bourgogne Brut NV Cave de Lugny £6.99
Although this just scraped through the super-selection process, it's heaps better than the Crémant de Bourgogne that did not even survive the tasting, so if you want the cheapest Burgundian fizz recommendable, this is it. [*France*]

Champagne Prince William Brut Reserve NV CM-836, Somerfield £11.95
Fresh, easy-drinking, uncomplicated. [*France*]

Champagne Prince William Blanc de Blancs Brut NV Michel Gonet £14.99
Luscious, creamy-rich Champagne that has the potential to develop stunning, creamy-biscuity complexity. [*France*]

Fortified Wines

Moscatel de Valencia NV Bodegas Vicente Gandia, Somerfield £3.39
Very fresh, raisiny-Muscat fruit aroma, very clean, rich, sweet fruit. This appears to be identical with the other bronze medal Spanish Moscatel recommended (*see* **Tesco**), and there is little to

separate either from the Castillo de Liria Moscatel (*see* **Co-operative Pioneer**). [*Spain*]

Frontignan Vin de Liqueur NV Frontignan Coopérative £5·49

Very fresh indeed, this is softer, more flowery and slightly sweeter than any French or Spanish Moscatel-type wine submitted. [*France*]

Beers

Banks's Bitter Per pint: £0.89

Distinctive flowery-hopped aromas follow through on to the palate. Very smooth. £3.15 per 4 x 500ml bottles. [*3.8%, Wolverhampton, UK*]

Double Maxim Premium Quality Ale Vaux Per pint: £0.98

Strong and malty. £3.45 per 4 x 440ml cans. [*4.7%, Sunderland, UK*]

Bavarian Wheat Beer Weizenbier, Somerfield Per pint: £1.01

Wheat beer in a can with a perfectly homogenized haze deserves a medal for innovation alone. £0.89 per 500ml can. [*5.3%, Bavaria, Germany*]

John Smith's Bitter Per pint: £1.09

Nothing to get excited about, but this is refreshing and dry with a clean bitter-hop finish, and is the cheapest bitter or ale to deserve a medal. £3.39 per 4 x 440ml cans. [*4.0%, Yorkshire, UK*]

Faxe Premium Danish Export Lager Per pint: £1.11

Like drinking sweet, slightly fizzy water; you have little idea that it contains 5 per cent alcohol, which no doubt explains the success of this litre-sized can at parties. Party-goers should be aware, however, that it has the original ring-pull, which sliced up many a foot in outdoor pools when it first appeared in the 1960s – which was why the current, integral opener was invented. So if you see Faxe at a party, don't dance bare-footed. £1.95 per one-litre can. [*5.0%, Denmark*]

French Premium Lager Bière d'Alsace, Somerfield

Per pint: £1.13

Good, unpretentious lager style that's easy to drink and sharp to the bottom of the glass. £4.99 per 10 x 25cl bottles. [*5.0%, France*]

Genuine Irish Stout Somerfield Per pint: £1.20

(S) This Cork-brewed own-label Irish Stout could be either Murphy's or Beamish, as both breweries are based there, but from the smoky aroma, smoky-bitter flavour and hoppy finish, it has to be Beamish. £3.75 per 4 x 440ml widgetized cans. [*4.1%, Cork, Ireland*]

Draught Premium Bitter Somerfield Per pint: £1.20

An easily drinkable brew with a peppery-hopped touch that stands shoulder to shoulder with branded brews at this price point. £3.75 per 4 x 440ml widgetized cans. [*4.2%, UK*]

Boddingtons Draught Per pint: £1.27

(B) A nicely hopped beer, this is much fruitier than John Smith's, the other best-performing widgetized bitter at this price point, and has a correctly crisp finish with some real bitterness on the aftertaste. £3.95 per 4 x 440ml widgetized cans. [*3.8%, Manchester, UK*]

Guinness Original Per pint: £1.29

Dense, dark, bitter chocolate, coffee and liquorice. Quite stern, but great with a Stilton ploughman. £2.99 per 4 x 330ml bottles. [*4.3%, Ireland/UK*]

Gillespie's Draught Malt Stout Per pint: £1.29

This may be the cheapest of the widgetized stouts, but it is certainly one of the most distinctive. Gillespie's is more malty-mellow than its Irish counterparts, and under blind tasting conditions has a smoky 'Camp Coffee' creaminess that I must admit I had not noticed when simply drinking it (and I often have a few tins in the fridge). £3.99 per 4 x 440ml widgetized cans. [*4.0%, Edinburgh, UK*]

Kronenbourg 1664 Courage Per pint: £1.29

Its deep gold colour belies the fresh, hoppy aroma and crisp flavour beneath. Considering that this is canned, not bottled, and brewed in the UK by Courage rather than by Kronenbourg in Strasbourg, it is surprisingly good, with a very authentic character. £3.99 per 4 x 440ml cans. [*5.0%, UK*]

German Pilsener Somerfield Per pint: £1.29

Light, refreshing, hoppy aroma, with a very refreshing taste that stands out amid the heavy, over-rich flavours that can spoil a lager or Pilsner at this price point. £4.49 per 6 x 33cl bottles. [*5.0%, Hamburg, Germany*]

Adnams Suffolk Strong Ale Per pint: £1.33

I'm all for better-quality beer, but if you have to pay the

equivalent of £1.30 a pint, it does not make much sense buying it in two-litre plastic bottles. That said, this good, strong ale does get my vote as the best quality party-sized beer on the market. £4.69 per 2-litre party-size plastic bottle. [*4.5%, UK*]

John Smith's Extra Smooth Bitter Per pint: £1.38

Unless you're into creamy-sweet, ultra-soft brews, the nicely perfumed hops and a decent bitter taste will make this one of the two best widgetized beers at this price point. £4.29 per 4 x 440ml widgetized cans. [*4.0%, Yorkshire, UK*]

Tetley's Draught Yorkshire Bitter Per pint: £1.45

The least widget-affected: the widget delivers a creamy head, but has little effect on the overall taste, which is less creamy than any other widgetized beer. For some, this might be a godsend. £4.49 per 4 x 440ml widgetized cans. [*3.6%, Leeds, UK*]

Marston's Pedigree Bitter Per pint: £1.45

Classic coppery colour with a smooth, dry complex taste highlighted by perfumed hoppy aromas. £1.45 per 568ml bottle. [*4.5%, Burton-on-Trent, UK*]

Budweiser Budvar Per pint: £1.47

Genuine Czech Budweiser has been made since the thirteenth century, and the only remaining example is instantly recognizable from the Budvar part of its name. It is a classic beer: whereas American Budweiser is just bland-tasting, perfumed water made primarily from rice, Budvar is made from pure, top-quality malt. Compare the two beers for yourself and you'll be pleasantly surprised, not the least because the superior, authentic product also happens to be cheaper. £1.29

per 50cl bottle. [*5.0%, Ceske Budejovice, Czech Republic*]

Draught Guinness Per pint: £1.51

G The king of stouts is also the inventor of the widget, which most beer writers abhor and most draught stout drinkers adore. Guinness stands out from the rest by the intensity of its smoky-toasty-malty aroma. It is every bit as smoky as Beamish, but has a greater depth of other top-quality ingredients so that smokiness is not perceived as its main characteristic. Lovely roasted-barley tones echo through malty-rich, smoky-toasty aromas on the mid-palate to give a satisfying edge other stouts lack. £4.69 per 4 x 440ml widgetized cans. [*4.1%, Dublin/London, Ireland/UK*]

☞ THE BEST VALUE DARK BEER OF THE YEAR

Caffrey's Draught Irish Ale Per pint: £1.61

B This light, fresh, creamy-sweet brew is brilliantly marketed. It is not as good as from the tap, even if that is connected to a pressurized keg, but the same could be said for Guinness Draught, and those who like this soft, easy beer will simply be thankful they can keep a reasonable replica ready-chilled in the fridge. Any Caffrey's drinker who has not tasted Wethered's Draught from M&S should do so. It's in a similar style, some will actually prefer it, and it costs 49 pence per pint less. £4.99 per 4 x 440ml widgetized cans. [*4.8%, County Antrim, UK*]

Stella Artois Premium Lager Beer Per pint: £1.63

Really quite a decent lunchtime lager considering the brand's naff reputation amongst serious beer drinkers and the fact that it is brewed in the UK by Whitbread, rather than in Belgium by Stella Artois itself. Light, flowery-Pilsner style. £5.69 per 6 x 330ml bottles. [*5.2%, UK*]

Murphy's Draught Irish Stout Per pint: £1.69

Murphy's is the lightest of the three Irish stouts, and it would not be unfair to describe it as the nearest to Caffrey's, although its smoky-malty aroma gives a far more distinctive edge to its creamy-smoky flavour. Not as dry or as bitter as the other two stouts, it does however fall into the dry, bitter category when tasted in isolation. The bottles used to be less creamy than the cans until Murphy's introduced floating widgets into the latter; now they are both very lightly widgetized. £1.49 per 500ml widgetized bottle. [*4.0%, Ireland/ UK*]

6X Export Wadworth Per pint: £1.69

I do not believe that anyone can seriously enjoy the almost salty richness of sour, sultana-malt taste in this beer, but 6X is so popular that I include it for those who obviously do. £1.49 per 500ml bottle. [*5.0%, Devizes, UK*]

Staropramen Beer Per pint: £1.70

Very elegant, with perfumed hops, this is a truly dry Pilsner style that is soft and so delicately aromatic that it can easily be consumed by those who do not usually like their beers so dry. £0.99 per 330ml bottle. [*5.0%, Prague, Czech Republic*]

'Old Speckled Hen' Strong Pale Ale Morland

Per pint: £1.76

Fresh and tasty with a characterful maltiness in both the aroma and on the palate, which finishes with the barest hint of smoke. Not as good as the cask-conditioned draught, but what bottled beer is? £1.55 per 500ml bottle. [*5.2%, Oxfordshire, UK*]

Beck's Per pint: £1.92

This beer is too popular for its own good. Its clean, fresh taste deserves a recommendation, not a medal, at this price point. If you're in a pub and want to be seen drinking a premium beer, why not go for a Bitburger or Budweiser Budvar and show your Beck's-swilling friends you know something they don't? £5.59 per 6 x 275ml bottles. [*5.0%, Germany*]

Grolsch Premium Lager Per pint: £2.13

G The perfect lager (in bottles anyway). £1.69 per 450ml bottle. [*5.0%, Netherlands*]

☞ THE BEST QUALITY LIGHT BEER OF THE YEAR

Prices

Prices were correct at the time of tasting. You should expect some changes due to exchange-rate fluctuations, prices rising at source, possible increases in VAT and other variables, but these should be within reason, and the historical price in this book will help you to spot any excessive increases.

Please note that prices were not updated prior to publication because all the wines and beers were tasted within their own price category and to change that would be to make a mockery of the blind tasting, the notes made and the medals awarded.

SPAR

Number of stores *'Nearly 2,000'*
Opening hours *All open 8a.m.–10p.m. on a convenience basis, and a small percentage (mostly city-centre stores) open 24 hours a day*
Maximum range *158 wines, 12 beers, 7 spirits*
Alternative methods of payment *At owner-members' discretion, but most recognize every major method of payment and all accept cheque with card and Visa*
Local delivery *Not provided, but will help carry goods to car if requested*
Discounts *It's up to the individual retailers, so try haggling*
Other services *Some shops offer sale-or-return terms, and free loan of glasses*

Comment This really is a case of the least said the better. Spar's young buyer Liz Aked is hard working and a good taster. It is not a case of the products not coming up to standard, but of not submitting enough. Fifteen qualifying out of twenty-four submitted is not a bad percentage. It's three times better than this symbol group did last year, as a matter of fact, but when others are submitting eighty to a hundred wines and thirty-odd beers, Spar is bound to look disappointing in comparison. I tried telling both Liz and Ray this, but although I got some good noises from the latter, nothing materialized.

Red Wines

Sicilian Red Table Wine NV Spar £2.45
Lots of fruit, some grip and a clean, characterful flavour. What more could you want from a cheap Italian red? [*Italy*]

Campo Rojo NV Bodega Coop. San José £3·35

A really tasty mouthful of soft, supple, characterful fruit that makes easy drinking on its own, yet has enough structure and depth to accompany food. [*Spain*]

Chianti 1994 AMF, Spar £4·25

(B) Very fresh and fruity. [*Tuscany, Italy*]

☞ SPAR'S BEST VALUE RED WINE

Merlot Vin de Pays d'Oc 1994 Les Vignerons du Val d'Orbieu, Spar £4·49

Oozing fruit, but with a nice dry tannic finish that makes it more of a food wine than an easy guzzler. One could not expect much more from a *vin de pays*, but it's just a pity it's not a pound cheaper and a gold medal winner! [*Languedoc-Roussillon, France*]

Canepa Merlot 1994 £4·49

Soft berry fruits with a creamy tea and tobacco finish. [*Chile*]

La Fortuna Malbec 1994 Lontue Valley £4·79

(B) Soft, violety-cherry mid-palate fruit with a chewy food wine finish. [*Chile*]

White Wines

Czech White Wine NV Moravian Vineyards, Spar £3·25

This lightly rich, smooth and very clean white wine indicates that if the Czech Republic has any future in winemaking, it will be for easy-drinking dry white wines. [*Czech Republic*]

Chardonnay Vin de Pays d'Oc 1995 Les Vignerons du Val d'Orbieu, Spar £3.89

(S) Delicious richness of fresh, tropical fruits. [*Languedoc-Roussillon, France*]

☞ SPAR'S BEST VALUE WHITE WINE

South African Classic White 1995 W.O. Robertson £3.99

(B) A sort of Ozzified South African wine, although no Australians are involved in the making of this wine as far as I am aware. [*South Africa*]

Canepa Chardonnay 1995 Rancagua £4.49

(B) Lovely, fresh, rich, thirst-quenching fruit. [*Chile*]

Chardonnay Vin de Pays d'Oc 1993 Les Vignerons du Val d'Orbieu, Spar £4.49

Very fresh for a three-year-old Chardonnay, with nice fruit and a hint of underlying oak. [*Languedoc-Roussillon, France*]

Fortified Wines

Old Cellar Late Bottled Vintage Port 1989 Smith Woodhouse £7.15

(B) Very soft, easy and smooth, this makes the ideal premium quality tawny for those who do not (yet?) like the fire and spice in the belly of a great Port. [*Portugal*]

Beers

Spar Extra Lager Per pint: £0.76

The best cheapest lager for those who like a richer, more mellow style. £2.35 per 4 x 440ml cans. [*4.2%, EU*]

Spar Premium Gold Bier Per pint: £0.89

The delicate, wheat-like richness stands out at this price point. £2.75 per 4 x 440ml cans. [*5.0%, EU*]

Joseph Jones Strong Ale Knotty Ash Ales Per pint: £0.96

Perfumed and flowery, with a liquorous texture – if that's the sort of thing you like. £2.99 per 4 x 440ml cans. [*5.0%, Liverpool, UK*]

Different Vintages

Wines recommended in this book are specific to the vintages indicated. Follow-on vintages might be of a similar quality and character, but are likely to be either better or worse. Wines of real interest are seldom exactly the same from one year to the next. Cheap fruity wines, whether white or red, are often better the younger they are, and the difference between vintages is generally less important for bulk wines produced in hotter countries, but even these will vary in some vintages. The difference in vintage is usually most noticeable in individually crafted wines produced the world over. Don't be put off a wine because it is a different vintage, as you could be missing an even greater treat, but do try a bottle before laying out on a case or two.

STOP & SHOP

STOCK ME AND BUY ONE

A chain of 311 off-licensed convenience stores run by CRS (Co-operative Retail Service), which also operates 289 stores currently changing from Leo's, Lo-Cost and Pioneer to Co-operative Pioneer. By virtue of the size and nature of a Stop & Shop, the range of products is far more limited (77 wines, 26 spirits and 40 beers on average) and prices slightly higher. All stores do however have access to the much larger Co-operative Pioneer range, but as most receive just one delivery per week, it may take that long to acquire a product (*see* **Co-operative Pioneer**, page 47).

TESCO

Number of stores *520*
Opening hours *Most open Monday–Friday 8.30a.m.–6p.m., Saturday 9a.m.–6p.m., Sunday 12 noon–4p.m.*
Maximum range *800 wines, 100 beers, 300 spirits*
Alternative methods of payment *Cheque with card, Switch, Access, Visa*
Local delivery *Through Tesco Direct (Freephone 0800 403403)*
Discounts *Last year it was an unspecified quantity discount 'in some stores', but this year you are advised to 'contact head office for details' – what have you got to lose?*
Other services *Loan of glasses in larger stores; permanent tasting area in larger stores*

Comment Currently outpacing Sainsbury's, Tesco has had a knack of getting everything right over the last twelve months, whereas the country's premier supermarket (for how long?) seems to have been floundering. I cannot see Sainsbury's continuing in its current uncertain mood, and Tesco will not give up the lead easily, so we're set for a head-on battle between these two giants over the next twelve months, which can only be good news for the consumer. Sit back and enjoy!

Red Wines

Grenache Vin de Pays d'Oc NV Tesco £2.99

Surprisingly soft and gentle rendition of one of the Rhône's most fiery grapes, with a long finish pushing it above most other wines of this price and type. [*Languedoc-Roussillon, France*]

JP Barrel Selection Red Wine 1991 Vinho Regional Terras do Sado £3·59

(B) There's no mistaking the Portuguese origin of the dry, spicy fruit in this wine, but it has real depth of flavour too and a positive dry tannin finish that would be ideal with a nice juicy roast. [*Portugal*]

☞ TESCO'S BEST VALUE RED WINE

Le Trulle Primitivo del Salento 1994 £3·99

Rich, raspberry-flavoured, full-bodied red wine made by flying winemaker Kym Milne MW and local winemaker Augusto Càntele. [*Italy*]

Italian Merlot del Trentino NV Concilio Vini, Tesco £4·29

(B) Lovely pure fruit aromas follow into a pure fruit richness on the palate, and good, dry, grippy tannins on the finish. It would be difficult to find a dish too powerfully flavoured to partner this wine. [*Italy*]

Chianti Classico 1994 Tesco £4·49

(B) Very tangy, fruit-driven Chianti. [*Tuscany, Italy*]

Fairview Shiraz 1994 £4·49

(S) Absolutely packed with fruit. A touch jammy, perhaps, but fruit-driven with totally delicious, purple-coloured, plummy fruit. Deep, tasty. [*Paarl, South Africa*]

Robertson Shiraz Cabernet Sauvignon 1995 Johann de Wet, Tesco £4·49

(B) So fresh and tangy, there is even a sherbetty character here that is more usually a feature of a white, rather than red, wine. Made for very fresh, easy drinking. [*South Africa*]

Viña Mara Rioja Alavesa NV Tesco £4.89

Although I agree that the oak on most of even the best traditional Riojas is overstated, I am not one of those who want Rioja stripped of its veneer, because when you take it away there is precious little of interest underneath. But for those who do, this is very well made, with ultra-clean, smooth fruit. [*Spain*]

New Zealand Cabernet Sauvignon NV Huapai, Tesco £4.99

Nice to come across a light-coloured, light to medium-bodied red that deserves a medal, as this very fresh, elegant, creamy-oaky wine does. It proves that a red wine does not have to be big and deep coloured to have flavour. [*New Zealand*]

Beyers Truter Pinotage NV Stellenbosch, Tesco £4.99

Creamy-smooth berry fruits underpinned by supple tannins. Good food wine. [*South Africa*]

Vintage Claret 1993 Bordeaux Supérieur, Tesco £4.99

Very soft, smooth, youthful fruit with a lovely hint of oak that builds on the finish. [*Bordeaux, France*]

Spanish Merlot Reserva 1991 Tesco £5.49

Big coconut-oak job to please those who like their wines as thick as two planks. [*Costers del Segre, Spain*]

Viña Mara Rioja Reserva 1988 Tesco £5.49

Attractive plummy fruit and oak concoction. [*Spain*]

Coonawarra Cabernet Sauvignon 1994 Rymill Winery, Tesco £5.99

The berry fruits and firm tannins in this wine are not terribly Australian at first taste, but are very appealing in a food-wine style. [*Australia*]

Barossa Valley Merlot 1993 Tesco £5·99

B Tastes like oak-matured Ribena with a good dollop of blackberry jam. [*Australia*]

Kingston Estate Mataro 1994 Murray Valley £5·99

G Mataro is better known in the Rhône as the Mourvèdre, one of the three best of the thirteen varieties that may be used in Châteauneuf-du-Pape, where it often has a silky Syrah-like quality. In this pure varietal Antipodean version, the Mataro comes across as full and dense, with smooth fruit and smoky-spice complexity. A serious wine of some class. [*Australia*]

Chianti Classico Riserva 1991 Tesco £5·99

S An elegant wine of real depth and class; the fruit has a lovely plummy finesse and a nice dry finish. [*Italy*]

Old Penola Estate Cabernet Sauvignon 1991 Coonawarra £6.99

Recommended more for instruction than pleasure, this meaty, chunky red wine is a textbook example of old-fashioned Coonawarra Cabernet. [*Australia*]

Châteauneuf-du-Pape 1994 Tesco £6.99

S Not as big as some Châteauneuf-du-Pape, but that makes its silver medal all the more well deserved, recognizing its elegance rather than being besieged by its size. Attractive spicy fruit on nose and palate, with a long, dry, grippy tannin finish. [*Rhône Valley, France*]

Maglieri Shiraz 1993 McLaren Vale £6.99

S An immensely attractive wine with oodles of fresh, sweet cedary-spicy fruit and a lovely long finish. [*Australia*]

Kanonkop Pinotage 1994 Stellenbosch £7.99

Ⓑ Big, gutsy, oaky fruit with a long, intense, berry-fruit and grippy tannin finish. [*South Africa*]

Châteauneuf-du-Pape 1993 Les Arnevals £8.29

Ⓖ A gold medal for the pure hedonistic pleasure of deliciously soft, ripe, mellow fruit. [*Rhône Valley, France*]

White Wines

Santa Carolina 1995 White Wine £3.29

Ⓖ Rich and ripe, with peach-flesh and peach-stone fruit of a depth no one could reasonably expect at this price. [*Chile*]

☞ TESCO'S BEST VALUE WHITE WINE

Dry Vinho Verde NV Tesco £3.29

One of only two Vinhos Verdes that just scraped in, this won some admiration for its genuinely dry, barely perceptible spritzy style, which is a blessed relief from the sugared-up, fizzed-up concoctions this country has been fed for twenty years. The difference between the two recommended wines is that this one has a soapy character, which is an indication of its freshness and will disappear, while the other (*see* **Asda**) has a more exotic, lavender style. [*Portugal*]

Orvieto Classico Abboccato NV Tesco £3.89

Ⓑ This wine has been deliberately bottled with residual CO_2 to give a spritz that is absolutely essential to lift the lush fruit of such ripe grapes – which is eminently preferable to the tasteless fruit and peardrop aroma of cool-fermented, barely ripe grapes that most Orvieto is made from. [*Italy*]

Le Trulle Chardonnay del Salento 1994 £3·99

B It's surprising how many wines made by Kym Milne, the flying MW from Oz, survive the tastings and super-selection process. This one has a lovely, invigorating sherbetty richness on the nose and gorgeously fresh, oaky fruit penetrating the palate through to the aftertaste. [*Italy*]

Chenin Blanc Barrel Fermented 1995 Stellenbosch, Pacific Wine £3·99

B I tasted Chenin Blanc from £2.99 upwards, and although I found one under £3.99 to be fresh, clean and drinkable (Great Trek from Littlewoods at £3.49), it did not survive my super-selection process, making this one the cheapest I could recommend. It well deserves a medal: flying Aussie winemaker Kym Milne manages to capture the real flavour of Chenin in this very clean, well-focused wine with its elegantly understated oak. [*South Africa*]

Chilean Sauvignon Blanc NV Talca, Tesco £3·99

B There is a lovely richness about the Sauvignon fruit in this wine, which is also very fresh – if not quite crisp – on the finish. [*Chile*]

Best's Colombard 1994 Victoria £4·49

S Very, very green and crisp, but with such fresh fruit that it is as thirst-quenching as old-fashioned lemonade. [*Australia*]

Chardonnay Réserve 1995 Vin de Pays d'Oc £4·49

Fresh, elegant Chardonnay fruit gently supported by

understated oak. [*Languedoc-Roussillon, France*]

Domaine de la Source Muscat 1995 Vin de Pays de l'Hérault, Tesco £4.49

B Wonderfully fresh, floral-peachy-orange Muscat fruit in a totally dry yet very accessible style, lifted on the finish with a definite spritz. [*Languedoc-Roussillon, France*]

New Zealand Sauvignon Blanc 1995 Gisborne, Tesco £4.49

Very fresh, suck-a-stone, gooseberry fruit. [*New Zealand*]

New Zealand Chardonnay NV Gisborne, Tesco £4.99

S Lovely toasty aromas fill out the crisp, ripe, precise kiwi fruit, which gives way to a long, rich finish. [*New Zealand*]

Hunter Valley Semillon 1994 Tesco £4.99

B Less intense, but fresher, more breezy fruit than the M&S own-label Honey Tree version of this wine. [*Australia*]

McLaren Vale Chardonnay 1995 Tesco £5.99

B Rich, toasty fruit. [*Australia*]

Tim Adams Semillon 1994 Clare Valley £8.99

G Amazing stuff: pure lime aroma and penetrating, pure lime fruit. Like Rose's Lime Cordial with a kick! [*Australia*]

Sparkling Wines

Asti NV Perlino, Tesco £4.99

Vibrantly fresh, delicious, flowery-peachy richness of fruit. [*Italy*]

Robertson Sparkling Wine Brut NV Kangra Farms, Tesco £6.99

Attractive tangy-fruity fizz. [*South Africa*]

Tesco Champagne Brut NV CM-803 £12.95

Rich creamy-biscuity fruit supported by a lovely smooth mousse. Inexpensive, serious quality Champagne made to go with food. [*France*]

Tesco Vintage Champagne Brut 1985 CVC Chouilly £19.99

Lots of fruit and potential to improve, this *cuvée* is a vast improvement on Tesco's 1982 (which was from Cattier, not CVC). [*France*]

Fortified Wines

Moscatel de Valencia NV Tesco £3.49

Very fresh, raisiny-Muscat fruit aroma, very clean, rich sweet fruit. This appears to be identical to the other bronze medal Spanish Moscatel recommended (*see* **Somerfield**), and there is little to separate either from the Castillo de Liria Moscatel (*see* **Co-operative Pioneer**). [*Spain*]

Beers

Ruddles Strong County Traditional Ale Per pint: £0.99

Not as good as from the cask (but what beer is?), this does, however, have a very strong, peppery-malty-hoppy flavour that, up to this price point, is more distinctive than most bottle versions of cask ales. £2.89 per 4 x 275ml bottles. [*4.9%, Rutland, UK*]

Vratislav Lager Tesco Per pint: £1.24

Just as smooth and flowery as last year, but softer and without that toasty-malt flavour that filled out the mid-palate. £1.09 per 500ml bottle. [*5.0%, Vratislavice, Czech Republic*]

Spanish Lager Export Tesco Per pint: £1.29

Crisp, fruity-style lager with correct, flowery-hop fragrance. £2.99 per 4 x 33cl bottle. [*5.5%, Spain*]

German Pilsener Bier Tesco Per pint: £1.35

Fragrant, hoppy aroma with a distinctive long, mellow flavour and crisp, hoppy finish. £4.69 per 6 x 33cl bottles. [*4.9%, Germany*]

Tesco Traditional Premium Ale Caledonian Brewery Per pint: £1.42

This seems to fall closer to Caledonian's 70/- brew than its 80/-, having some sweetness, notably on the finish, and a similar malty taste dominated by perfumed-hops. £1.25 per 500ml bottle. [*4.1%, Edinburgh, UK*]

Bavarian Wheat Beer Tesco Per pint: £1.47

Excellent own-label wheat beer (for people who

like hazy, spiced-apple-flavoured brews) with an assertive, citrus complexity. £1.29 per 500ml bottle. [*4.9%, Germany*]

DAB Original German Beer Dortmunder Actien-Brauerei Per pint: £1.48

(S) Pale, attractive, flowery-hopped aroma, fragrant and elegant on the palate, with a long, smooth, gently rich flavour, just a hint of bitterness, and lifted by a correctly crisp finish. £0.65 per 250ml bottle. [*5.0%, Germany*]

Marston's Pedigree Bitter Draught Per pint: £1.50

(B) The combination of can and widget converts the elegantly perfumed hoppy aromas that make the bottled version so classic into more mellow, somewhat toasty aromas with a creamy-smoky taste. Taste the two side by side and you will see that this brew has nothing in common with the bottled version, but it nevertheless makes one of the most distinctive widgetized brews on the market. £4.65 per 4 x 440ml widgetized cans. [*4.5%, Burton-on-Trent, UK*]

Kronenbourg 1664 Premium Bière Per pint: £1.51

(B) The bottled, Strasbourg-brewed version does have the edge over the British brewed can, but they both represent the same value for money at their respective price points. £3.99 per 6 x 25cl bottles. [*5.0%, France*]

Black Sheep Ale Paul Theakston Per pint: £1.53

(G) Made by Paul Theakston, whose family brewery is now part of Scottish & Newcastle. He alone was determined to maintain an independent status, hence the name Black Sheep. This is classy, distinctive, soft and yet completely dry, with a delicious nutty-hoppy complexity. Although there was a time when M&S's own-label version was better than the original (smokier, with a more mellow bitterness), they are almost identical this year – but why doesn't Paul Theakston market a bottle-conditioned version? £1.35 per 500ml bottle. [*4.4%, Yorkshire, UK*]

☞ THE BEST VALUE BITTER OF THE YEAR

Thurn und Taxis Kristall Weizen Bavarian Weizen Beer Per pint: £1.53

I prefer the assertive style and complexity of Tesco's own-label Bavarian Wheat Beer, with its authentic sediment haze, to this cleaned-up, crystal-clear, bland-tasting peardrop brew from the aristocratic Thurn und Taxis brewery. £1.35 per 500ml bottle. [*5.3%, Germany*]

Bottle Conditioned India Pale Ale Tesco Select Ales, Marston Thompson Evershed Per pint: £1.58

Ⓢ So clean and fresh, with a lovely wisp of smoke drifting through a crisp pale ale bitterness. £1.39 per 500ml bottle. [*5.0%, Burton-on-Trent, UK*]

Caffrey's Draught Irish Ale Per pint: £1.61

Ⓑ This light, fresh, creamy-sweet brew is brilliantly marketed. It is not as good as from the tap, even if that is connected to a pressurized keg, but the same could be said for Guinness Draught, and those who like this soft, easy beer will simply be thankful they can keep a reasonable replica ready-chilled in the fridge. Any Caffrey's drinker who has not tasted Wethered's Draught from M&S should do so. It's in a similar style, some will actually prefer it, and it costs 49 pence per pint less. £4.99 per 4 x 440ml widgetized cans. [*4.8%, County Antrim, UK*]

'Old Speckled Hen' Strong Pale Ale Morland
Per pint: £1.62

Fresh and tasty with a characterful maltiness in both the aroma and on the palate, which finishes with the barest hint of smoke. Not as good as the cask-conditioned draught, but what bottled beer is? £4.29 per 3 x 500ml bottles. [*5.2%, Oxfordshire, UK*]

Fuller's ESB Export Extra Special Bitter
Per pint: £1.64

Not my sort of beer, but its powerful, malty-rich flavour is adored by many. £1.59 per 550ml bottle. [*5.9%, London, UK*]

Hoegaarden White Beer Per pint: £1.70

This has a classic, soapy-spicy aroma and stewed, spiced-apple flavour, but is it worth 23 pence a pint more than Tesco's extraordinarily good own-label? £0.99 per 330ml bottle. [*5.0%, Belgium*]

Moretti Birra Friulana Italian Pilsner Beer
Per pint: £1.70

Crisp, apple-sharp, light-but-not-lacking, Italian lager-style beer with a clean finish. £0.99 per 330ml bottle. [*4.5%, Italy*]

Cobbold's 250 Special Year 1996 Beer Per pint: £1.70

Rich and smooth, with an attractive hint of celery. £0.99 per 330ml bottle. [*6.0%, Suffolk, UK*]

Fischer Tradition Bière Blonde Spéciale d'Alsace
Per pint: £1.74

Perfumed hop aromas, smooth tasting with citric

undertones, in a traditional flip-top bottle that can be resealed if you cannot manage the entire contents. £1.99 per 650ml bottle. [*6.5%, France*]

Fuller's 1845 Bottle Conditioned Celebration Strong Ale Per pint: £1.75

B Give me Fuller's London Pride any day, but others much prefer this bottle-conditioned beer, and even I cannot help admiring its rich, liquorous malty taste and complex coffee-caramel-burnt-toffee aromas. £1.69 per 550ml bottle. [*6.3%, London, UK*]

Bishops Finger Kentish Strong Ale Shepherd Neame Per pint: £1.76

S Taste this next to the canned version and you will realize why the premium charged for bottled beers is well worth paying. Beautifully fresh and crisp with a powerful true-bitter flavour and long, hoppy aftertaste. £1.55 per 500ml bottle. [*5.4%, Kent, UK*]

Spitfire Bottle Conditioned Bitter Shepherd Neame Per pint: £1.76

G A great bitter with an elegant fruity-yeasty fullness, delicate bitter-hop flavours and a beautifully dry, understated finish. One bottle of Spitfire tasted was unbelievably fizzy and aggressively tasteless as a result. The sediment looked to be twice the norm, so I can only imagine that it was a faulty batch, as can sometimes happen with a live beer. If you have a similar experience, be advised that Spitfire should not be like that – but buy another bottle to satisfy yourself. £1.55 per 500ml bottle. [*4.7%, Kent, UK*]

☞ THE BEST QUALITY BITTER OF THE YEAR

Staropramen Beer Per pint: £1.98

Very elegant, with perfumed hops, this is a truly dry Pilsner style that is soft and so delicately aromatic that it can easily be consumed by those who do not usually like their beers so dry. £1.15 per 330ml bottle. [*5.0%, Prague, Czech Republic*]

Jenlain Bière de Garde Ambrée Brasserie Duyck
Per pint: £2.03

Very perfumed, flowery Belgian hops with a sweetish but satisfying spritzy taste. £1.79 per 500ml bottle. [*6.5%, France*]

Norman's Conquest Extra Strong Ale Per pint: £2.05

Dark nut-brown colour with a very rich, firm flavour and lots of citrussy-spice. Well worth a bronze, but the fact that it was CAMRA's Supreme Champion Beer in 1995 illustrates how beer tasters are as prone to biggest-is-best as wine tasters are. £1.19 per 330ml bottle. [*7.0%, Somerset, UK*]

Desperados Tequila Beer Brasserie Fischer
Per pint: £2.05

This is made from lemon and cactus juice – honest – and is thoroughly recommended for anyone who likes paying over £2 a pint for something that tastes like a lager shandy. £1.19 per 330ml bottle. [*5.9%, France*]

Chimay Pères Trappistes 1996 Scourmont Abbey
Per pint: £3.43

Blue Cap, as this particular 9 per cent brew is called (as opposed to 8 per cent White and 7 per cent Red), really has a delightful, hoppy perfume. It is less malty, crisper and not quite so sweet as the heartily recommended La Trappe (*see* **Waitrose**), which makes it preferable in my book, but it could be the other way round if I had a sweeter tooth, as both are excellent quality and value, despite the not inconsiderable price. £1.99 per 330ml bottle. [*9.0%, Belgium*]

Is a £3 Gold medal as good as a £6 Gold medal?

It *is* possible, and no doubt there are some in this edition – but remember that a medal is awarded for style and price category, thus the higher the price the harder it is to earn one and the probability of a significantly cheaper product being just as good is a slim one.

WAITROSE

Number of stores *113*
Opening hours *Vary from store to store, but majority are open Monday and Tuesday 8.30a.m.–6p.m., Wednesday and Thursday 8.30a.m.–8p.m., Friday 8.30a.m.–9p.m., Saturday 8.30a.m.–6p.m., Sunday 10a.m.–4p.m. or 11a.m.–5p.m. (80 branches)*
Maximum range *550 wines, 280 beers, 150 spirits*
Alternative methods of payment *Cheque with card, Switch and Delta debit cards, Access, Visa*
Local delivery *Not provided, except through* Waitrose Direct, *a mail-order service provided under the auspices of its sister company Findlater Mackie Todd (phone 0181 543 0966 for details) and you can pay for this service with a Lewis Partnership Account Card, as well as Visa, Mastercard or cheque; Waitrose supermarket staff will help carry goods to car if requested*
Discounts *5 per cent off a whole case of any wine not subject to another offer, and 12 bottles for the price of 11 on any Wines of the Month*
Other services *Sale or return on party purchases. Free loan of glasses. Gift vouchers for use in either Waitrose or John Lewis stores.*

Comment Despite being fourth on the straight-gold principle and second when weighted, Waitrose could do even better. Perhaps it is because they're down to just three MWs when they are used to five. In any case, however Waitrose performs in my blind tastings (and let's not forget that they did extremely well), it is the most interesting, eclectic and even bizarre range of wines that any supermarket has to offer. On my travels through the north of the country I was often accosted by people who felt frustrated that southern wine writers are always going on about how good Waitrose wines are, yet the nearest branch is hundreds of miles away. Although I think the time is overdue for Waitrose to expand further into the north, the reality is that it is a small, high-quality supermarket group, and there will never be one at every corner south of Watford, let alone north. There is, however, the simplest of solutions: order wines through Waitrose Direct, delivered to your doorstep at supermarket prices.

Red Wines

Winter Hill 1995 Vin de Pays de l'Aude £3·29

If you've often wondered why and how so many wines are acquiring such anglicized names as Winter Hill, the why is always very logical – to attract English-speaking customers who might not know what a *vin de pays* is, let alone anything about the *vin de pays* in question. As to how they acquire their particular anglicized name, each has a different story, and this just happens to be where the importer lives. It's a sturdy red made by modern technology without being Ozzified. [*Languedoc-Roussillon, France*]

Mavrud Reserve 1991 Assenovgrad £3·49

(B) Lovely dry-peppery fruit food wine. [*Bulgaria*]

Waitrose Côtes-du-Rhône 1995 £3·49

(S) Soft, easy, dangerously easy to drink and all for less than £3.50 – what more could you ask from own-label Côtes-du-Rhône? [*Rhône Valley, France*]

☞ WAITROSE BEST VALUE RED WINE

Deer Leap Cabernet Sauvignon/Cabernet Franc 1995 Sopron Region £3·65

Good depth of crisp, grippy raspberry fruit. [*Hungary*]

Good Ordinary Claret NV Waitrose £3.65

Wonderfully understated marketing: this is indeed a Good Ordinary Claret, with soft, fruit-led palate and good, supple tannin structure. Ideal luncheon claret. [*Bordeaux, France*]

Sangiovese Vino da Tavola di Toscana 1994 Fiordaliso £3.75

S A very elegant wine with sweet, plummy fruit and a hint of spice on the finish. [*Italy*]

Waitrose Australian Malbec/Ruby Cabernet 1995 £3.79

B The blood-orange taste of Ruby Cabernet bleeds through the Malbec to dominate this blend. This is one of the best Ruby Cabernet wines, pure or blended, I have tasted. Ruby Cabernet is a cross between Carignan and Cabernet Sauvignon developed for the sweltering heat of California's Central Valley; the Carignan's rustic character tends to coarsen the grape's blood-orange flavour, but not in this case. [*Australia*]

Ermitage du Pic St. Loup 1995 Coteaux du Languedoc £3.99

B The 1994 was still available at the time of tasting and had gained length, creaminess and some spicy finesse since I tasted it for the first edition of *SuperBooze*; the 1995 promises to be even better. [*Languedoc-Roussillon, France*]

Barbera d'Alba di La Morra 1994 Cantina Terre del Barolo £4.75

S Extremely elegant Barbera, fine fruit-acidity balance and well-focused varietal character. [*Piedmont, Italy*]

Graves 1994 Ginestet £4·75

Has the violety aroma of a true Graves and builds slowly in the glass, which makes it an excellent food wine, although a taster could be forgiven for not noticing this when motoring past on auto-palate. [*Bordeaux, France*]

Agramont 1992 Navarra, Bodegas Príncipe de Viana £4·75

Big, rustic, oaky mouthful with plenty of fruit. [*Spain*]

Valdivieso Barrel-Fermented Cabernet-Merlot 1994 Lontue £4·99

Very elegant, although there's definitely some residual sweetness on the finish of this ripe, fruity red. [*Chile*]

Château Saint Auriol 1993 Corbières £4·99

Full-bodied, traditionally structured in the food-wine mould, with a classy nose for its modest appellation, deep, inky fruit and a concentrated flavour that is neither fat nor too rich. [*Languedoc-Roussillon, France*]

Avontuur Pinotage 1995 Stellenbosch £4·99

Inky-coloured wine with just enough *macération carbonique* to bring out the ultra-creamy rich fruit without going bubble-gummy. Excellent grippy tannins, to drink on its own or with food. [*South Africa*]

Red Burgundy 1994 Bourgogne Passetoutgrains, Jean-Claude Boisset £4·99

Tasted in the company of Gamay wines, very elegant Pinot fruit comes through with a gentle touch of oak, but tasted against Pinot Noirs, the Pinot character is submerged. In both cases, however, the fruit is very soft, juicy and attractive, making this unmistakably top-quality Passetoutgrains. [*France*]

Cartlidge & Browne Zinfandel NV £4·99

A really flavoursome, jammy-jello style of Zinfandel with a kick on the finish. [*California, USA*]

Vale do Bomfim Reserva 1990 Douro £5·35

Soft, elegant and clean as a whistle, this wine is chock-a-block full of flavour. [*Portugal*]

Château La Favière 1994 Bordeaux Supérieur £5·35

Sweet-perfumed aroma and elegant fruit with a dry tannic finish. [*Bordeaux, France*]

Yaldara Grenache Reserve 1995 Whitmore Old Vineyard, Barossa £5·75

Chewy, creamy-rich, jammy fruit. [*Australia*]

Tatachilla Cabernet Sauvignon 1994 McLaren Vale & Langhorne Creek £5·99

A gorgeous wine full of intense, blackcurranty fruit in a creamy-rich style with bags of ripe acidity. A beautiful wine, but so complete all you need is a knife and fork – no food! [*Australia*]

Fetzer 1993 Valley Oaks Cabernet Sauvignon £5·99

It is easy to make soft, luscious Cabernet in California, but they are all too often everyday drinking wines; it is difficult to make a wine as soft and ripe as this with such elegance and class. [*California, USA*]

Crozes Hermitage 1992 Cave des Clairmonts £6.45

Fresh raspberry fruit with a peppery finish. [*Rhône Valley, France*]

Gigondas 1994 Domaine Sainte Lucie £6.95

This tasty mouthful supported by good grippy tannins would have been a medal contender if a pound cheaper. In fact, at the annual Waitrose tasting I had speculated bronze going on silver in my notes, but under blind conditions it simply could not hack it at this price level with medal-winning wines from other supermarkets – which proves not only how essential blind tasting is, but tasting like with like within the same price category. [*Rhône Valley, France*]

Bourgogne Hautes-Côtes de Beaune Tête de Cuvée 1992 Les Caves des Hautes-Côtes £6.99

Rich, plummy-redcurranty Pinot fruit of some complexity. [*France*]

Browns of Padthaway Shiraz 1994 £6.99

You might think this deserves a gold medal, but a good many people will loathe it and wonder why it receives a mention at all. Even those who loathe it will agree that its smooth, warm, cedary-oaky bouquet is very attractive, but where they will come unstuck with this wine is its strange balance, which almost makes it taste salty or like iodine. Almost, but not quite: rather than actually *tasting* of salt or iodine, it has a curious salty feel in the mouth. It is as if oak sap – not essence – has been added. What the heck! I cannot describe this most unusual characteristic, which falls somewhere between texture and taste. You'll just have to buy a bottle and taste it yourself to see what I mean, and no doubt a few of you will be intrigued enough to do just that. [*Australia*]

Avignonesi 1992 Vino Nobile di Montepulciano £7.95
(S) Excellent richness and typicity of fruit, deft balance and a long, lingering finish. [*Tuscany, Italy*]

Fleurie 1995 Château des Déduits, Waitrose £7.99
(S) Real Beaujolais that's worth the money? Must be a scam . . . but no, this has true Gamay flavour and elegance, yet gluggy-creamy fruit, which is something that very few of even the best Beaujolais can boast. [*Burgundy, France*]

Chorey-les-Beaune 1993 Domaine Maillard £9.75
Apricot and plums with a touch of oak. [*Burgundy, France*]

Beaune Premier Cru 1993 Edouard Delaunay £9.95
(B) Pure Pinot fruit of some class in an easy-drinking style. [*Burgundy, France*]

Clos Saint Michel Châteauneuf-du-Pape 1994 Guy Mousset £9.95
(G) The most deliciously perfumed, elegantly spiced fruit in the entire Châteauneuf-du-Pape tasting. [*Rhône Valley, France*]

Le Pergole Torte 1987 Monte Vertine £9.95
(S) The lush sweetness of very ripe fruit gently supported by beautifully integrated oak. [*Tuscany, Italy*]

White Wines

Deer Leap Dry White 1995 Hárslevelu £2.99
(B) Easy to drink crisp white wine with very fresh and zesty fruit. [*Hungary*]

Diamond Hills Chenin Blanc/Chardonnay 1995 £3·75
Very fresh, crisp aperitif style with an attractive richness of fruit on the finish. [*South Africa*]

Deer Leap Gewürztraminer 1995 Mór Region £3.85
Were it not for the Romanian Gewurztraminer more than a pound cheaper (*see* **Co-operative Pioneer**), I would be going wild about this wine, simply because it has a real spiciness seldom found outside Alsace. This wine also has high acidity and the pungency of its spice will increase over the next year or two in bottle, whereas the Romanian wine is designed more for immediate consumption. [*Hungary*]

Santa Julia Chardonnay 1995 £3·99
This one is for those who like a leesy Chardonnay style. [*Argentina*]

Fairview Chenin Blanc 1995 Paarl £3·99
Creamy-rich tropical fruits with a smack of sweetness on the finish. [*South Africa*]

Cuvée d'Alban Barrique Fermented 1995 Bordeaux £3·99
Excellent richness of pure Semillon fruit with upfront, oaky overtones and a lovely, dry, oaky-tannin finish. A great food wine now, it should be even better by Christmas; it will be interesting to see how it develops with another year in bottle. Ridiculously cheap for a serious white Bordeaux. [*France*]

Longuicher Probstberg Riesling Spätlese 1988 Moselland £4·45
Good, ripe and well rounded with age, a fresh eight-

year-old Mosel for under a fiver cannot be bad. [*Mosel-Saar-Ruwer, Germany*]

Le Voyageur Sauvignon 1995 Bordeaux £4·45

(B) Gentle, ripe fruit with a perfumed aftertaste. Lovely old-fashioned label. [*Bordeaux, France*]

Agramont Viura Chardonnay 1995 Navarra £4·75

(B) Fresher and not as fat as the 1994 (*see* **Safeway**), this is just as rich and oaky, and even fresher. Delicious drinking for the money, particularly if you go for more oaky wines. [*Spain*]

Roussanne Vin de Pays d'Oc 1995 Hugh Ryman £4·75

(S) Even under blind conditions, it was easy to discern the Australian influence on this gently oaked wine. Although it turned out to be made by Hugh Ryman, a Brit, he was Australian-trained. [*Languedoc-Roussillon, France*]

Soave Classico 1995 Vigneto Colombara, Zenato £4·95

(B) Fresh, ripe fruity flavour of exceptional sherbetty finesse for Soave. [*Italy*]

Chardonnay/Sauvignon Blanc Vin de Pays d'Oc 1995 Domaine Bousquet £4·99

(S) So fresh, ripe and succulently rich, I do not even want to contemplate how sweet this supposedly dry wine is: drink and enjoy. Made by Australian-trained, English-born Hugh Ryman. [*Languedoc-Roussillon, France*]

Erdener Treppchen Riesling 1991 Mönchhof £4·99

The diffused petrolly aroma indicates that this wine is going through a transition and the odds are that it will emerge as a medal-winner. Very good sherbetty-petroly-lime fruit mid-palate, with a grassy aftertaste that needs some bottle-mature, mellowing honey. [*Mosel-Saar-Ruwer, Germany*]

Cuckoo Hill Viognier 1995 Vin de Pays d'Oc £4·99

(B) Very juicy fruit, extremely fresh and long. [*Languedoc-Roussillon, France*]

Gewürztraminer Vin d'Alsace 1993 Waitrose, C.V.B. £5·79

(B) Nice fruit with a touch of honeyed spice, but not showing as well as it did last year, when it won a silver medal. However, it still promises to develop more pungency of spice, so it is probably going to be much better next year. The three MWs at Waitrose spell Gewurztraminer with a u-umlaut, although French Alsace no longer adopts this German practice. [*France*]

Geisenheimer Mönchspfad Riesling Spätlese 1990 Schumann-Nägler £5·99

(G) A racy, petroly nose that's more Mosel than Rheingau, but absolutely Riesling, no doubt about that. The palate is, however, unmistakably Rheingau, with ripe peaches and even a strawberry-like succulence on the finish. Sensational quality – and brilliant value, considering it's from such a top-performing estate. [*Rheingau, Germany*]

Tokay Pinot Gris Vin d'Alsace 1994 Cave de Beblenheim £3·39 (half-bottle)

(B) A bit of a gamble, this, but its lovely bouquet is so reminiscent of the richness of a Vendange Tardive Pinot Gris that I am willing to bet that it will fill out on the palate, which is curiously devoid of fruit, never mind varietal character. I just cannot believe that the richness on the nose comes from absolutely nothing – there must be fruit waiting to burst through on the palate, and its genuinely dry style does not help in trying to discern where it is. Keep for up to two years. [*France*]

Bacharacher Schloss Stahleck Riesling Kabinett 1992 Weingut Toni Jost **£6.95**

(S) This Kabinett is sweeter than some Spätlesen, has a nice hint of petrol on the nose and luscious Riesling fruit on the palate, lifted by a pleasing spritz on the finish. [*Mittelrhein, Germany*]

Saltram Mamre Brook Chardonnay 1994 **£6.99**

(S) Luscious creamy-tangy fruit that drinks beautifully on its own. [*Australia*]

Penfolds Organic Wine 1994 Chardonnay-Sauvignon Blanc, Clare Valley **£6.99**

(B) Mouthwatering lemony-lime fruit on nose and palate with a refreshing crispness, rather than taste, of Sauvignon on the finish. Only gets a bronze because it's available elsewhere at £1 less. [*Australia*]

Pouilly-Fumé 1995 Domaine J.M. Masson-Blondelet **£7.49**

(B) The intense fruit character is more Sancerre than Pouilly Fumé, but it has true Fumé finesse. [*Loire, France*]

Ninth Island Chardonnay 1995 Tasmania Wine Company **£7.99**

(G) Rich, classic Chardonnay from Australia's ultimate cool-climate vineyards. As it happens, this was tasted side by side with the 1994 vintage (submitted by another supermarket), and it is interesting to note that I had written 'absolutely *à point*' for this beautiful wine and 'starting to go over' for the 1994. It would do no harm to drink this up by Christmas or New Year's Day, and it would certainly be a pleasure to do so. [*Australia*]

Ungsteiner Honigsäckel Gewürztraminer Spätlese 1994 Pfälz, Weingut Pfeffingen £7·99

Ⓢ Lovely, sweet-mellow, spicy Gewurztraminer. Soft and fruity. [*Germany*]

Lawson Dry Hills Sauvignon Blanc 1995 Marlborough £7·99

Ⓢ This delicious wine demonstrates how much finesse New Zealand's climate can bring to this hit-you-between-the-eyes grape variety. [*New Zealand*]

Rosemount Estate Show Reserve Chardonnay 1994 Hunter Valley £8.95

Ⓢ Rich, classy Chardonnay fruit. Impeccably balanced for current drinking. [*Australia*]

Passito di Pantelleria 1994 Pellegrino £5·45 (half-bottle)

Ⓖ For some reason I wrote 'all warm thoughts' about this sweet straw wine. Perhaps you will have to taste it to find out why, but I can still remember the wonderful honeyed-coffee aftertaste that went on and on. [*Italy*]

Rosé Wines

Nagyréde Cabernet Sauvignon Rosé 1995 £3·25

Ⓢ An exceptionally deep flavour for such a cheap wine, with elegant rose petal and strawberry aromas for easy supping on a balmy summer afternoon. The surprising quality of this wine is, however, its fine, ripe acidity, which makes it an ideal accompaniment to most tomato-based dishes. Serve it blind with a *tricolore* of tomato, mozzarella and avocado or tomato baked in cream, and your guests will never imagine this wine to be Hungarian, and will think it cost three times the price! [*Hungary*]

Sparkling Wines

Waitrose Cava Brut NV Castellblanch £4.95

The cheapest fizz in the tasting also turned out to be one of the most outstanding bargains in the book. Cava has been on a roll for at least eighteen months, and this is the best example I have tasted in a long while. Although a couple of other Cavas from the same producer showed a similar fresh, zesty style with truly excellent acidity and depth, they could not quite match the sensationally fresh lime-peel aromas in this *cuvée*. [*Spain*]

Clairette de Die Tradition 1993 Comtesse de Die, Première Cuvée £6.45

Definitely a sweet wine, although nowhere near as sweet as an Asti, it has the most heavenly peachy-Muscat fruit aroma and flavour of all the wines tasted, and a certain class and finesse that puts it on a completely different quality level. [*Rhône Valley, France*]

☞ THE BEST VALUE SPARKLING WINE OF THE YEAR

Krone Borealis Brut 1993 Twee Jonge Gezellen £6.99

Ⓑ Soft, easy, deliciously gentle fruit that falls somewhere between New and Old World in character. The previous vintage (1992) developed a nice malty-biscuity complexity by the spring of 1996, so you should be able to keep this one for up to twelve months with no worries. [*South Africa*]

Waitrose Champagne Blanc de Blancs Brut NV NM 143 £13.95

Ⓢ The classic, creamy-nutty *blanc de blancs* complexity in this Champagne comes from good landed-age. [*France*]

Waitrose Champagne Brut Rosé NV CM 806 £14.95

Ⓑ This attractive rosé is made by Vve Devaux in the Aube, which has a certain reputation for producing excellent value, fruity rosé. [*France*]

Waitrose Champagne Brut 1989 NM 123 £14.95

Ⓢ Lovely richness of fruit, beginning to drink well now, but quite capable of improving over the next year or two, picking up a creamy-biscuity finesse along the way. [*France*]

Fortified Wines

Southbrook Farms Framboise NV Canada

£7.99 (half-bottle)

This is not really a wine in the sense of fruit of the vine, let alone a fortified wine – but this sweet Canadian liqueur has such a heady, powerful, concentrated raspberry aroma that I simply had to include it. God knows what you can do with it: you could add it to a dry white Burgundy to make it palatable, but I don't keep such astringent wines and it would not enhance the Framboise. Pour it over ice-cream perhaps? Why not buy a bottle and see what you think – answers on a postcard and a case of wine to the best or wittiest! [*Canada*]

Beers

Waitrose Czech Lager Per pint: £1.12

Soft, delicate, perfumed Pils style. £0.99 per 500ml bottle. [*5.0%, Vratislavice, Czech Republic*]

Waitrose German Lager Per pint: £1.14

Flowery Pilsner-style aroma and flavour with a soft, fragrant finish. £3.99 per 6 x 330ml bottles. [*4.8%, Germany*]

Waitrose Westphalian Lager Per pint: £1.29

Even better than last year's brew, the current one has a lovely hop-pillow aroma and its bright, light-lemon colour perfectly expresses the crisp, flowery-hopped flavour, which remains sharp to the bottom of the glass. £2.99 per 4 x 330ml bottles. [*5.0%, Germany*]

Waitrose Very Strong Lager Per pint: £1.29

I must admit that these super-strong lagers are not for me, but if that's what turns you on, this has an elegance most others lack, with fragrant, perfumed hop aromas and a fresh finish. £3.99 per 4 x 440ml cans. [*8.5%, UK*]

Enigma Draught Lager Guinness Per pint: £1.29

A bronze within the context of a widgetized lager, I hasten to add, although for a brewery that is responsible for Harp lager, I'm almost inclined to give Enigma a knighthood! This rises above the other widgetized lagers because, like Guinness, it has a touch – just a touch – more CO_2 than other brands. In a lager this spritz gives a certain crispness to the finish, which is refreshing after the creaminess. The perfumed hops also add some much-needed authenticity to a widgetized lager. £3.99 per 4 x 440ml widgetized cans. [*5.0%, UK*]

Adnams Suffolk Strong Ale Per pint: £1.30

I'm all for better-quality beer, but if you have to pay the equivalent of £1.30 a pint, it does not make much sense buying it in two-litre plastic bottles. That said, this good, strong ale does get my vote as the best quality party-sized beer on the market. £4.59 per 2-litre party-size plastic bottle. [*4.5%, UK*]

Murphy's Draught Irish Stout Per pint: £1.51

Scrapes in at silver because the new metallic floating widgets seem to be less effective than the plastic floating widgets Murphy's use in their bottles. I picked out the can under blind conditions every time (well OK, I only tried it twice, but three cans to one bottle each time is statistically impressive) and assume this to be because the metallic device floats with its pinhole facing upwards, and hence releases its contents into the nitrogen-filled space rather than into the beer itself. £4.69 per 4 x 440ml widgetized cans. [*4.0%, UK/Ireland*]

Fuller's ESB Export Extra Special Bitter
Per pint: £1.64

(B) Not my sort of beer, but its powerful, malty-rich flavour is adored by many. £1.59 per 550ml bottle. [*5.9%, London, UK*]

Fuller's 1845 Bottle Conditioned Celebration Strong Ale
Per pint: £1.75

(B) Give me Fuller's London Pride any day, but others much prefer this bottle-conditioned beer, and even I cannot help admiring its rich, liquorous malty taste and complex coffee-caramel-burnt-toffee aromas. £1.69 per 550ml bottle. [*6.3%, London, UK*]

Bishops Finger Kentish Strong Ale Shepherd Neame
Per pint: £1.76

(S) Taste this side by side with the canned version, and you will realize why the premium charged for bottled beers is well worth paying. Beautifully fresh and crisp, with a powerful true-bitter flavour and long, hoppy aftertaste. £1.55 per 500ml bottle. [*5.4%, Kent, UK*]

Edinburgh Strong Ale Caledonian Brewery
Per pint: £1.87

(B) Strong malty aromas with fruity-spicy hints, a nice dry, rich taste and a long, peppery-hop finish. £1.65 per 500ml bottle. [*6.4%, Edinburgh, UK*]

Pete's Wicked Ale Per pint: £1.90

Pete must have been brought up in a very strict household if this is his idea of wicked, but it does have an interesting, chocolaty-coffee edge to the aroma. £1.19 per 355ml bottle. [*5.1%, USA*]

La Trappe Koningshoeven Trappiste Brune

Per pint: £3.40

A bronze medal despite the price for this sweet, fresh, characterful Trappist ale with its exquisitely clean, ripe-fruity-malty flavour, but how bottle-conditioned is it? After congratulating myself on pouring so much from the bottle in crystal-clear condition, I opened another, having first given it a good shake, only to find a slight haze. It does not detract one iota from the quality of the beer, but I think this Holy Order is being economical with the truth! A smidgen of yeast, perhaps? £2.99 per 500ml bottle. [*6.5%, Netherlands*]

SPECIAL FEATURE: THE HARD SOFT-DRINK BOOM

SuperBooze gives its verdict on the controversial alcoholic lemonade issue

It all started in an Australian pub, when licensee Duncan MacGillivray served a local lemon-grower who was looking to offload his surplus crop. Why not ferment them? he thought. A good job no winemakers were present, because they might have told him that fermentation requires sugar – and there's precious little of it in a mouth-puckering lemon. According to one story, a couple of winemakers *were* present when Old Dunc had his bright idea. Apparently they gave each other wicked grins, winked, sank the beers in front of them, one burped and the other just said, 'That'll be another two pints, Dunc.'

Well, Old Dunc had the last laugh. Quite how much sugar he had to shovel into his brew is unclear, but the result was such a success that he now buys up a third of all the lemons grown in South Australia. His product? Two Dogs, and the retail value of his sales currently stands at more than £13 million per year.

The first alcoholic lemonade to be sold in this country was Hoopers Hooch as recently as June 1995, and the paradox is that while 80 per cent of the population is unaware of its existence, it has quickly become a runaway success, with sales for 1996 estimated at some ten million cases! How come?

It was launched just before the so-called Silly Season, during which the media traditionally has nothing better to do than to hype up any story that appears. Without putting a team of researchers on the job, it would be very difficult to discern who first made the allegation that Hoopers Hooch and Two Dogs were directly targeting young children by calling these products 'alcoholic lemonade', but it was probably a TV consumer programme. The programme reported how it had successfully sent children into supermarkets to buy these alcoholic products.

Producers have since agreed to drop the word lemonade and label these products as 'alcoholic lemon drinks'. It does not, however, require much thought to realize what a media-generated farce this whole alcoholic lemonade story has been. Surely no one would swallow the idea that a multi-million pound investment would deliberately hinge its success on targeting children? What's their disposable income, for God's sake? If it was not deliberate targeting, then perhaps it was accidental? The only problem with that suggestion is that the stuff never did appeal to children anyway. Ask any cheeky small boy likely to have a guzzle whether he would like a beer or some alcoholic lemonade, and guess which most would opt for? The beer, of course. Not much to feel grown-up about in drinking alcoholic lemonade, is there? But a beer, like his dad drinks – or one of the older boys who passes for being 18 in a pub – now *that's* different.

At the heart of the under-age drinking problem is the simple fact that children want to act big, to be like grown-ups. This is why the idea that you could target children by calling such a product lemonade is totally ridiculous. The irony is that those who created this myth did not sink the product, but actually made it the phenomenal success it has so quickly become. Those who picked up the idea of alcoholic lemonade from the television reports could not possibly be children, unless they are children who prefer consumer and news-oriented programmes to Beavis and Butthead. No, they are exactly the audience the producers of these drinks wanted to target. They are young but not children. They are in the 18 to 24 age group, and do you know what? They do not like the taste of alcohol. That's right, but they do enjoy the effect that alcohol provides, quite legally of course, which is why these soft drinks with a hard kick have become so successful. It's true that you cannot taste the alcohol, but if those reporters visit clubs and theme pubs all over the country, they'll see exactly who is drinking the stuff.

Another ironic twist was that the media fuss forced producers to change the word lemonade to lemon. This was no hardship. It was in fact a godsend for the marketing people, who were at that very moment trying to work out how they could sell other flavours on the back of the lemonade name, which was proving a hard nut to crack.

What about the TV reporters who proved that supermarkets were selling this stuff to kids, I hear you ask. Obviously I do not condone such a practice, but we will never know how successful the children would have been had they been told to buy a six-pack of Budweiser from the same stores. The issue was not selling alcoholic lemonade to kids, but selling any alcoholic product to them.

In the following table I indicate the level of fizziness, sweetness and zest on a scale of 1 to 5 (the higher the rating, the more fizzy, sweet or zesty it is), as these seem to be important to the style of this sort of product. Remember this is a scale, not a score, meaning that high numbers in all of these columns might not necessarily be to your taste. The scales will probably be more useful once you have purchased one of the products listed below, as you can then decide whether you would like something, say, more zesty or less fizzy, and then check which will be the best candidates for your own taste.

Rating	Product	Alcohol	Fizz	Sweetness	Zest	Supermkt.
☆☆	Lemon Lightning Alcoholic Lemonade, Inch's Cider Ltd	4.7%	1	2	2	Co-op
☆	Lemon Lips Alcoholic Lemonade	5.0%	3	2	1	Asda
☆☆☆☆	Barker's Liquid Gold Sparkling Alcoholic Cola	4.3%	4	4	2	Morrisons
☆☆☆	Two Dogs Alcoholic Lemon Australian Original, Merrydown	4.0%	2	3	3	Co-op
☆☆	Decoda Alcoholic Soda, Western Soda Company	5.3%	4	4	1	Londis
☆☆	Memphis Mist Premium Alcoholic Cola	4.9%	3	2	2	Londis
☆☆☆☆	Hooch Alcoholic Lemon, Hooper's	4.7%	2	2	4	Co-op
☆☆☆	Hooch Alcoholic Orange, Hooper's	5.1%	4	4	4	Co-op
☆☆	Hooch Alcoholic Blackcurrant, Hooper's	5.1%	3	4	4	Co-op
☆☆	Woody's Alcoholic Pink Grapefruit Drink	4.7%	3	3	3	Co-op
☆	Woody's Alcoholic Lemon Fruit Drink	4.7%	2	3	3	Co-op
☆☆☆	Woody's Alcoholic Strawberry & Lemon Fruit Drink	4.7%	4	3	4	Co-op

Price	Per Alc.[1]	Per Litre[2]	Comment
2.29	0.49	2.29	Clear water-white, hint of ginger to less than natural lemon aroma and flavour.
1.99	0.53	2.65	Old-fashioned lemonade appearance (like lemon barley) with lots of fresh lemon aroma when poured, but this fades quicker than with other fresh lemon brands. Very zesty flavour at first, but quickly turns watery in the mouth. Not the freshest finish.
0.89	0.63	2.70	Actually smells and tastes like a famous brand of real cola.
0.89	0.68	2.70	Looks like murky water, as if you've just rinsed out a milk bottle. Very fresh lemon aroma. Softer, sweeter and slightly less zesty than Hooch.
0.89	0.51	2.70	A hint of ginger and citrus aromas followed by a slight citrus flavour.
0.89	0.55	2.70	If you like cola with ginger and vanilla, this Bourbon-boosted carbonate is for you.
0.99	0.64	3.00	Old-fashioned lemonade appearance (like lemon barley) with piercing fresh lemon aroma and fresh, zesty, old-fashioned lemonade flavour. The sweetness is balanced by zest, making it very zingy. Richer, longer lasting, with more flavour than most brands.
0.99	0.59	3.00	Deepest orange in colour, this carbonate has an Orangina-like aroma and flavour. The most concentrated of the alcoholic orange drinks and really quite sweet, but a good zestiness prevents it from being too cloying.
0.99	0.59	3.00	Pungent blackcurrant aroma and flavour. If you're used to drinking lager and blackcurrant, this should make an ideal 'short', but most people will find it difficult to drink a single glass.
0.99	0.64	3.00	The aroma is so powerfully grapefruit that it actually loses the true character of this fruit. Initially it tastes nice and grapefruity, but the excessively citrus aromatics catch at the back of the throat.
0.99	0.64	3.00	Old-fashioned lemonade appearance and, initially, fresh lemon aroma, but this quickly tires. Artificial lemon flavouring type of taste, lifted by a zesty finish.
0.99	0.64	3.00	A pale, milky-pink colour with the aroma and tangy flavour of strawberry-flavoured Opal Fruits.

Rating	Product	Alcohol	Fizz	Sweetness	Zest	Supermkt.
☆	Woody's Alcoholic Orange Fruit Drink	4.7%	2	5	3	Co-op
☆☆	Mog Original Alcoholic Cream Soda, Shack Beverage Co.	4.0%	5	3	0	Co-op
☆☆☆☆☆	Lemonhead Alcoholic Lemon, Waverley Beer Co	4.9%	4	1	5	Co-op
☆	Vault Alcoholic Soda, Waverley Beer Company	5.3%	3	3	1	Asda
☆☆	Max Black Cider with Blackcurrant Flavouring, Bulmers Ltd	5.0%	3	2	3	Morrisons
☆☆☆	Shott's Vanilla Heist Alcoholic Seltzer	5.3%	2	4	0	Co-op
☆☆☆☆	Shott's Lemon Jag Alcoholic Seltzer	5.3%	2	2	4	Co-op
☆☆	Diamond Zest Lemon Cider Cooler, Taunton Cider	5.0%	3	2	4	Asda
☆	Mrs Pucker's Alcoholic Cola Citrus Brew	4.0%	4	4	1	Co-op
☆☆	Mrs Pucker's Alcoholic Lemon Citrus Brew	5.5%	3	4	2	Co-op
☆☆	Skinny Pucker's Alcoholic Lemonade Low Cal Citrus Brew	4.0%	3	4	2	Co-op

Notes

1 Per Alcohol is the price for a litre at 1%ABV, which may be higher than the Per Alcohol price of a seemingly more expensive product if the alcohol level is lower.
2 Per Litre is the straight price per litre without taking into account the different alcoholic degrees.

Price	Per Alc.[1]	Per Litre[2]	Comment
0.99	0.64	3.00	Fresh orange aroma and quite a fresh taste too, but watery with very little flavour.
0.99	0.75	3.00	The distinctive aroma and flavour reminds me of the sweet, vanilla-caramel chunks found in some toffee ice-creams. I cannot imagine who would drink this, but you could try thickening it with arrowroot and pouring it over a chocolate nut sundae
0.99	0.61	3.00	Aptly named, this is for lemonheads – and you'll end up looking like the lemonhead on the label if you drink too much of this stuff. Piercing fresh lemon aroma, very tart fresh lemon taste, fizzy and acid.
0.99	0.57	3.00	Watery-sweet with a hint of citrus.
0.85	0.62	3.09	This pale pink, blackcurranty concoction is the most successful of all the cider-based carbonates, but I wouldn't drink it.
1.09	0.62	3.30	Like a creamier version of Mog Original. Why not use it to flavour milk shakes?
1.09	0.62	3.30	Bright lemon colour, absolutely clear, with fresh, zesty lemon aroma and flavour. Lively and fresh.
0.95	0.69	3.45	If you want a cider-based, lemon-flavoured carbonate, this is the one to buy. A milky-white colour with fresh, zesty lemon aroma and flavour.
0.99	0.90	3.60	Quite like cola on the nose, but doesn't taste like it. Very sweet and frothy.
0.99	0.65	3.60	Looks, smells and tastes like the cheap, sweet, water-white lemonade that comes in two-litre plastic bottles, and in that sense it could be judged the most successful of all these products, although it's not the freshest, zestiest or tastiest.
0.99	0.90	3.60	Unlike Skinny Pucker's Cola, Skinny Pucker's Lemon is very similar to Mrs Pucker's fully fledged version.

I am indebted to Colin Emmins's *Soft Drinks, Their Origins and History* (Shire Publications) for some of the background material used in this feature.

THE WINE & BEER RANKINGS

Virtually all the wines found under each supermarket entry can be found here, listed in ascending order of price by type, style, region and country. Do not ignore non-medal wines or beers, as they too survived the rigorous tasting and are highly recommended. Indeed, if this book is to be judged on anything, it must be the quality of the products that carry no medals. If they are truly outstanding, then the reader will be reassured about the superiority of all the other wines and beers in the guide.

Where a price seems to be out of logical order, this will be because of a non-standard bottle size (such as half-bottles or 2-litre and 3-litre wine boxes).

RED WINES

Argentina

The Falklands War upset things for the Argentinians just as their wines were about to become established on the UK market, but they are creeping back on to the shelf. The country still has a lot to prove in the medium-price range and above, but being the fifth-largest wine-producing country in the world should enable it to satisfy our more basic needs. Prices ranged from £2.99 to £4.99.

Bronze	Mission Peak Red NV	£2.99	**Co-op**
	Argentine Country Red NV Somerfield	£2.99	**Somerfield**
Silver	Trapiche Malbec Oak Cask Reserve 1992 St Michael	£4.99	**Marks & Spencer**

Bordeaux

These wines are not made from a single grape but blended from various varieties, most importantly Cabernet Sauvignon for flavour and structure and Merlot for softness. Contrary to popular belief, however, the Cabernet Sauvignon is not the staple of all fine Bordeaux, as it accounts for only 18 per cent of the vines cultivated in the region. The choice and quality was much better this year, although it would have been nice to find a gold medal winner under a fiver from the most famous red wine region in the world. Prices of wines tasted ranged from £2.69 to £15.95.

	Claret Cuvée VE Bordeaux 1995 Calvet/ Guy Anderson	£3.19	**Kwik Save**
	Claret NV Paul Barbe, Asda	£3.29	**Asda**
	Good Ordinary Claret NV Waitrose	£3.65	**Waitrose**
	Sainsbury's Cuvée Prestige Bordeaux Rouge NV	£4.49	**Sainsbury's**

	Graves 1994 Ginestet	£4.75	**Waitrose**
Bronze	Château Saint Galier 1993 Graves	£4.85	**Morrisons**
Bronze	Saint Emilion NV Paul Barbe, Asda	£4.99	**Asda**
Bronze	Vintage Claret 1993 Bordeaux Supérieur, Tesco	£4.99	**Tesco**
Bronze	Claret Aged in Oak NV Etienne Lalande, Safeway	£4.99	**Safeway**
	Claret Oak Aged NV Peter A. Sichel, Somerfield	£4.99	**Somerfield**
Silver	Domaine de Sours 1993 Rouge	£4.99	**Sainsbury's**
	Château La Favière 1994 Bordeaux Supérieur	£5.35	**Waitrose**
	Booths Oak Aged Vintage Claret 1990	£5.49	**Booths**
Silver	Château Marquis de Terme 1992 3ème Cru Classé Margaux	£12.95	**Sainsbury's**
Gold	Château Lagrange 1992 3ème Cru Classé Margaux	£13.95	**Sainsbury's**
	Château Ferrière 1993 3ème Cru Classé Margaux	£15.95	**Sainsbury's**

Bulgaria

Since the collapse of Communism the consistency of these wines has suffered, but amongst the dullards and dross more individual wines can also be found. Prices ranged from £2.69 to £3.79.

Bronze	Sliven Merlot & Pinot Noir NV The Bulgarian Vintners'	£2.69	**Co-op**
	Bulgarian Merlot & Cabernet Sauvignon 1995 Domaine Boyar	£2.79	**Kwik Save**
	Bulgarian Country Wine Merlot & Pinot Noir NV Sliven Region, Vini Sliven, Somerfield	£2.89	**Somerfield**
	Bulgarian Cabernet Sauvignon 1989 Melnik Region, Vinprom Damianitza, Somerfield	£2.95	**Somerfield**
Bronze	Bulgarian Cabernet Sauvignon 1992 Elhovo Winery	£2.99	**Kwik Save**
	Bulgarian Cabernet Sauvignon 1991 Vinprom Svischtov, St Michael	£2.99	**Marks & Spencer**

	Gamza Reserve 1992 Lovico Suhindol	£3.09	**Kwik Save**
Bronze	Oriachovitza Cabernet Sauvignon Reserve 1991 Stara Zagora Region	£3.19	**Co-op Pioneer**
Bronze	Mavrud Reserve 1991 Assenovgrad	£3.49	**Waitrose**
Bronze	Stambolovo Merlot 1990 The Bulgarian Vintners' Reserve	£3.55	**Morrisons**
	Sainsbury's Reserve Cabernet Sauvignon 1992 Iambol Region	£3.69	**Sainsbury's**
Bronze	The Bulgarian Vintners' Merlot Aged in Oak 1995 Rousse Region	£3.79	**Safeway**

Cabernet Sauvignon

Although it is the noblest variety of Bordeaux grape, you will rarely find a Bordeaux wine made entirely from Cabernet Sauvignon. It has a greater ability than any other variety to transplant its essential characteristics into the wines it produces, hence its proliferation throughout the world. Great quality Cabernet Sauvignon can be made in every New World country, not to mention the great value wines which stretch much further to encompass the mass-producing vineyards of Spain, Eastern Europe and elsewhere. Romania has overtaken Bulgaria as the cheapest source of Cabernet Sauvignon, and Chile is also mounting a strong challenge. Prices ranged from £2.29 to £11.99.

	Bulgarian Cabernet Sauvignon 1989 Melnik Region, Vinprom Damianitza, Somerfield	£2.95	**Somerfield**
Bronze	Chilean Cabernet Sauvignon NV Viña Cornellana, Somerfield	£2.95	**Somerfield**
	Cabernet Sauvignon 1995 François Dulac, Vin de Pays d'Oc	£2.99	**Budgens**
Bronze	Bulgarian Cabernet Sauvignon 1992 Elhovo Winery	£2.99	**Kwik Save**
	Bulgarian Cabernet Sauvignon 1991 Vinprom Svischtov, St Michael	£2.99	**Marks & Spencer**
Bronze	Cabernet Sauvignon Special Reserve 1986 Rovit	£3.15	**Morrisons**
Bronze	Oriachovitza Cabernet Sauvignon Reserve 1991 Stara Zagora Region	£3.19	**Co-op Pioneer**

	La Source Cabernet Sauvignon 1993 Vin de Pays d'Oc	£3.35	**Morrisons**
Bronze	Cabernet Sauvignon Special Reserve 1986 Rovit	£3.39	**Co-op Pioneer**
	Chilean Cabernet Sauvignon NV Curicó, Co-op	£3.69	**Co-op**
	Sainsbury's Reserve Cabernet Sauvignon 1992 Iambol Region	£3.69	**Sainsbury's**
Bronze	Chilean Cabernet Sauvignon 1995 Lontue Region, Safeway	£3.79	**Safeway**
Bronze	Eagle Ridge Cabernet Sauvignon 1992 The California Winery	£3.89	**Littlewoods**
Bronze	Casa Leona Cabernet Sauvignon 1994 Rapel, St Michael	£3.99	**Marks & Spencer**
	South African Cabernet Sauvignon NV Somerfield	£3.99	**Somerfield**
	South Australia Cabernet Sauvignon 1994 Angove's, Co-op	£4.29	**Co-op**
Bronze	Miguel Torres Cabernet Sauvignon 1993 Santa Digna, Curico	£4.49	**Co-op Pioneer**
Bronze	Caliterra Cabernet Sauvignon 1993 Maipo Valley	£4.49	**Co-op Pioneer**
	Sutter Home Cabernet Sauvignon 1993 Napa	£4.49	**Co-op Pioneer**
	Carmen Cabernet Sauvignon 1994 Maipo, St Michael	£4.49	**Marks & Spencer**
Bronze	Caliterra Cabernet Sauvignon 1993 Maipo Valley	£4.49	**Littlewoods**
Bronze	Sainsbury's Australian Cabernet Sauvignon 1994	£4.49	**Sainsbury's**
Silver	Casablanca Cabernet Sauvignon 1991 Miraflores Estate	£4.69	**Budgens**
Bronze	Hardys Nottage Hill Cabernet Sauvignon Shiraz 1993 South Eastern Australia	£4.79	**Co-op Pioneer**
Bronze	Hardys Nottage Hill Cabernet Sauvignon 1992 South Eastern Australia	£4.89	**Littlewoods**
Bronze	Lindemans Bin 45 Cabernet Sauvignon 1994	£4.99	**Morrisons**
Bronze	New Zealand Cabernet Sauvignon NV Huapai, Tesco	£4.99	**Tesco**

	Casa Porta Cabernet Sauvignon 1993 Valle del Chachapoal	£4.99	**Londis**
Bronze	Montana Cabernet Sauvignon 1994	£4.99	**Littlewoods**
Bronze	Stonybrook Cabernet Sauvignon 1993 California	£4.99	**Safeway**
	Orlando RF Cabernet Sauvignon 1992	£5.39	**Co-op Pioneer**
	Orlando RF Cabernet Sauvignon 1992	£5.39	**Londis**
Bronze	Montana Cabernet Sauvignon 1994	£5.49	**Londis**
Bronze	Lindemans Bin 45 Cabernet Sauvignon 1994	£5.99	**Londis**
Bronze	Carmen Cabernet Sauvignon Reserve 1994 Maipo, St Michael	£5.99	**Marks & Spencer**
Silver	Canyon Road Cabernet Sauvignon 1994 St Michael	£5.99	**Marks & Spencer**
Bronze	Coonawarra Cabernet Sauvignon 1994 Rymill Winery, Tesco	£5.99	**Tesco**
Gold	Tatachilla Cabernet Sauvignon 1994 McLaren Vale & Langhorne Creek	£5.99	**Waitrose**
Silver	Fetzer 1993 Valley Oaks Cabernet Sauvignon	£5.99	**Co-op**
Silver	Fetzer 1993 Valley Oaks Cabernet Sauvignon	£5.99	**Waitrose**
Bronze	Quinta da Bacalhôa Cabernet Sauvignon 1993	£6.25	**Sainsbury's**
Silver	Hardys Coonawarra Cabernet Sauvignon 1993	£6.49	**Littlewoods**
Silver	Miranda Rovalley Ridge Cabernets 1992 Barossa Valley	£6.99	**Booths**
	Old Penola Estate Cabernet Sauvignon 1991 Coonawarra	£6.99	**Tesco**
Bronze	Jamiesons Run 1992 Coonawarra	£7.65	**Morrisons**
Bronze	Wynns Coonawarra Cabernet Sauvignon 1991 South Australia	£7.95	**Sainsbury's**
Bronze	Gallo Sonoma Cabernet Sauvignon 1992	£7.99	**Budgens**
Silver	Hardys Coonawarra Cabernet Sauvignon 1993	£7.99	**Safeway**
Gold	Penfolds Bin 407 Cabernet Sauvignon 1992 South Australia	£7.99	**Somerfield**
Gold	James Halliday Coonawarra Cabernet Sauvignon 1992 St Michael	£11.99	**Marks & Spencer**

Cabernet-based Blends

Mostly Bordeaux, Australian Cabernet-Shiraz and New World Bordeaux-type blends involving the juicy Merlot, the Cabernet Franc – which is firm and herbaceous in Europe but like a softer version of Cabernet Sauvignon in Australia – and the Malbec, which was once used to produce the famous 'black wines' of Cahors and is favoured as blending-fodder in the New World. Prices ranged from £2.69 to £15.95

	Claret Cuvée VE Bordeaux 1995 Calvet/ Guy Anderson	£3.19	**Kwik Save**
	Claret NV Paul Barbe, Asda	£3.29	**Asda**
	Sainsbury's Chilean Cabernet Sauvignon Merlot NV Curico	£3.49	**Sainsbury's**
Bronze	Tocornal Chilean Cabernet-Malbec NV Central Valley	£3.49	**Safeway**
	Deer Leap Cabernet Sauvignon/ Cabernet Franc 1995 Sopron Region	£3.65	**Waitrose**
Bronze	New Zealand Cabernet-Merlot Co-op	£4.29	**Co-op**
	Good Ordinary Claret NV Waitrose	£3.65	**Waitrose**
	Sainsbury's Cuvée Prestige Bordeaux Rouge NV	£4.49	**Sainsbury's**
	Graves 1994 Ginestet	£4.75	**Waitrose**
Bronze	Château Saint Galier 1993 Graves	£4.85	**Morrisons**
Bronze	Saint Emilion NV Paul Barbe, Asda	£4.99	**Asda**
Bronze	Vintage Claret 1993 Bordeaux Supérieur, Tesco	£4.99	**Tesco**
Bronze	Claret Aged in Oak NV Etienne Lalande, Safeway	£4.99	**Safeway**
	Claret Oak Aged NV Peter A. Sichel, Somerfield	£4.99	**Somerfield**
Silver	Domaine de Sours 1993 Rouge	£4.99	**Sainsbury's**
Bronze	Kaituna Hills Cabernet Merlot 1994 Averill Estate, St Michael	£4.99	**Marks & Spencer**
	Hardys Nottage Hill Cabernet Sauvignon Shiraz 1994 South Eastern Australia	£4.99	**Somerfield**
	Penfolds Rawsons Retreat Bin 35 1994 Cabernet Sauvignon-Shiraz	£4.99	**Somerfield**

	Valdivieso Barrel-Fermented Cabernet-Merlot 1994 Lontue	£4.99	**Waitrose**
	Château La Favière 1994 Bordeaux Supérieur	£5.35	**Waitrose**
	Booths Oak Aged Vintage Claret 1990	£5.49	**Booths**
Bronze	Gran Calesa Costers del Segre 1991 Raimat, St Michael	£5.50	**Marks & Spencer**
Bronze	Mitchelton Cabernet Shiraz 1992 South Eastern Australia	£5.69	**Co-op Pioneer**
Bronze	Hardys Barossa Valley Cabernet Sauvignon Merlot 1993	£5.99	**Safeway**
Silver	Saints Cabernet Merlot 1994 Montana	£6.99	**Marks & Spencer**
Gold	Leasingham Cabernet Sauvignon Malbec 1992 Clare Valley	£6.99	**Co-op**
Silver	Penfolds Bin 389 Cabernet Shiraz 1993 South Australia	£9.95	**Sainsbury's**
Silver	Château Marquis de Terme 1992 3ème Cru Classé Margaux	£12.95	**Sainsbury's**
Gold	Château Lagrange 1992 3ème Cru Classé Margaux	£13.95	**Sainsbury's**
	Château Ferrière 1993 3ème Cru Classé Margaux	£15.95	**Sainsbury's**

Cabernet Franc

Most of these wines were Bourgueil, Chinon and so on from the Loire Valley and although a couple were decent enough, they were mostly not that good and were grossly overpriced. Many were simply green and unpleasant. Prices ranged from £3.39 to £7.99.

Gold	Pepperwood Grove Cabernet Franc 1994 California	£3.99	**Budgens**
Silver	Tim Knappstein The Franc 1994 Clare Valley	£6.95	**Sainsbury's**

Chianti

And other Sangiovese-dominated blends

Last year was a pig of a tasting, but my comments obviously served to concentrate minds, as the wines submitted this year were much better, even at the cheap end. The chief Chianti grape variety is Sangiovese, which is also used for various other Italian wines including Brunello di Montalcino and Vino Nobile di Montepulciano. Like most of Italy's most famous wines, the quality can range from dire to stunning. Some of the most exciting Sangiovese wines are the so-called 'super-Tuscan' Cabernet/Sangiovese blends. New World Sangiovese is an up-and-coming, if relatively rare, category of wine, particularly in supermarkets (owing to the premium prices charged), but Booths Coriole Sangiovese from Australia's McLaren Vale illustrates just how exciting they can be. Prices from £3.29 to £12.99.

Bronze	Sangiovese di Romagna NV Somerfield	£3.49	**Somerfield**
Silver	I Grilli di Villa Thalia 1993 Calatrasi	£3.65	**Somerfield**
Silver	Sangiovese Vino da Tavola di Toscana 1994 Fiordaliso	£3.75	**Waitrose**
	Chianti 1994 Rocca Delle Macie Castellina, Safeway	£3.79	**Safeway**
Bronze	Chianti 1994 AMF, Spar	£4.25	**Spar**
Gold	Uggiano Chianti Classico 1992	£4.39	**Morrisons**
Bronze	Chianti Classico 1994 Tesco	£4.49	**Tesco**
Silver	Chianti Classico 1994 Montecchio	£4.69	**Somerfield**
	Tenuta San Vito Chianti 1994	£5.49	**Safeway**
Gold	Chianti Classico Conti Serristori 1995 Villa Primavera, Somerfield	£5.49	**Somerfield**
Silver	Chianti Classico Riserva 1991 Tesco	£5.99	**Tesco**
Bronze	Chianti Classico 1994 Basilica Cafaggio, St Michael	£5.99	**Marks & Spencer**
Gold	Uggiano Chianti Riserva 1990	£6.15	**Morrisons**
Silver	Avignonesi 1992 Vino Nobile di Montepulciano	£7.95	**Waitrose**
Gold	Coriole Sangiovese 1993 McLaren Vale	£8.25	**Booths**
Silver	Le Pergole Torte 1987 Monte Vertine	£9.95	**Waitrose**
Silver	Brunello di Montalcino 1990 Val di Suga, St Michael	£12.99	**Marks & Spencer**

French Vins de Pays

Hugely varied range of styles and quality, including some of the most exciting new developments in French winemaking. Great for bargain hunters. Prices ranged from £2.79 to £5.99.

	Cabernet Sauvignon 1995 François Dulac, Vin de Pays d'Oc	£2.99	**Budgens**
	Winter Hill 1995 Vin de Pays de l'Aude	£2.99	**Morrisons**
	Saint-Laurent 1995 Vin de Pays de l'Hérault	£2.99	**Asda**
	Grenache Vin de Pays d'Oc NV Tesco	£2.99	**Tesco**
	Vin de Pays des Coteaux de l'Ardèche NV Vignerons Ardéchois, Somerfield	£2.99	**Somerfield**
	Winter Hill 1995 Vin de Pays de l'Aude	£3.29	**Waitrose**
	La Source Cabernet Sauvignon 1993 Vin de Pays d'Oc	£3.35	**Morrisons**
	Sainsbury's Vin de Pays de l'Aude NV Rouge	£3.39	**Sainsbury's**
Bronze	La Baume Cuvée Australe 1994 Vin de Pays d'Oc	£3.99	**Co-op Pioneer**
Bronze	Terrasses de Landoc Carignan 1995 Vin de Pays de l'Hérault	£3.99	**Booths**
	Domaine Mandeville Merlot 1995 Vin de Pays d'Oc, St Michael	£3.99	**Marks & Spencer**
Bronze	Domaine Mandeville Syrah 1995 Vin de Pays d'Oc, St Michael	£3.99	**Marks & Spencer**
	Domaine de Picheral Merlot 1995 Vin de Pays d'Oc	£3.99	**Safeway**
Bronze	La Baume Cuvée Australe 1994 Vin de Pays d'Oc	£3.99	**Safeway**
	Merlot Vin de Pays d'Oc 1994 Les Vignerons du Val d'Orbieu, Spar	£4.49	**Spar**
Bronze	Pinot Noir Vin de Pays d'Oc 1994 Domaine Virginie, St Michael	£4.99	**Marks & Spencer**
Silver	James Herrick Cuvée Simone 1995 Vin de Pays d'Oc	£4.99	**Asda**
Silver	James Herrick Cuvée Simone 1995 Vin de Pays d'Oc	£4.99	**Sainsbury's**

Bronze	Domaine Joseph de Bel Air 1994 Pinot Noir	£5.45	Sainsbury's
Bronze	Domaine de la Baume 1994 Estate Merlot	£5.95	Sainsbury's
Gold	La Cuvée Mythique 1993 Vin de Pays d'Oc	£5.99	Safeway

Gamay

Mostly Beaujolais, with a few Mâcon thrown in. They say the soil is not right for Gamay in Mâcon, but whatever the reason Mâcon never makes anything red worth drinking. The soil is right in Beaujolais, but most of its wines are simply a rip-off when you consider what you can get from virtually every other region in the world. I am amazed to have found as many as three to recommend, and astounded that two were worthy of medals. Prices ranged from £3.69 to £7.99.

	Morgon 1994 Georges Duboeuf	£5.95	Sainsbury's
Bronze	Fleurie Cru du Beaujolais 1995 Cellier des Samsons, St Michael	£7.99	Marks & Spencer
Silver	Fleurie 1995 Château des Déduits, Waitrose	£7.99	Waitrose

Italy

Other than Chianti (*see* earlier). Prices ranged from £2.45 to £9.99.

	Sicilian Red Table Wine NV Spar	£2.45	Spar
Bronze	Montepulciano d'Abruzzo 1995 Venier	£2.99	Kwik Save
	Vino da Tavola Rosso NV Co-op	£2.99	Co-op
Bronze	Eclisse NV Vino da Tavola di Puglia	£3.29	Morrisons
	Cardillo Rosso di Sicilia 1995 Casa Vinicola Calatrasi, St Michael	£3.49	Marks & Spencer
	Montepulciano d'Abruzzo 1994 Co-op	£3.49	Co-op
Silver	Villa Mantinera Montepulciano NV Vino da Tavola del Molise Rosso	£3.59	Co-op
	Montepulciano d'Abruzzo 1994 Umani Ronchi	£3.79	Somerfield
	Le Trulle Primitivo del Salento 1994	£3.99	Tesco

Bronze	Zagara Nero d'Avola 1995 Vino da Tavola di Sicilia	£3.99	**Safeway**
Bronze	Italian Merlot del Trentino NV Concilio Vini, Tesco	£4.29	**Tesco**
Silver	Barbera d'Alba di La Morra 1994 Cantina Terre del Barolo	£4.75	**Waitrose**
Bronze	Taurino Salice Salentino Riserva 1990 Rosso	£5.49	**Somerfield**
Gold	Primitivo di Manduria 1993 Giordano, St Michael	£6.99	**Marks & Spencer**

Malbec

Responsible for the once-famed 'black wines' of Cahors, the Malbec is usually utilized in a secondary blending role these days, although it is occasionally allowed to dominate a blend and a few pure varietals can be found. Prices ranged from £3.49 to £4.99.

Bronze	Waitrose Australian Malbec/Ruby Cabernet 1995	£3.79	**Waitrose**
Bronze	La Fortuna Malbec 1994 Lontue Valley	£4.79	**Spar**
Silver	Trapiche Malbec Oak Cask Reserve 1992 St Michael	£4.99	**Marks & Spencer**

Merlot

Pure and blended

The Merlot is a great Bordeaux grape capable of luscious, velvety red wine, and is currently very fashionable. Although traditionally perceived as a relatively light, supple grape that will soften a Cabernet-dominated blend, it can also be one of the biggest, richest and most majestically structured of all grape varieties, as Château Pétrus proves. Prices ranged from £2.69 to £6.99.

Bronze	Sliven Merlot & Pinot Noir NV The Bulgarian Vintners'	£2.69	**Co-op**
	Bulgarian Merlot & Cabernet Sauvignon 1995 Domaine Boyar	£2.79	**Kwik Save**

	Bulgarian Country Wine Merlot & Pinot Noir NV Sliven Region, Vini Sliven, Somerfield	£2.89	Somerfield
	Gandia Merlot 1993 Hoya Valley	£3.39	Co-op Pioneer
Bronze	Stambolovo Merlot 1990 The Bulgarian Vintners' Reserve	£3.55	Morrisons
Bronze	The Bulgarian Vintners' Merlot Aged in Oak 1995 Rousse Region	£3.79	Safeway
	Domaine Mandeville Merlot 1995 Vin de Pays d'Oc, St Michael	£3.99	Marks & Spencer
Bronze	Merlot Tannat 1995 Juanico, St Michael	£3.99	Marks & Spencer
Bronze	Stellenbosch Merlot 1995 St Michael	£3.99	Marks & Spencer
	Domaine de Picheral Merlot 1995 Vin de Pays d'Oc	£3.99	Safeway
Bronze	Glen Ellen Merlot 1993 Proprietor's Reserve, Sonoma	£4.29	Morrisons
Bronze	Italian Merlot del Trentino NV Concilio Vini, Tesco	£4.29	Tesco
	Merlot Vin de Pays d'Oc 1994 Les Vignerons du Val d'Orbieu, Spar	£4.49	Spar
	Canepa Merlot 1994	£4.49	Spar
Bronze	Fiuza Merlot 1994 Vinho Regional Ribatejo	£4.49	Safeway
Bronze	Spanish Merlot Reserva 1991 Tesco	£5.49	Tesco
Bronze	Domaine de la Baume 1994 Estate Merlot	£5.95	Sainsbury's
Bronze	Barossa Valley Merlot 1993 Tesco	£5.99	Tesco

New Zealand

It is the leafy or herbaceous nature of these wines that generally stands out in a blind tasting. Prices ranged from £4.29 to £6.99.

Bronze	New Zealand Cabernet-Merlot NV Co-op	£4.29	Co-op
Bronze	Waimanu Premium Dry Red Wine NV Corbans	£4.39	Budgens
Bronze	Kaituna Hills Cabernet Merlot 1994 Averill Estate, St Michael	£4.99	Marks & Spencer

Bronze	New Zealand Cabernet Sauvignon NV Huapai, Tesco	£4.99	**Tesco**
Bronze	Montana Cabernet Sauvignon 1994	£4.99	**Littlewoods**
Bronze	Montana Cabernet Sauvignon 1994	£5.49	**Londis**
Silver	Saints Cabernet Merlot 1994 Montana	£6.99	**Marks & Spencer**

New World Southern Rhône Style

This consisted mainly of Grenache and Grenache- or Mourvèdre-based blends. Prices ranged from £2.99 to £8.99.

Bronze	Pieters Drift Cinsaut Ruby Cabernet NV Western Cape	£2.99	**Littlewoods**
Bronze	Landskroon Cinsaut Shiraz 1995 Paarl	£3.59	**Safeway**
Silver	Mount Hurtle Grenache Shiraz 1994 Geoff Merrill	£4.49	**Asda**
Silver	Breakaway Grenache Shiraz 1994 South Australia	£4.99	**Safeway**
Bronze	Yaldara Grenache Reserve 1995 Whitmore Old Vineyard, Barossa	£5.75	**Waitrose**
Gold	Kingston Estate Mataro 1994 Murray Valley	£5.99	**Tesco**
Silver	Penfolds Old Vine Shiraz Grenache Mourvèdre 1993 Barossa Valley	£8.99	**Booths**

Other Reds

One of the most interesting, if taxing, categories to taste, this included red wines that could not be conveniently labelled, or those that could but not enough were submitted to make a viable tasting – although a few wines were in fact tasted in other categories (I like to give all wines every chance). The wines in this section had to fight it out on a purely price-per-price basis and because there were so many different styles, it took me twice as long. I constantly had to consider what sort of a wine each product was supposed to be. Prices ranged from £2.39 to £7.99.

	Macedonian Country Red NV	£2.39	**Kwik Save**
	Sicilian Red Table Wine NV Spar	£2.45	**Spar**
	Soveral Tinto NV Vinho de Mesa	£2.49	**Morrisons**
Silver	Alto Plano Chilean Red Wine NV	£10.99	**Asda**
Bronze	Don Darias Tinto NV Vino de Mesa, Bodegas Vitorianas	£2.75	**Asda**
Bronze	Marino El Vino Tinto del Mediterráneo NV Bodegas Berberana	£2.79	**Kwik Save**
Silver	Alta Mesa Tinto 1994 Estremadura	£2.79	**Booths**
	Promesa Tinto NV Cosecheros y Criadores	£2.89	**Kwik Save**
Gold	Ramada NV Vinho de Mesa Tinto	£2.89	**Co-op**
Bronze	Montepulciano d'Abruzzo 1995 Venier	£2.99	**Kwik Save**
Bronze	Leon 1992 Castilla-Leon, Asda	£2.99	**Asda**
Silver	Alta Mesa Tinto 1994 Estremadura	£2.99	**Kwik Save**
Bronze	Mission Peak Red NV	£2.99	**Co-op**
Bronze	Marqués de la Sierra 1994 Garnacha Puro	£2.99	**Co-op**
	Vino da Tavola Rosso NV Co-op	£2.99	**Co-op**
Bronze	Remonte 1995 Navarra	£2.99	**Asda**
	Argentine Country Red NV Somerfield	£2.99	**Somerfield**
Bronze	Australian Dry Red Wine NV Darlington	£11.99	**Littlewoods**
	Gamza Reserve 1992 Lovico Suhindol	£3.09	**Kwik Save**
Bronze	Vin de Crete 1995 Kourtaki	£3.15	**Morrisons**
Bronze	Eclisse NV Vino da Tavola di Puglia	£3.29	**Morrisons**
	Misty Mooring Australian Dry Red Wine NV Angove's	£3.29	**Littlewoods**
	Côtes du Lubéron 1995 Cellier de Marrenon, Safeway	£3.29	**Safeway**
	Campo Rojo NV Bodega Coop San José	£3.35	**Spar**
	Bush Vine Grenache 1995 Coteaux du Languedoc	£3.39	**Sainsbury's**
Gold	Domaine des Bruyère 1994 Côtes de Malepère	£3.49	**Kwik Save**
	Domaine de Borios 1994 Saint-Chinian	£3.49	**Co-op Pioneer**
	Cardillo Rosso di Sicilia 1995 Casa Vinicola Calatrasi, St Michael	£3.49	**Marks & Spencer**
Bronze	Mavrud Reserve 1991 Assenovgrad	£3.49	**Waitrose**
	Wallaby Ridge Australian Dry Red Wine NV	£3.49	**Littlewoods**

Bronze	Eagle Ridge California Red NV The California Winery	£3·49	**Littlewoods**
	Montepulciano d'Abruzzo 1994 Co-op	£3·49	**Co-op**
Bronze	Château Jougrand Saint Chinian 1994 Cuvée Réservée à la Gastronomie	£3·59	**Morrisons**
Bronze	JP Barrel Selection Red Wine 1991 Vinho Regional Terras do Sado	£3·59	**Tesco**
Silver	Villa Mantinera Montepulciano NV Vino da Tavola del Molise Rosso	£3·59	**Co-op**
Bronze	Blossom Hill Collection Red NV	£3·69	**Morrisons**
	Dornfelder Qualitätsrotwein 1994 Rheinhessen, Gustav Adolf Schmitt	£3·79	**Budgens**
Bronze	Vin de Crete 1995 Kourtaki	£3·79	**Budgens**
	Terra Alta Old Vines Garnacha 1995 Pedro Rovira S.A.	£3·79	**Asda**
	Montepulciano d'Abruzzo 1994 Umani Ronchi	£3·79	**Somerfield**
Bronze	Blossom Hill Collection Red NV	£3·89	**Londis**
	Côtes du Brulhois 1990 Cave de Donzac	£3·99	**Booths**
Bronze	Terrasses de Landoc Carignan 1995 Vin de Pays de l'Hérault	£3·99	**Booths**
	Domaine Saint-Germain Minervois 1994 St Michael	£3·99	**Marks & Spencer**
	Le Trulle Primitivo del Salento 1994	£3·99	**Tesco**
Bronze	Ermitage du Pic St. Loup 1995 Coteaux du Languedoc	£3·99	**Waitrose**
Bronze	Zagara Nero d'Avola 1995 Vino da Tavola di Sicilia	£3·99	**Safeway**
Bronze	David Wynn Red 1993 South Eastern Australia	£4·25	**Booths**
Bronze	Waimanu Premium Dry Red Wine NV Corbans	£4·39	**Budgens**
Bronze	Château Valoussière 1993 Coteaux-du-Languedoc	£4·49	**Somerfield**
Silver	Torres Sangre de Toro 1993	£4·59	**Co-op Pioneer**
Silver	Barbera d'Alba di La Morra 1994 Cantina Terre del Barolo	£4·75	**Waitrose**
	Guelbenzu Jardin 1995 Navarra	£4·99	**Booths**
Bronze	Castel Pujol Tannat 1992 Las Violetas	£4·99	**Booths**
Silver	Palacio De La Vega 1992 Navarra	£4·99	**Londis**
Bronze	Vale do Bomfim Reserva 1990 Douro	£5·35	**Waitrose**

	Duque de Viseu Dão 1991 Vinhos Sogrape	£5.49	**Co-op**
Bronze	Taurino Salice Salentino Riserva 1990 Rosso	£5.49	**Somerfield**
Gold	Domaine de l'Hortus Classique 1994 Coteaux du Languedoc	£5.99	**Booths**
Silver	Mas Champart 1994 Saint-Chinian	£5.99	**Booths**
Bronze	Château de Canterrane 1980 Côtes du Roussillon	£6.25	**Booths**
Gold	Primitivo di Manduria 1993 Giordano, St Michael	£6.99	**Marks & Spencer**
Bronze	Chateau Musar 1988 Gaston Hochar	£7.99	**Somerfield**

Pinotage

This grape is to South Africa what Zinfandel is to California and Shiraz to Australia, although it does not have half their potential and winemakers are in a bit of quandary about how it should be produced. Prices ranged from £3.19 to £7.99

	Kumala Cinsault Pinotage 1995 Western Cape	£3.39	**Booths**
	South African Pinotage 1995 Coastal Region, Teltscher Brothers	£3.49	**Co-op Pioneer**
	Kumala Cinsault Pinotage 1995 Western Cape	£3.99	**Somerfield**
Bronze	Simonsvlei Wynkelder Pinotage Reserve 1995 Paarl	£4.49	**Safeway**
Bronze	Beyers Truter Pinotage NV Stellenbosch, Tesco	£4.99	**Tesco**
Silver	Avontuur Pinotage 1995 Stellenbosch	£4.99	**Waitrose**
Bronze	Kanonkop Pinotage 1994 Stellenbosch	£7.99	**Tesco**

Pinot Noir

The world's most elusive classic red wine grape. More Pinot Noirs disappoint than excite, even in Burgundy, but it is capable of producing a red wine of incomparable finesse and grace. Prices ranged from £2.89 to £16.95.

Bronze	Romanian Pinot Noir 1993 River Route Selection	£2.89	**Asda**
Bronze	Posta Romana Classic Pinot Noir 1991 Dealul Mare Region, Valea Calugareasca	£2.99	**Littlewoods**
Bronze	Posta Romana Classic Pinot Noir 1991 Dealul Mare Region, Valea Calugareasca	£3.29	**Londis**
Silver	Pinot Noir Special Reserve 1990 Valea Mieilor Vineyards, Dealul Mare	£3.39	**Morrisons**
Bronze	Romanian Pinot Noir Special Reserve 1993 Dealul Mare, Safeway	£3.49	**Safeway**
Bronze	Pinot Noir Vin de Pays d'Oc 1994 Domaine Virginie, St Michael	£4.99	**Marks & Spencer**
Silver	Red Burgundy 1994 Bourgogne Passetoutgrains, Jean-Claude Boisset	£4.99	**Waitrose**
Silver	South Bay Vineyards Pinot Noir NV Sainsbury's	£4.99	**Sainsbury's**
Silver	Redwood Trail Pinot Noir 1994 By Sterling Vineyards	£4.99	**Somerfield**
Bronze	Domaine Joseph de Bel Air 1994 Pinot Noir	£5.45	**Sainsbury's**
Bronze	Red Burgundy Pinot Noir 1994 Somerfield	£5.49	**Somerfield**
Bronze	Bourgogne Hautes-Côtes de Beaune 1994 Georges Désire	£6.49	**Somerfield**
Silver	Bourgogne Hautes-Côtes de Beaune Tête de Cuvée 1992 Les Caves des Hautes-Côtes	£6.99	**Waitrose**
Gold	Willamette Valley Vineyards 1994 Oregon Pinot Noir	£7.49	**Morrisons**
	Chorey-les-Beaune 1993 Domaine Maillard	£9.75	**Waitrose**
Bronze	Beaune Premier Cru 1993 Edouard Delaunay	£9.95	**Waitrose**
Bronze	Château de Rully 1993 Rodet	£9.95	**Sainsbury's**
Bronze	Beaune 1er Cru Clos de la Féguine 1992 Domaine Jacques Prieur	£16.95	**Sainsbury's**

Portugal

Things are buzzing in Portugal at the moment, with real fruit being found in what used to be astringently dry and unappealing wines. Prices ranged from £2.49 to £6.25.

	Soveral Tinto NV Vinho de Mesa	£2.49	**Morrisons**
Silver	Alta Mesa Tinto 1994 Estremadura	£2.79	**Booths**
Gold	Ramada NV Vinho de Mesa Tinto	£2.89	**Co-op**
Silver	Alta Mesa Tinto 1994 Estremadura	£2.99	**Kwik Save**
Bronze	JP Barrel Selection Red Wine 1991 Vinho Regional Terras do Sado	£3.59	**Tesco**
Bronze	Fiuza Merlot 1994 Vinho Regional Ribatejo	£4.49	**Safeway**
Bronze	Vale do Bomfim Reserva 1990 Douro	£5.35	**Waitrose**
	Duque de Viseu Dão 1991 Vinhos Sogrape	£5.49	**Co-op**
Bronze	Quinta da Bacalhôa Cabernet Sauvignon 1993	£6.25	**Sainsbury's**

Rhône

Southern Rhône to be precise (*see* Syrah/Shiraz for Northern Rhône), and mainly consisting of Côtes-du-Rhône, Châteauneuf-du-Pape, Côtes-du-Ventoux and various Southern Rhône village wines such as Gigondas and Vacqueyras. Not many of the basic Côtes-du-Rhône wines got through, and that is, after all, where most of the bargains from this region should reside. That said, the results are a huge improvement, with a great clutch of gongs compared to just one medal earned last year. Prices ranged from £2.99 to £9.95.

Bronze	Côtes du Rhône 1995 Le Cellier des Trois Couronnes, Asda	£2.99	**Asda**
Bronze	Côtes du Rhône 1995 F. Dubessy	£3.29	**Kwik Save**
Bronze	Côtes du Ventoux 1995	£3.35	**Sainsbury's**
Silver	Waitrose Côtes-du-Rhône 1995	£3.49	**Waitrose**
Bronze	Château Malijay 'Fontanilles' 1994 Côtes du Rhône	£4.35	**Budgens**

Bronze	Domaine de Grangeneuve Cuvée Tradition 1994 Coteaux-du-Tricastin	£4.49	**Asda**
Bronze	Vieux Clocher 1994 Vacqueyras	£4.99	**Somerfield**
	Domaine La Réméjeanne Les Arbousiers 1994 Côtes du Rhône	£5.49	**Booths**
	Gigondas 1994 Domaine Sainte Lucie	£6.95	**Waitrose**
Silver	Châteauneuf-du-Pape 1994 Tesco	£6.99	**Tesco**
Bronze	Châteauneuf-du-Pape 1995 Les Maitres Goustiers, Jacques Mousset	£7.99	**Londis**
Gold	Châteauneuf-du-Pape 1993 Les Arnevals	£8.29	**Tesco**
Bronze	Châteauneuf-du-Pape 1992 Cellier des Princes	£8.49	**Co-op**
Gold	Châteauneuf-du-Pape 1993 Château des Fines Roches	£8.99	**Asda**
Silver	Domaine de la Solitude 1994 Châteauneuf-du-Pape	£8.99	**Somerfield**
Gold	Clos Saint Michel Châteauneuf-du-Pape 1994 Guy Mousset	£9.95	**Waitrose**

Rioja

And other Tempranillo-dominated blends

Rioja had its own way for a long time, then Tempranillo from Navarra got some attention and now it's even coming from Valdepeñas in La Mancha, although this is one quality grape variety the New World has been slow in coming forward with. Prices ranged from £2.75 to £9.99.

Bronze	Tempranillo La Mancha NV Wine Selection, St Michael	£10.99	**Marks & Spencer**
Silver	Stowells of Chelsea Tempranillo NV	£12.49	**Asda**
	Peñascal Vino de Mesa Tinto NV Castilla y Leon, St Michael	£3.99	**Marks & Spencer**
Bronze	Valdepeñas Reserva Aged in Oak 1989 Bodegas Felix Solis, Safeway	£3.99	**Safeway**
Bronze	Berberana Tempranillo 1993 Rioja	£4.29	**Co-op**
	Agramont 1992 Navarra, Bodegas Príncipe de Viana	£4.75	**Waitrose**
	Viña Mara Rioja Alavesa NV Tesco	£4.89	**Tesco**
	Campillo Rioja 1991	£4.99	**Asda**

	Viña Mara Rioja Reserva 1988 Tesco	£5.49	**Tesco**
Silver	Enate Tempranillo-Cabernet Sauvignon 1993 Somontano	£5.99	**Co-op**
Gold	Baron de Ley Reserva 1991 Rioja	£6.79	**Asda**
Bronze	Faustino V Reserva 1991 Rioja	£6.89	**Safeway**
Bronze	Sainsbury's Classic Selection Rioja 1990	£7.95	**Sainsbury's**
Silver	Marqués de Murrieta Ygay 1989 Rioja	£9.99	**Booths**

Romania

This country very quickly acquired something of a reputation for Pinot Noir, which in itself is not an easy thing to do, and other red wines are now starting to show promise. Prices ranged from £2.89 to £3.49.

Bronze	Romanian Pinot Noir 1993 River Route Selection	£2.89	**Asda**
Bronze	Posta Romana Classic Pinot Noir 1991 Dealul Mare Region, Valea Calugareasca	£2.99	**Littlewoods**
Bronze	Cabernet Sauvignon Special Reserve 1986 Rovit	£3.15	**Morrisons**
Bronze	Posta Romana Classic Pinot Noir 1991 Dealul Mare Region, Valea Calugareasca	£3.29	**Londis**
Silver	Pinot Noir Special Reserve 1990 Valea Mieilor Vineyards, Dealul Mare	£3.39	**Morrisons**
Bronze	Cabernet Sauvignon Special Reserve 1986 Rovit	£3.39	**Co-op Pioneer**
Bronze	Romanian Pinot Noir Special Reserve 1993 Dealul Mare, Safeway	£3.49	**Safeway**

Spain

Other than Rioja and other Tempranillo-based wines. Prices ranged from £2.75 to £6.99.

Bronze	Don Darias Tinto NV Vino de Mesa, Bodegas Vitorianas	£2.75	**Asda**
Bronze	Marino El Vino Tinto del Mediterráneo NV Bodegas Berberana	£2.79	**Kwik Save**

	Promesa Tinto NV Cosecheros y Criadores	£2.89	**Kwik Save**
Bronze	Leon 1992 Castilla-Leon, Asda	£2.99	**Asda**
Bronze	Marqués de la Sierra 1994 Garnacha Puro	£2.99	**Co-op**
Bronze	Remonte 1995 Navarra	£2.99	**Asda**
	Campo Rojo NV Bodega Coop San José	£3.35	**Spar**
	Gandia Merlot 1993 Hoya Valley	£3.39	**Co-op Pioneer**
	Terra Alta Old Vines Garnacha 1995 Pedro Rovira S.A.	£3.79	**Asda**
Silver	Torres Sangre de Toro 1993	£4.59	**Co-op Pioneer**
	Guelbenzu Jardin 1995 Navarra	£4.99	**Booths**
Silver	Palacio De La Vega 1992 Navarra	£4.99	**Londis**
	Viña Mara Rioja Reserva 1988 Tesco	£5.49	**Tesco**
Bronze	Spanish Merlot Reserva 1991 Tesco	£5.49	**Tesco**
Bronze	Gran Calesa Costers del Segre 1991 Raimat, St Michael	£5.50	**Marks & Spencer**

Syrah/Shiraz

As last year, this primarily involves Australian Shiraz and Northern Rhônes (such as Crozes Hermitage), but blended Syrah and Shiraz-dominated blends have been separated this year (*see* next category). In France, youthful Syrah has a raspberry character, but can develop plummy-blackcurrant fruit and silky-spicy finesse, particularly in the best vintages after a couple of years in bottle. Prices ranged from £3.29 to £12.95.

Bronze	Angove's Shiraz Classic Reserve 1994	£3.69	**Kwik Save**
Bronze	Peter Lehmann Vine Vale Shiraz 1994 Barossa	£3.99	**Asda**
Bronze	Domaine Mandeville Syrah 1995 Vin de Pays d'Oc, St Michael	£3.99	**Marks & Spencer**
Bronze	Peter Lehmann Vine Vale Shiraz 1994 Barossa	£4.49	**Co-op Pioneer**
Bronze	Peter Lehmann Vine Vale Shiraz 1994 Barossa	£4.49	**Booths**
Silver	Fairview Shiraz 1994	£4.49	**Tesco**

Bronze	Simonsvlei Wynkelder Shiraz Reserve 1994 Paarl	£4.49	Safeway
Bronze	L.A. Cetto Petite Sirah 1993	£4.49	Co-op
Silver	Lindemans Bin 50 Shiraz 1993 South Eastern Australia	£4.99	Co-op Pioneer
Silver	Shiraz South Eastern Australia 1993 Lindemans, St Michael	£4.99	Marks & Spencer
Silver	Parrots Hill Shiraz 1992 Barossa Valley	£4.99	Littlewoods
Bronze	McLarens Shiraz 1993 South Eastern Australia	£4.99	Littlewoods
Silver	Honey Tree Shiraz Cabernet 1995 Rosemount Estate, St Michael	£4.99	Marks & Spencer
Silver	James Herrick Cuvée Simone 1995 Vin de Pays d'Oc	£4.99	Asda
Silver	James Herrick Cuvée Simone 1995 Vin de Pays d'Oc	£4.99	Sainsbury's
Gold	Rosemount Estate Shiraz 1994 St Michael	£5.99	Marks & Spencer
Bronze	Bankside Shiraz 1993 Hardys, Padthaway Clare Valley	£5.99	Safeway
Bronze	Bankside Shiraz 1992 Hardys	£5.99	Somerfield
Bronze	Andrew Garrett Black Shiraz 1993 McLaren Vale	£6.29	Littlewoods
	Crozes Hermitage 1992 Cave des Clairmonts	£6.45	Waitrose
Silver	Leasingham Domaine Shiraz 1993 Clare Valley	£6.99	Booths
Silver	Maglieri Shiraz 1993 McLaren Vale	£6.99	Tesco
Bronze	Browns' of Padthaway Shiraz 1994	£6.99	Waitrose
Silver	Crozes-Hermitage Les Jalets 1994 Paul Jaboulet Ainé	£7.95	Sainsbury's
Silver	Saint-Joseph Cuvée Médaille d'Or 1991 Cave de Saint-Désirat	£8.25	Somerfield
Gold	Capel Vale Shiraz 1993 Western Australia, St Michael	£9.99	Marks & Spencer
Silver	Rosemount McLaren Vale Shiraz 1993 St Michael	£9.99	Marks & Spencer
Silver	Cornas 1990 Les Serras	£12.95	Sainsbury's

Syrah/Shiraz-dominated Blends

Almost entirely an Australian category. Without decrying the best pure Shiraz, blending this grape really does enable the wine wizards of Oz to produce better quality, better balanced wines at significantly cheaper prices. Prices ranged from £3.37 to £6.29.

Silver	Angove's Butterfly Ridge Shiraz/ Cabernet NV South Australia	£3.69	**Kwik Save**
Gold	Kingston Shiraz Mataro 1995 Murray Valley	£3.79	**Co-op**
Bronze	Hardys Shiraz Cabernet Sauvignon 1994 Stamps of Australia	£3.99	**Littlewoods**
Bronze	La Baume Cuvée Australe 1994 Vin de Pays d'Oc	£3.99	**Co-op Pioneer**
Bronze	La Baume Cuvée Australe 1994 Vin de Pays d'Oc	£3.99	**Safeway**
Silver	Bin No. 60 Shiraz Ruby Cabernet 1995 H. G. Brown	£3.99	**Safeway**
Bronze	Robertson Shiraz Cabernet Sauvignon 1995 Johann de Wet, Tesco	£4.49	**Tesco**
Bronze	Shiraz Cabernet Bin 505 1994 Southcorp Wines, St Michael	£4.49	**Marks & Spencer**
Bronze	Rosemount Estate Shiraz Cabernet 1995	£4.99	**Co-op Pioneer**
Bronze	Rosemount Estate Shiraz Cabernet 1995	£5.29	**Safeway**
Silver	Penfolds Koonunga Hill Shiraz-Cabernet Sauvignon 1994 South Australia	£5.99	**Co-op Pioneer**
Silver	Penfolds Koonunga Hill Shiraz-Cabernet Sauvignon 1994 South Australia	£5.99	**Somerfield**
Bronze	Wolf Blass Shiraz/Cabernet Sauvignon 'Red Label' 1994 South Australia	£6.29	**Londis**

Zinfandel

Primarily a Californian category, because this grape is as American as cherry pie – even if it is the same variety as the Italian Primitivo. What makes the Zinfandel so full of stars and stripes is the use of all-American oak, whereas French is traditionally used for Cabernet Sauvignon and other classic varieties. As a style, Zinfandel is hard to pin down. Each bunch ripens unevenly, and depending on where and how it's grown, the yield can vary by as much as tenfold, thus Zinfandel is used for everything from sparkling and blush to red and fortified, and there is a tremendous variation in styles of red wine produced, with berry fruits and some spiciness being the only common denominators. Prices ranged from £3.99 to £11.99.

	Le Trulle Primitivo del Salento 1994	£3.99	**Tesco**
Bronze	Pepperwood Grove Zinfandel 1994 California	£3.99	**Budgens**
Bronze	Sutter Home Zinfandel 1993 Napa	£4.05	**Morrisons**
Bronze	Sutter Home Zinfandel 1993 Napa	£4.29	**Co-op Pioneer**
Bronze	Sutter Home Zinfandel 1993 Napa	£4.49	**Londis**
Bronze	Cartlidge & Browne Zinfandel NV	£4.99	**Waitrose**
Bronze	Fetzer Vineyards Zinfandel 1993 Mendocino	£5.49	**Safeway**
Gold	Primitivo di Manduria 1993 Giordano, St Michael	£6.99	**Marks & Spencer**
Silver	Frog's Leap Zinfandel 1993 Napa Valley	£11.99	**Booths**

WHITE WINES

Bordeaux

Dry Style

The world's most famous red wine region is a minefield when it comes to dry white wines, but the cheapest got through, proving it can be very rewarding if you know what to pick. Prices ranged from £3.19 to £16.95.

Bronze	Bordeaux Blanc Sec Aged in Oak 1995 Union Prodiffu Landerrouat, Safeway	£3.19	**Safeway**
Bronze	Entre Deux Mers Sec 1994 G.V.A. Ets Fleury	£3.39	**Morrisons**
Bronze	Entre Deux Mers NV Yvon Mau, Somerfield	£3.99	**Somerfield**
Silver	Château Carbonnieux 1993 Pessac-Léognan	£16.95	**Sainsbury's**

Chardonnay

Pure and blended

More Chardonnays than ever before, starting off at 50 pence a bottle cheaper than last year, and the cheapest wine collects a bronze medal in the process. Hungary is singing and even Bulgaria is getting it right (strange it took so long), but when you examine where the medal-winning Chardonnays are made, it's the same as last year, with Burgundy hardly getting a look in. Perhaps they should employ a couple of flying winemakers? Prices ranged from £2.49 to £11.99.

Bronze	Hungarian Chardonnay Private Reserve 1995 Neszmély Winery	£2.49	**Asda**
Silver	Vintage Blend Chardonnay Sauvignon Blanc 1995 Domaine Boyar	£2.79	**Kwik Save**

Bronze	Hungarian Chardonnay 1995 Mór Region, Neszmély Winery	£2.89	**Kwik Save**
Bronze	The Gyöngyös Estate Chardonnay 1995 Mátraalja	£2.99	**Somerfield**
Bronze	Chapel Hill Chardonnay Oaked NV Balatonboglár Estate Bottled	£3.05	**Morrisons**
	Eagle Ridge California Chardonnay 1993 The California Winery	£3.49	**Littlewoods**
Silver	Kirkwood Chardonnay 1994 Vitis Hincesti	£3.49	**Safeway**
Bronze	Mátra Mountain Chardonnay Oaked 1995 Nagyréde	£3.49	**Safeway**
	Chilean Long Slim White 1994 Chardonnay Semillon	£3.49	**Co-op**
	La Source Chardonnay 1995 Vin de Pays d'Oc	£3.69	**Morrisons**
Bronze	Reserve Chardonnay Aged in Oak 1993 Rousse, The Bulgarian Vintners'	£3.79	**Safeway**
Silver	Chardonnay Vin de Pays d'Oc 1995 Les Vignerons du Val d'Orbieu, Spar	£3.89	**Spar**
Bronze	Glen Ellen Chardonnay 1994 Proprietor's Reserve, Sonoma	£3.99	**Budgens**
	Chapel Hill Chardonnay Barrique Aged 1993 Balatonboglár Estate Bottled	£3.99	**Londis**
	South Australia Chardonnay 1995 Asda	£3.99	**Asda**
Silver	Montagne Noire Chardonnay 1995 Vin de Pays d'Oc	£3.99	**Asda**
	Casa Leona Chardonnay 1995 Rapel, St Michael	£3.99	**Marks & Spencer**
Bronze	Le Trulle Chardonnay del Salento 1994	£3.99	**Tesco**
	Santa Julia Chardonnay 1995	£3.99	**Waitrose**
	Chardonnay Vin de Pays d'Oc NV Cellier du Grangeon, Londis	£3.99	**Londis**
	Oak Village Chardonnay 1994 Stellenbosch, Cape Selection	£3.99	**Co-op**
Bronze	Cuckoo Hill Chardonnay 1995 Vin de Pays d'Oc	£3.99	**Co-op Pioneer**
	Cono Sur Chardonnay 1995 Rapel Region	£3.99	**Asda**
Bronze	Glen Ellen Chardonnay 1994 Proprietor's Reserve, Sonoma	£4.29	**Morrisons**

Bronze	Sutter Home Chardonnay 1994 Napa	£4.49	**Co-op Pioneer**
Bronze	Caliterra Chardonnay 1995 Curico	£4.49	**Co-op Pioneer**
Bronze	Kaituna Hills Chardonnay Semillon 1995 Averill Estate, St Michael	£4.49	**Marks & Spencer**
Bronze	Canepa Chardonnay 1995 Rancagua	£4.49	**Spar**
	Chardonnay Vin de Pays d'Oc 1993 Les Vignerons du Val d'Orbieu, Spar	£4.49	**Spar**
	Chardonnay Réserve 1995 Vin de Pays d'Oc	£4.49	**Tesco**
	Gold Label Chardonnay Vin de Pays d'Oc 1995 Domaine Virginie, St Michael	£4.49	**Marks & Spencer**
Bronze	Caliterra Chardonnay 1995 Curico	£4.49	**Somerfield**
	Berri Estates Unwooded Chardonnay 1995 South Australia	£4.49	**Somerfield**
Bronze	Philippe de Baudin Chardonnay 1994 La Baume, Vin de Pays d'Oc	£4.69	**Co-op**
Bronze	Miguel Torres Chardonnay de la Cordillera 1995	£4.99	**Co-op Pioneer**
Bronze	Hungarian Chardonnay 1995 Mór Region, Asda	£4.99	**Asda**
Bronze	Hardys Nottage Hill Chardonnay 1995 South Eastern Australia	£4.99	**Asda**
Bronze	Hardys Nottage Hill Chardonnay 1995 South Eastern Australia	£4.99	**Somerfield**
Silver	Penfolds Koonunga Hill Chardonnay 1995 South Australia	£4.99	**Asda**
Bronze	James Herrick Chardonnay 1995 Vin de Pays d'Oc	£4.99	**Somerfield**
Bronze	Carmen Chardonnay Semillon Oak Aged 1995 St Michael	£4.99	**Marks & Spencer**
Bronze	Kaituna Hills Chardonnay 1995 Averill Estate, St Michael	£4.99	**Marks & Spencer**
Silver	New Zealand Chardonnay NV Gisborne, Tesco	£4.99	**Tesco**
Silver	Chardonnay/Sauvignon Blanc Vin de Pays d'Oc 1995 Domaine Bousquet	£4.99	**Waitrose**
	Stonybrook Chardonnay 1994 California	£4.99	**Safeway**
Silver	Alasia 1994 Chardonnay del Piemonte	£4.99	**Co-op**
Bronze	Casillero del Diablo Chardonnay 1994 Casablanca Valley, Concha y Toro	£4.99	**Safeway**

Silver	Penfolds Koonunga Hill Chardonnay 1995 South Australia	£4.99	Somerfield
	Orlando RF Chardonnay 1994	£5.39	Co-op Pioneer
	Orlando RF Chardonnay 1994	£5.39	Londis
	Danie de Wet Chardonnay 1995 Robertson	£5.45	Sainsbury's
	Canyon Road Chardonnay 1994 St Michael	£5.99	Marks & Spencer
Bronze	McLaren Vale Chardonnay 1995 Tesco	£5.99	Tesco
	Hunter Valley Chardonnay 1994 Rosemount	£5.99	Safeway
Silver	Penfolds Organic Wine 1994 Chardonnay-Sauvignon Blanc, Clare Valley	£5.99	Safeway
Bronze	Rosemount Estate Chardonnay 1995 Hunter Valley	£6.49	Co-op
Bronze	Rosemount Estate Chardonnay 1995 Hunter Valley	£6.49	Asda
	Saint-Véran 1994 Domaine des Deux Roches	£6.49	Asda
	Chablis 1994 Guy Mothe, Asda	£6.89	Asda
Gold	Saint-Véran Les Terres Noires 1994 Domaine des Deux Roches	£6.95	Booths
	Petit Chablis 1995 CVC, St Michael	£6.99	Marks & Spencer
Bronze	Saints Chardonnay 1995 Montana, St Michael	£6.99	Marks & Spencer
Silver	Saltram Mamre Brook Chardonnay 1994	£6.99	Waitrose
Bronze	Rosemount Estate Chardonnay 1995 Hunter Valley, St Michael	£6.99	Marks & Spencer
Silver	Penfolds Padthaway Chardonnay 1992	£6.99	Somerfield
Bronze	Penfolds Organic Wine 1994 Chardonnay-Sauvignon Blanc, Clare Valley	£6.99	Waitrose
Silver	Angove's Chardonnay Classic Reserve 1995	£3.99	Kwik Save
Gold	Lindemans Padthaway Chardonnay 1994 South Australia	£7.95	Sainsbury's
Silver	Gallo Sonoma Chardonnay 1993	£7.99	Budgens
Gold	Ninth Island Chardonnay 1995 Tasmania Wine Company	£7.99	Waitrose

Silver	Rosemount Estate Show Reserve Chardonnay 1994 Hunter Valley	£8.95	**Waitrose**
Silver	Rosemount Orange Vineyard Chardonnay 1994 St Michael	£9.99	**Marks & Spencer**

Chenin Blanc

Dry style

The Loire Valley's most famous grape variety, but not a single one survived, leaving the New World (primarily South Africa) to pick up the credits, few though they may be. Most of the Loire wines were dullards at best, foul-smelling at worst, and even those that appeared to be fresh and clean on the nose left something unpleasant at the back of the throat. If Burgundy needs flying winemakers, the Loire needs flying doctors. Prices were all £3.99.

Bronze	Fairview Chenin Blanc 1995 Paarl	£3.99	**Waitrose**
Bronze	Long Mountain Chenin Blanc 1995 Western Cape	£3.99	**Londis**
Bronze	Chenin Blanc Barrel Fermented 1995 Stellenbosch, Pacific Wines	£3.99	**Tesco**
Bronze	McGregor Chenin Blanc 1996 KWV, St Michael	£3.99	**Marks & Spencer**

French Vins de Pays

Chardonnay dominates, but it is not the only grape available. Prices ranged from £2.99 to the equivalent of £5.98.

Bronze	Skylark Hill Very Special White NV Vin de Pays d'Oc, Kwik Save	£2.99	**Kwik Save**
Bronze	Vin de Pays des Côtes de Gascogne 1995 Somerfield	£2.99	**Somerfield**
	Vin de Pays du Gers 1995 Patrick Azcué, St Michael	£2.99	**Marks & Spencer**
	Vin de Pays des Côtes de Gascogne NV Dry White, Co-op	£2.99	**Co-op**

	Vin de Pays du Gers NV Wine Selection, St Michael	£11.99	**Marks & Spencer**
Silver	Vin de Pays des Côtes de Gascogne 1995 Patrick Azcué, St Michael	£3.49	**Marks & Spencer**
Bronze	La Coume de Peyre 1995 Vin de Pays des Côtes de Gascogne	£3.49	**Safeway**
Bronze	Viognier Chais Cuxac 1995 Vin de Pays d'Oc	£3.49	**Somerfield**
	La Source Chardonnay 1995 Vin de Pays d'Oc	£3.69	**Morrisons**
Gold	Domaine du Rey 1994 Vin de Pays des Côtes de Gascogne	£3.69	**Morrisons**
	Domaine du Rey 1995 Vin de Pays des Côtes de Gascogne	£3.75	**Safeway**
Bronze	Fair Martina Vermentino NV Vin de Pays d'Oc, Co-op	£3.79	**Co-op**
Silver	Chardonnay Vin de Pays d'Oc 1995 Les Vignerons du Val d'Orbieu, Spar	£3.89	**Spar**
Silver	Montagne Noire Chardonnay 1995 Vin de Pays d'Oc	£3.99	**Asda**
	Roussanne Vin de Pays d'Oc 1995 Domaine Virginie, St Michael	£3.99	**Marks & Spencer**
	Chardonnay Vin de Pays d'Oc NV Cellier du Grangeon, Londis	£3.99	**Londis**
Bronze	Cuckoo Hill Chardonnay 1995 Vin de Pays d'Oc	£3.99	**Co-op Pioneer**
	Chardonnay Vin de Pays d'Oc 1993 Les Vignerons du Val d'Orbieu, Spar	£4.49	**Spar**
Bronze	Domaine de la Source Muscat 1995 Vin de Pays de l'Hérault, Tesco	£4.49	**Tesco**
	Chardonnay Réserve 1995 Vin de Pays d'Oc	£4.49	**Tesco**
	Gold Label Chardonnay Vin de Pays d'Oc 1995 Domaine Virginie, St Michael	£4.49	**Marks & Spencer**
Bronze	Philippe de Baudin Sauvignon Blanc 1994 La Baume, Vin de Pays d'Oc	£4.49	**Safeway**
Bronze	Sauvignon Blanc Vin de Pays d'Oc 1995 Le Vieux Mas	£4.49	**Somerfield**
Bronze	Philippe de Baudin Chardonnay 1994 La Baume, Vin de Pays d'Oc	£4.69	**Co-op**

Silver	Roussanne Vin de Pays d'Oc 1995 Hugh Ryman	£4.75	**Waitrose**
Bronze	Cuckoo Hill Viognier 1995 Vin de Pays d'Oc	£4.99	**Co-op Pioneer**
Bronze	Cuckoo Hill Viognier 1995 Vin de Pays d'Oc	£4.99	**Waitrose**
Bronze	James Herrick Chardonnay 1995 Vin de Pays d'Oc	£4.99	**Somerfield**
Bronze	Domaine Mandeville Viognier 1995 Vin de Pays d'Oc, St Michael	£4.99	**Marks & Spencer**
Silver	Chardonnay/Sauvignon Blanc Vin de Pays d'Oc 1995 Domaine Bousquet	£4.99	**Waitrose**
Gold	Muscat Petits Grains 1993 Vin de Pays des Collines de la Moure	£2.99	**Booths**

Gewurztraminer

These wines should be big, fat and spicy with relatively low acidity, and they often have more than a touch of sweetness to enhance the fruit. If I was disappointed about this category in the first edition, I would be over the moon this year if only one of the following wines had got through: the Co-op's quite extraordinary Posta Romana. Gewurztraminer is second only to Pinot Gris in being the most disappointing grape when cultivated beyond the borders of Alsace. It simply lacks spice, and I have never found pungent spice in any Gewurztraminer beyond Alsace and, perhaps, Germany's Rheinpfalz. Until now, that is. And the fact that it costs just £2.79 and comes from Romania is even more amazing. I hope I can be equally ecstatic about future vintages, but there is no track record to base any hopes on, so buy the 1993 while you can! Prices ranged from £2.79 to £9.49.

Gold	Posta Romana Classic Gewurztraminer 1993 Tarnave Region, Transylvania, Blaj Winery	£2.79	**Co-op Pioneer**
Bronze	Deer Leap Gewürztraminer 1995 Mór Region	£3.85	**Waitrose**
Bronze	Vin d'Alsace Gewurztraminer 1995 Cave des Vignerons Turckheim, Somerfield	£5.25	**Somerfield**

Bronze	Preiss-Zimmer Gewurztraminer 1994 Vin d'Alsace Tradition	£5.29	**Morrisons**
Bronze	Gewürztraminer Vin d'Alsace 1993 Waitrose, C.V.B.	£5.79	**Waitrose**
	Gewurztraminer Vin d'Alsace 1994 Cave des Vignerons Turckheim	£5.79	**Safeway**
Gold	Mader Gewurztraminer Cuvée Théophile 1994 Alsace	£9.49	**Booths**

Medium-dry

This did not include Riesling or indeed any German wines, but did encompass medium-dry wines that do not belong to any other white wine category and a Bordeaux simply because it tasted more medium than dry. A number of wines were flabby, but too many simply lacked freshness. Prices ranged from £2.75 to £4.49.

Bronze	Cape White NV Simonsvlei Winery, Asda	£10.99	**Asda**
	Hungarian Muscat 1994 Aszár-Neszmély Region, Asda	£2.79	**Asda**
Bronze	Bordeaux Blanc NV Paul Barbe	£2.99	**Asda**
	Carden Vale 1995 Three Choirs	£3.99	**Asda**
Bronze	Australian Medium Dry NV Lindemans, St Michael	£3.99	**Marks & Spencer**
Bronze	Nobilo White Cloud NV Gisborne	£4.39	**Co-op**

Medium-sweet

This included German wines (except Riesling) and a number of Vouvrays, but I'm not sure which were the smelliest, the Germans or the Vouvrays. The Vouvrays, I suppose, as none qualified. I don't know why supermarkets stock such awful Vouvray, except that although most of the appellation is rubbish, the punters keep returning to buy more. I cannot be too harsh on non-Riesling medium-sweet wines, but is it too much to ask for freshness? And the cheaper the wine, the more benefit having the very latest vintage would bring, as Somerfield's Niersteiner Spiegelberg proved. Prices ranged from £2.49 to £7.99.

Bronze	Hock NV Deutscher Tafelwein Rhein, Littlewoods	£2.49	**Littlewoods**
	Bereich Nierstein 1994 Schmitt Söhne, Littlewoods	£2.99	**Littlewoods**
Silver	Niersteiner Spiegelberg Kabinett 1995 Rheinhessen	£3.99	**Somerfield**
Silver	Ungsteiner Honigsäckel Gewürztraminer Spätlese 1994 Pfälz, Weingut Pfeffingen	£7.99	**Waitrose**

Muscadet

Quite a number were submitted last year, but not one was worth buying, which probably explains the relatively small number entered this year. The quality was, however, much higher. Prices ranged from £2.99 to £5.99.

Silver	Sainsbury's Classic Selection 1995 Muscadet de Sèvre et Maine Sur Lie	£5.95	**Sainsbury's**
Silver	Muscadet de Sèvre et Maine Sur Lie 1994 Domaine de l'Ecu	£5.99	**Safeway**

Muscat

Dry Style

Although just one Muscat survived the tastings, the fact that it earned a bronze medal is better than last year. This happens to be far and away the best vintage of Domaine de la Source Muscat produced so far.

Bronze	Domaine de la Source Muscat 1995 Vin de Pays de l'Hérault, Tesco	£4.49	**Tesco**

Other Whites

This included wines that could not be conveniently labelled – or those that could but not enough were submitted to make a viable tasting – plus a few that were tasted in other categories but where I needed to see how they performed on a purely price-per-price basis. Prices ranged from £2.49 to £9.75.

Bronze	Windmill Hill Bulgarian Dry White Wine NV The Lyaskovets Region	£2.49	**Asda**
Silver	Khan Krum Riesling & Dimiat NV Bulgarian Country White Wine	£2.59	**Kwik Save**
	Coltiva il Bianco NV Vino da Tavola Bianco	£2.69	**Asda**
	Bela Fonte NV Vinho de Mesa Branco	£2.69	**Asda**
	Jun Carillo White 1995 Navarra	£2.89	**Kwik Save**
Bronze	Entre Rios NV Chilean White Wine	£2.99	**Morrisons**
Gold	Santa Carolina 1995 White Wine	£2.99	**Booths**
Bronze	Deer Leap Dry White 1995 Hárslevelu	£2.99	**Waitrose**
	Wallaby Ridge Australian Dry White Wine NV	£11.99	**Littlewoods**
Silver	Uggiano Orvieto Classico 1994	£3.19	**Morrisons**
	Retsina NV Boutari	£3.19	**Co-op Pioneer**
	Czech White Wine NV Moravian Vineyards, Spar	£3.25	**Spar**
Bronze	Eclisse NV Vino da Tavola di Puglia	£3.29	**Morrisons**
Bronze	Conca de Barbera 1995 Bodegas Concavins, St Michael	£3.29	**Marks & Spencer**
Gold	Santa Carolina 1995 White Wine	£3.29	**Tesco**
Silver	Viña Malea Viura Lightly Oak Aged 1995 Vino de la Tierra Manchuela	£3.29	**Safeway**
Bronze	Murrumbidgee Estate NV Fruity Australian White Wine	£3.49	**Co-op**
Bronze	Kretikos Vin de Pays de Crete 1994 Boutari	£3.69	**Co-op Pioneer**
Bronze	Bright Brothers Fernão Pires/ Chardonnay 1994 Vinho Regional Ribatejo	£3.69	**Safeway**
	Diamond Hills Chenin Blanc/ Chardonnay 1995	£3.75	**Waitrose**
	August Sebastiani White 1995 California	£3.89	**Co-op Pioneer**
Bronze	Orvieto Classico Abboccato NV Tesco	£3.89	**Tesco**
Bronze	Etchart Cafayate Torrontes 1994 Vino Fino Blanco	£3.99	**Co-op Pioneer**
	Waimanu Premium Dry White Wine NV Corbans	£3.99	**Londis**

	Sant'Antonio Frascati Superiore 1994 Colli di Catone	£3.99	**Booths**
Bronze	South African Classic White 1995 W.O. Robertson	£3.99	**Spar**
	Waimanu Premium Dry White Wine NV Corbans	£3.99	**Budgens**
	David Wynn Dry White 1994 South Eastern Australia	£4.25	**Booths**
	Frascati Superiore 1995 Azienda Vinicola, St Michael	£4.49	**Marks & Spencer**
Silver	Best's Colombard 1994 Victoria	£4.49	**Tesco**
Bronze	Agramont Viura Chardonnay 1994 Navarra	£4.75	**Waitrose**
	Agramont Viura Chardonnay 1994 Navarra	£4.79	**Safeway**
Bronze	Soave Classico 1995 Vigneto Colombara, Zenato	£4.95	**Waitrose**
	Ca' del Solo Malvasia Bianca NV Monterey White Table Wine	£7.99	**Booths**
	Pazo de Barrantes Albariño 1994 Rias Baixas	£9.75	**Booths**

Pinot Blanc

Better than last year, but a lot failed to qualify. Pinot Blanc is such a fast-improving Chardonnay alternative that this category should have shown more potential than it did. Prices ranged from £3.29 to £4.99.

Bronze	Nagyréde Estate Pinot Blanc 1995 Szoloskert Co-operative	£3.29	**Londis**
Bronze	Pinot Blanc Vin d'Alsace 1995 Cave des Vignerons Turckheim	£4.49	**Somerfield**

Pinot Gris

Another grape that is at its absolute best in Alsace, where it has a rich, heady, spicy character not normally found in Pinot Gris wines made elsewhere. Generally the spice is not so pungent as Gewurztraminer, but the acidity is much higher. Prices ranged from £2.99 to the equivalent of £6.78 per bottle.

	Hungarian Pinot Gris 1995 Neszmély Region	£2.99	**Kwik Save**
Bronze	Hungaroo Pinot Gris 1995 Neszmély Winery	£3.49	**Co-op**
Bronze	Tokay Pinot Gris Vin d'Alsace 1994 Cave de Beblenheim	£3.39	**Waitrose**

Riesling

Dry style

No medals for German Riesling? This doesn't surprise me, but it is sad. The Riesling has no peers when it comes to high sugar-acidity levels, providing the crispest, most intensely flavoured and yet most delicate of wines. For the second year running this is a category that could, and should, do much better. Prices ranged from £2.99 to £6.99.

	Stony Ridge Riesling Pfälz 1995 St. Ursula	£2.99	**Kwik Save**
	Devil's Rock Riesling 1994 St. Ursula	£2.99	**Sainsbury's**
	Devil's Rock Riesling 1994 St. Ursula	£3.49	**Morrisons**
Bronze	Penfolds Bin 202 Riesling 1994	£3.99	**Co-op Pioneer**
	Devil's Rock Riesling 1994 St. Ursula	£3.99	**Co-op**
	Johannisberg Riesling 1995 Klosterhof, St Michael	£4.99	**Marks & Spencer**
Silver	Mader Riesling Muhlforst 1994 Alsace	£6.99	**Booths**

Riesling

Medium-to-sweet style

In its medium-to-sweet style, the Riesling is supreme, providing wines that are at once luscious and electrifying. The succulence of sweet Riesling fruit underpinned by startlingly fresh, crisp, ripe acidity cannot be matched by any other grape in the world. Although this is Germany's forte and the supermarkets did even better this year than last, there were a number of dirty German wines that should never have been purchased, let alone submitted to *SuperBooze.* Prices ranged from £2.99 to £7.75.

Bronze	Cape Afrika Rhine Riesling 1995 Co-op	£3.99	**Co-op**
Bronze	Ruppertsberger Nussbien Riesling Kabinett 1992 Pfälz	£4.15	**Safeway**
	Longuicher Probstberg Riesling Spätlese 1988 Moselland	£4.45	**Waitrose**
	Zell Castle Riesling Spätlese 1995 Klosterhof, St Michael	£4.99	**Marks & Spencer**
	Erdener Treppchen Riesling 1991 Mönchhof	£4.99	**Waitrose**
	Erdener Treppchen 1985 Riesling Spätlese	£5.45	**Sainsbury's**
Gold	Geisenheimer Mönchspfad Riesling Spätlese 1990 Schumann-Nägler	£5.99	**Waitrose**
Silver	Bacharacher Schloss Stahleck Riesling Kabinett 1992 Weingut Toni Jost	£6.95	**Waitrose**
Bronze	Piesporter Goldtröpfchen Riesling Spätlese 1990 Reichsgraf von Kesselstatt	£7.75	**Sainsbury's**

Rhône Style

What is a Rhône-style white? Good question, but for the purposes of this category it included, of course, any white wines made in the Rhône Valley with the exclusion of Viognier (*see* separate entry). Prices ranged from £3.49 to £6.19.

Bronze	Côtes du Rhône Cuvée Spéciale 1995 Domaine Vieux Manoir de Maransan	£4.49	**Safeway**
	Roussanne Vin de Pays d'Oc 1995 Domaine Virginie, St Michael	£3.99	**Marks & Spencer**
Silver	Roussanne Vin de Pays d'Oc 1995 Hugh Ryman	£4.75	**Waitrose**
Silver	Chateau Tahbilk Marsanne 1994 Victoria	£5.99	**Co-op Pioneer**

Sauvignon Blanc

There were almost as many Sauvignon as Chardonnay, but match the size of the following entry to the number of Chardonnay recommended and you will see why that grape is so popular – reliability. Most of the Sauvignon that did not survive the tasting assault course were French and mostly Loire, including a lot of Sancerre and Pouilly Fumé, such is the depth that those once great appellations have descended to. I'm not myopically a New World devotee. I have in fact been described as a Francophile by fellow critics, and when the French get it right, they are almost impossible to beat. Trouble is, far too many bad French wines are sold on name alone, and a terrifying proportion of the worst and greediest winemakers seem to live in the Loire Valley. Whether French or New Zealand, Sauvignon Blanc should be fresh and zesty. New Zealand does have the advantage of being able to ripen Sauvignon Blanc to a beautiful degree, yet retain the most mouthwatering and refreshing acidity. Prices ranged from £2.89 to £8.89.

Bronze	Début Fumé Sauvignon Blanc 1995 Russe Region, The Bulgarian Vintners'	£2.89	**Co-op**
Bronze	Bordeaux Blanc NV Paul Barbe	£2.99	**Asda**
Bronze	Gaillac 1995 Cave de Labastide de Lévis	£3.89	**Booths**
Bronze	Chilean Sauvignon Blanc NV Talca, Tesco	£3.99	**Tesco**
Bronze	Le Voyageur Sauvignon 1995 Bordeaux	£4.45	**Waitrose**
	New Zealand Sauvignon Blanc 1995 Gisborne, Tesco	£4.49	**Tesco**
Bronze	Philippe de Baudin Sauvignon Blanc 1994 La Baume, Vin de Pays d'Oc	£4.49	**Safeway**
Bronze	Sauvignon Blanc Vin de Pays d'Oc 1995 Le Vieux Mas	£4.49	**Somerfield**
Gold	Casablanca Sauvignon Blanc 1994 Lontue Valley, Curico	£4.69	**Budgens**
Bronze	Cooks Sauvignon Blanc 1995 Gisborne	£4.99	**Co-op Pioneer**
Bronze	Cooks Sauvignon Blanc 1995 Gisborne	£4.99	**Londis**
Bronze	Château Pierrail 1995 Bordeaux	£4.99	**Booths**
Silver	Kaituna Hills Sauvignon Blanc 1995 Averill Estate, Marlborough, St Michael	£4.99	**Marks & Spencer**

	Saint Clair Sauvignon Blanc 1995 Marlborough	£6.49	**Asda**
Bronze	Pouilly-Fumé 1995 Domaine J.M. Masson-Blondelet	£7.49	**Waitrose**
Bronze	Sancerre La Vigne des Rocs 1995 Duc Etienne de Loury	£7.69	**Asda**
Bronze	Pouilly Fumé 1995 Domaine Mathilde de Favray, St Michael	£7.99	**Marks & Spencer**
Silver	Lawson Dry Hills Sauvignon Blanc 1995 Marlborough	£7.99	**Waitrose**

Semillon

The best dry Semillon are Australian, although quite why other countries have not got the hang of this grape is a bit of a mystery (except in Chile where they over-harvest it). Australian Semillon typically has a lime character, which true Riesling coincidentally has when grown Down Under: this probably explains why Semillon grown in the Hunter Valley used to be sold as Hunter Riesling. Prices ranged from £3.39 to £8.99.

Bronze	Semillon Chardonnay 1995 South Eastern Australia, Yaldara, Asda	£3.45	**Asda**
Bronze	Semillon Chardonnay 1995 South Eastern Australia, Barossa Winery, Safeway	£3.99	**Safeway**
Bronze	Château Haut Bonfils Sémillon 1994 Bordeaux Blanc	£4.49	**Safeway**
Silver	Peter Lehmann Semillon 1994 Barossa	£4.99	**Co-op Pioneer**
Silver	Peter Lehmann Semillon 1994 Barossa	£4.99	**Asda**
Bronze	Hunter Valley Semillon 1994 Tesco	£4.99	**Tesco**
Bronze	Honey Tree Semillon Chardonnay 1995 Rosemount Estate, St Michael	£4.99	**Marks & Spencer**
Gold	Saltram Classic Semillon 1994	£4.99	**Sainsbury's**
Bronze	Rosemount Estate Semillon 1995 Hunter Valley	£6.49	**Somerfield**
Gold	Tim Adams Semillon 1994 Clare Valley	£8.99	**Tesco**

Semillon-dominated Blends

Although Sauvignon is Semillon's traditional blending partner, there is a growing New World tendency to team this Bordeaux grape with Burgundy's Chardonnay – something the chauvinist Bordelais and Burgundians would not even allow themselves to consider.

Silver	Cuvée d'Alban Barrique Fermented 1995 Bordeaux	£3.99	**Waitrose**
Gold	New Zealand Semillon-Sauvignon NV Co-op	£4.29	**Co-op**
Bronze	Orlando Jacob's Creek Semillon Chardonnay 1995 South Eastern Australia	£4.39	**Asda**
Bronze	Penfolds Rawson's Retreat Bin 21 1995 Semillon Chardonnay Colombard	£4.49	**Co-op Pioneer**
Bronze	Penfolds Rawson's Retreat Bin 21 1995 Semillon Chardonnay Colombard	£4.49	**Safeway**
	Semillon Chardonnay Bin 501 1995 Southcorp Wines, St Michael	£4.49	**Marks & Spencer**
Bronze	Breakaway Sauvignon Blanc Semillon 1995 South Eastern Australia	£4.99	**Safeway**
Bronze	Rosemount Estate Semillon Sauvignon Blanc 1995 South Eastern	£4.99	**Co-op Pioneer**
	Rosemount Estate Semillon Chardonnay 1995	£5.29	**Safeway**
	Rosemount Estate Semillon Chardonnay 1995	£5.29	**Budgens**

Sweet or Dessert Wine Style

Everything from botrytised Riesling to non-sparkling (but spirity) Asti, taking in a 'straw wine' and the most unbelievable *vin de pays* dessert wine in the history of the universe. On the subject of the unbelievable, I do worry about the authenticity of any Beerenauslese that can retail for under a tenner, let alone as little as £5.95, and I am especially intrigued as I was unable even to buy it for my blind tasting (thus my tasting note was from the annual tasting and the wine was not considered for a medal), but as a wine it is certainly worth the money. Prices ranged from to £3.29 to £34.58 (not a typo – and it did not qualify!).

Gold	Moscato d'Asti 1995 Le Monferrine	£3.29	**Safeway**
	Wormser Liebfrauenmorgen 1994 Beerenauslese	£5.95	**Sainsbury's**
Silver	Ruppertsberger Nussbien Riesling Auslese 1991	£3.99	**Asda**
Gold	Muscat Petits Grains 1993 Vin de Pays des Collines de la Moure	£2.99	**Booths**
Gold	Passito di Pantelleria 1994 Pellegrino	£5.45	**Waitrose**

Vinho Verde

And its alternatives

It is nice to see that *vinho verde* is no longer souped up, fizzed up and sweetened for British palates, even if none could manage a medal (but to be honest, it would take a seriously good *vinho verde* to deserve one). The Pazo de Barrantes is the Spanish equivalent of *vinho verde* and if price did not count, would have to be a gold medal winner and nothing less. If you cannot afford Pazzo de Barrantes, but want a dry *pétillant* white superior to the two *vinhos verdes*, try Domaine de la Source Muscat at £4.49 from Tesco. Prices ranged from £2.99 to £9.75.

Dry Vinho Verde NV Aveleda	£2.99	**Asda**
Dry Vinho Verde NV Tesco	£3.29	**Tesco**
Pazo de Barrantes Albariño 1994 Rias Baixas	£9.75	**Booths**

Viognier

The Rhône Valley's very special and quite mysterious grape, Viognier is responsible for Condrieu, the Rhône's greatest white wines, the best of which are highly perfumed, wonderfully fresh, with delicate, peachy fruit. None of these Viognier have the peachy character of the grape, but do share Condrieu's quality of being best drunk young, and are nice, floral-fresh alternatives to Chardonnay.

Bronze	Viognier Chais Cuxac 1995 Vin de Pays d'Oc	£3.49	**Somerfield**
Bronze	Domaine Mandeville Viognier 1995 Vin de Pays d'Oc, St Michael	£4.99	**Marks & Spencer**
Bronze	Cuckoo Hill Viognier 1995 Vin de Pays d'Oc	£4.99	**Co-op Pioneer**
Bronze	Cuckoo Hill Viognier 1995 Vin de Pays d'Oc	£4.99	**Waitrose**

ROSÉ WINES

Dry and Off-dry

Technically the most difficult style in which to produce something that stands out. I always remember a description by (I think) Anthony Rose of *The Independent*, who said that a rosé is like a red wine without the tannin – a lovely thought, if only! On the other hand, Breakaway Grenache is the nearest I've come to it, and its winemaker Geoff Merrill is one of the most talented winemakers. Prices ranged from £2.99 to £4.99.

Silver	Nagyréde Cabernet Sauvignon Rosé 1995	£3.25	**Waitrose**
	Syrah Rosé Vin de Pays d'Oc 1995 Les Vignerons du Val d'Orbieu	£3.25	**Somerfield**
	La Source Syrah Rosé 1995 Vin de Pays d'Oc	£3.35	**Morrisons**
	Rosé de Valencia 1995 Vicente Gandia, St Michael	£3.49	**Marks & Spencer**
	Vin de Pays de l'Hérault Blush NV Co-op	£3.69	**Co-op**
	Blossom Hill Collection White Zinfandel NV Sonoma	£4.29	**Londis**
Bronze	High Ridge Pink 1994 Lamberhurst Vineyards	£4.49	**Budgens**
Gold	Breakaway Grenache 1995 Stratmer Vineyards	£4.99	**Safeway**

Medium to Medium-sweet

Technically the easiest rosé style to produce (the residual sugar hides mistakes, enhances the fruit and generally flatters the palate), but the most difficult in which to find anything drinkable, let alone interesting. Anjou Rosé should be the freshest, fruitiest and cheapest of these wines, but they're invariably the dirtiest. Prices ranged from £2.59 to £3.79.

Silver	August Sebastiani White Zinfandel 1994	£3.79	**Co-op Pioneer**

SPARKLING WINES

Brut or Dry Sparkling Wine

Champagnes will always dominate this category, but it has been difficult for those used to drinking good-quality Champagne to find an alternative they can be satisfied with. Most New World fizz will seem little more than a concoction of fruit and bubbles with a strange acidity balance. Even the handful of serious producers who manage to turn out something interesting do it at such a price level that it is just as easy to sort through the cheapest Champagnes for a genuine bargain. If all this rings a bell with you, you will be surprised to hear which sparkling wines have rocketed in quality – Cava! Suddenly they have a deeper flavour, higher acidity and attractive lemon, lime and citrussy-floral aromas. They have totally reshaped my concept of these wines – and that is from someone whose *bête noire* used to be Cava. And they are doing it for less than a fiver! Much better than last year. Prices ranged from £4.95 to £22.50.

Silver	Waitrose Cava Brut NV Castellblanch	£4.95	**Waitrose**
	Flinders Creek Brut Cuvée NV Savage	£4.99	**Budgens**
Bronze	Flinders Creek Rosé Cuvée NV Savage	£4.99	**Budgens**
Bronze	Cava Brut NV Sevisa, St Michael	£4.99	**Marks & Spencer**
Bronze	Cava Brut NV Safeway	£4.99	**Safeway**
	Australian Quality Sparkling Wine Brut NV Seppelt, Safeway	£4.99	**Safeway**
Bronze	Cava Brut Blanc de Blancs NV Coniusa, Somerfield	£4.99	**Somerfield**
	Sainsbury's Australian Sparkling	£4.99	**Sainsbury's**
	Australian Barramundi Sparkling Wine Brut NV	£5.49	**Co-op**
	Madeba Brut NV Robertson, Sainsbury's	£5.79	**Sainsbury's**
Bronze	Seaview Brut NV McLaren Vale	£5.79	**Co-op**
Bronze	Seaview Brut NV McLaren Vale	£5.99	**Co-op Pioneer**
Bronze	Seaview Brut NV McLaren Vale	£5.99	**Londis**

Bronze	Seaview Brut NV	£5.99	Somerfield
	Deinhard Yello NV	£5.99	Co-op
Bronze	Codorníu Première Cuvée NV Brut Chardonnay	£5.99	Somerfield
Bronze	Seaview Brut NV	£5.99	Somerfield
Bronze	Codorníu Première Cuvée NV Brut Chardonnay	£6.49	Co-op Pioneer
Bronze	Lindauer Brut NV Montana Wines	£6.95	Co-op Pioneer
Bronze	Bluff Hill Brut NV Averill Estate, Marlborough, St Michael	£6.99	Marks & Spencer
Bronze	Robertson Sparkling Wine Brut NV Kangra Farms, Tesco	£6.99	Tesco
Bronze	Krone Borealis Brut 1993 Twee Jonge Gezellen	£6.99	Waitrose
Bronze	Lindauer Brut NV	£6.99	Londis
	Crémant de Bourgogne Brut NV Cave de Lugny	£6.99	Somerfield
	Bouvet Brut NV Saumur	£7.79	Co-op Pioneer
	Seaview Pinot Noir Chardonnay NV	£7.95	Sainsbury's
Bronze	Australian Chardonnay Blanc de Blancs Brut 1993 Seppelt Great Western Winery, St Michael	£7.99	Marks & Spencer
Bronze	Yalumba Cuvée One Pinot Noir Chardonnay NV	£8.49	Sainsbury's
Bronze	Pongrácz Brut NV	£8.99	Co-op Pioneer
	Cuvée Napa by Mumm Brut NV	£8.99	Co-op Pioneer
Bronze	Cuvée Napa by Mumm Brut NV	£8.99	Londis
	Scharffenberger Brut NV Mendocino	£8.99	Asda
	Champagne Louis Raymond Brut NV	£9.45	Kwik Save
Bronze	Champagne Nicole d'Aurigny Réserve Brut NV	£9.49	Morrisons
Bronze	Champagne André Simon Brut NV NM-243	£10.29	Londis
	Champagne François Daumale Brut NV	£10.99	Littlewoods
	Champagne Prince William Brut Reserve NV CM-836, Somerfield	£11.95	Somerfield
Bronze	Sainsbury's Blanc de Noirs Champagne NV	£11.95	Sainsbury's
Silver	Champagne Booths Brut NV CM-835	£12.69	Booths
Silver	Tesco Champagne Brut NV CM-803	£12.95	Tesco
Silver	Sainsbury's Extra Dry Champagne NV	£12.95	Sainsbury's

Silver	Waitrose Champagne Blanc de Blancs Brut NV NM 143	£13.95	**Waitrose**
	Champagne Veuve de Medts Brut NV St Michael	£13.99	**Marks & Spencer**
Bronze	Waitrose Champagne Brut Rosé NV CM 806	£14.95	**Waitrose**
Silver	Waitrose Champagne Brut 1989 NM 123	£14.95	**Waitrose**
Silver	Sainsbury's Vintage Champagne 1990	£14.95	**Sainsbury's**
Bronze	Champagne Oudinot Brut 1989 St Michael	£14.99	**Marks & Spencer**
Bronze	Champagne Cattier 1er Cru NV	£14.99	**Littlewoods**
Silver	Champagne Albert Etienne Brut 1990 Safeway	£14.99	**Safeway**
Gold	Champagne Prince William Blanc de Blancs Brut NV Michel Gonet	£14.99	**Somerfield**
Bronze	Champagne Germain Brut Réserve NV	£14.99	**Budgens**
Bronze	Champagne Jeeper Brut Grande Réserve NV	£15.99	**Booths**
Bronze	Tesco Vintage Champagne Brut 1985 CVC Chouilly	£19.99	**Tesco**
Gold	Champagne Cuvée Orpale Blanc de Blancs Brut 1985 Union Champagne	£22.50	**Marks & Spencer**

Sweet Sparkling Wine

These need to be as fresh, pure and fruity as possible, which means getting the wine off its yeast as soon as the fermentation is over and drinking it as quickly as possible. Prices ranged from £3.29 to £6.95.

	Riviera Moscato Spumante NV Littlewoods	£3.69	**Littlewoods**
Silver	Asti NV Perlino, Tesco	£4.99	**Tesco**
Bronze	Sainsbury's Asti NV	£5.49	**Sainsbury's**
Bronze	Martini Asti NV	£5.99	**Littlewoods**
Gold	Clairette de Die Tradition 1993 Comtesse de Die, Première Cuvée	£6.45	**Waitrose**

FORTIFIED WINES

Port: Early-bottled Styles

This encompassed everything from cheap ruby through LBV and crusted to the most expensive vintage port. Although LBV stands for Late-Bottled Vintage, it's not out of place in the early-bottled category, as the emphasis is on vintage and vintage is an early-bottled style – so it's sort of late-early bottled! All early-bottled styles are ruby in colour and retain a fruitiness in bottle that tawny ports lack (although tawny has a smoothness and cask-matured complexity that early-bottled ports do not possess). There were no New World port-styles submitted for this edition, and the quality of the ports entered was nowhere near as high as last year. Prices ranged from £2.99 to £20.99.

Bronze	Sainsbury's L.B.V. Port 1989 Temilobos	£7.29	**Sainsbury's**
Gold	Booths Crusted Port 1989 Martinez Gassiot	£9.95	**Booths**
Bronze	Fonseca 1982	£17.95	**Sainsbury's**
Silver	Quarles Harris Vintage Port 1977	£18.99	**Booths**

Port: Late-bottled Styles

Essentially tawny ports. Cheap tawny ports are merely a blend of red and white ports: seldom exciting, but occasionally surprisingly good. Real tawny ports have a cask-aged colour, smoothness and complexity (often coffee-caramel) that can only be achieved through extended maturation in wood. The best tawnies are 10, 20 and 30 Year Old, but do not be mistaken – these are not the guaranteed minimum age. They merely represent a style that the wines must adhere to in an official blind tasting test. In theory, a 30 Year Old Tawny could be twelve months old, but in practice the composite age of most of these wines will be close to that indicated. Prices ranged from £5.69 to £14.99.

Bronze	Old Cellar Late Bottled Vintage Port 1989 Smith Woodhouse	£7.15	**Spar**
Silver	10 Years Old Port NV Morgan Brothers, St Michael	£9.99	**Marks & Spencer**
Silver	Sainsbury's 10 Year Old Tawny Port	£9.99	**Sainsbury's**
Silver	20 Years Old Port NV Morgan Brothers, St Michael	£14.99	**Marks & Spencer**

Sherry

Generally speaking, this was a disappointment after last year, when I wrote, 'I never thought I would be excited by a Sherry tasting – especially one consisting entirely of supermarket Sherry – but I was'. That said, Lustau Old East India was a revelation, or maybe even a revolution. Owing to the small number of wines surviving this tasting, the different styles have been lumped together. Prices ranged from £3.15 to the equivalent of £11.18 a bottle.

Gold	Lustau Old East India Sherry NV Emilio Lustau	£9.89	**Booths**
Gold	Pedro Ximenez NV Montilla	£5.59	**Sainsbury's**

Liqueur Muscat

Sweet, fortified Muscat is probably the oldest fortified wine style in the world. Prices ranged from £3.39 to the equivalent of £15.98 per bottle.

Bronze	Castillo de Liria Moscatel NV Vicente Gandia	£3.39	**Co-op Pioneer**
Bronze	Moscatel de Valencia NV Bodegas Vicente Gandia, Somerfield	£3.39	**Somerfield**
Bronze	Moscatel de Valencia NV Tesco	£3.49	**Tesco**
Bronze	Frontignan Vin de Liqueur NV Frontignan Coopérative	£5.49	**Somerfield**
Silver	Dom Brial Muscat de Rivesaltes 1995	£3.79	**Safeway**
Gold	Stanton & Killeen Liqueur Muscat NV Rutherglen, Victoria	£5.49	**Asda**

BEERS

Beer recommendations: an explanation

While there is some overlap of wine products throughout the various supermarket groups, it is far less significant than the overlap of branded beers. Most groups stock a fairly large range of branded beers that are common to all retailers. However, if a particular brand has not been submitted for tasting by a supermarket, it will not be included in that supermarket's *SuperBooze* entry. You can find which supermarket does include an entry on that brand by looking under the following section.

Unfortunately, although most supermarkets stock as many as 150–350 beers, most do not possess a full price list. Compiling a comprehensive list of brands stocked by each supermarket has, therefore, proved impossible.

Bitter or Traditional Ale Style

Without widgets

An English term for a well-hopped draught ale that is typically copper-coloured with ruddy glints and has a slight but distinctive bitter taste unspoilt by the fizziness of CO_2. It is unrealistic to expect the so-called bitter sold in a can or bottle to have any semblance of true draught-bitter character, unless the residual gas is reduced to a minimal level and the consumer urged to pour the bitter from a great height. Most bitter is 3.75–4 per cent ABV, although Best or Special will be 4–4.75 per cent, and some go as high as 5.5 per cent. Please note that Farm Stores Best Bitter is not recommended for anything other than force-feeding football hooligans (*see* **Asda**). Prices ranged from an equivalent of 32p per pint (almost half the cheapest price last year!) to £3.25.

	Farm Stores Best Bitter Asda	£0.32	**Asda**
	Special Northern Bitter Mansfield Brewery	£0.49	**Kwik Save**
	Best Bitter Londis	£0.56	**Londis**
Bronze	Banks's Bitter	£0.89	**Safeway**

Bronze	Banks's Bitter	£0.89	Somerfield
Bronze	John Smith's Bitter	£0.95	Kwik Save
	Double Maxim Premium Quality Ale Vaux	£0.96	Kwik Save
	Joseph Jones Strong Ale Knotty Ash Ales	£0.96	Spar
Bronze	John Smith's Bitter	£0.96	Safeway
	Double Maxim Premium Quality Ale Vaux	£0.98	Somerfield
Bronze	Ruddles Strong County Traditional Ale	£0.99	Tesco
Bronze	John Smith's Bitter	£1.09	Somerfield
Bronze	John Smith's Bitter	£1.13	Budgens
Bronze	Double Maxim Premium Quality Ale Vaux	£1.29	Booths
	Adnams Suffolk Strong Ale	£1.30	Waitrose
Bronze	Banks's Bitter	£1.31	Booths
Gold	Black Sheep Ale Paul Theakston	£1.31	Booths
	Adnams Suffolk Strong Ale	£1.33	Safeway
	Adnams Suffolk Strong Ale	£1.33	Somerfield
Bronze	Caledonian 70/- Amber Ale Caledonian Brewery	£1.35	Morrisons
Bronze	Caledonian 70/- Amber Ale Caledonian Brewery	£1.35	Safeway
Bronze	Masterbrew Premium Bitter Shepherd Neame	£1.35	Booths
Bronze	Masterbrew Premium Bitter Shepherd Neame	£1.35	Budgens
Bronze	Marston's Pedigree Bitter	£1.39	Booths
Bronze	Jennings Sneck Lifter	£1.42	Booths
Bronze	Tesco Traditional Premium Ale Caledonian Brewery	£1.42	Tesco
Silver	St. Andrews Ale Belhaven Brewery	£1.42	Co-op
Gold	Fuller's London Pride Premium Ale	£1.44	Booths
Silver	Waggle Dance Traditional Honey Beer Vaux	£1.44	Booths
Silver	Waggle Dance Traditional Honey Beer Vaux	£1.44	Kwik Save
Bronze	Marston's Pedigree Bitter	£1.45	Somerfield
	Bombardier Premium Bitter Charles Wells	£1.47	Booths
	Greenmantle Ale Broughton Ales	£1.47	Booths
Bronze	Merlin's Ale Broughton Ales	£1.47	Booths

Gold	Traditional Yorkshire Bitter St Michael	£1.47	**Marks & Spencer**
Bronze	Caledonian 80/- Export Ale St Michael	£1.47	**Marks & Spencer**
Bronze	Masterbrew Premium Bitter Shepherd Neame	£1.47	**Safeway**
Bronze	Bishops Finger Kentish Strong Ale Shepherd Neame	£1.48	**Asda**
Bronze	Marston's Pedigree Bitter	£1.49	**Morrisons**
Bronze	Marston's Pedigree Bitter	£1.49	**Co-op Pioneer**
	Batemans Victory Ale	£1.51	**Booths**
Bronze	Bishops Finger Kentish Strong Ale Shepherd Neame	£1.53	**Safeway**
	Merrimans Old Fart Merrimans Brewery	£1.53	**Morrisons**
Gold	Black Sheep Ale Paul Theakston	£1.53	**Morrisons**
Gold	Black Sheep Ale Paul Theakston	£1.53	**Tesco**
Silver	Jennings Cocker Hoop Golden Bitter	£1.53	**Booths**
Silver	Bishops Finger Kentish Strong Ale Shepherd Neame	£1.53	**Booths**
Gold	Spitfire Bottle Conditioned Bitter Shepherd Neame	£1.53	**Booths**
Bronze	Caledonian 80/- Export Ale Caledonian Brewery	£1.53	**Safeway**
Gold	Fuller's London Pride Premium Ale	£1.54	**Co-op Pioneer**
Bronze	Marston's Pedigree Bitter	£1.55	**Budgens**
	Bombardier Premium Bitter Charles Wells	£1.58	**Morrisons**
Bronze	Cains Formidable Ale	£1.58	**Booths**
Bronze	Deakin's Red Admiral Mansfield Brewery	£1.58	**Co-op**
Gold	Black Sheep Ale Paul Theakston	£1.58	**Safeway**
	Bombardier Premium Bitter Charles Wells	£1.58	**Safeway**
Bronze	Fuller's ESB Export Extra Special Bitter	£1.64	**Co-op Pioneer**
Bronze	Fuller's ESB Export Extra Special Bitter	£1.64	**Tesco**
Bronze	Fuller's ESB Export Extra Special Bitter	£1.64	**Waitrose**
Gold	Fuller's London Pride Premium Ale	£1.64	**Budgens**
Bronze	Merlin's Ale Broughton Ales	£1.65	**Safeway**
Silver	Waggle Dance Traditional Honey Beer Vaux Breweries	£1.69	**Morrisons**
	6X Export Wadworth	£1.69	**Booths**
	6X Export Wadworth	£1.69	**Co-op Pioneer**

	6X Export Wadworth	£1.69	**Morrisons**
	6X Export Wadworth	£1.69	**Somerfield**
Silver	Directors Live Ale Courage	£1.69	**Co-op Pioneer**
Silver	Directors Live Ale Courage	£1.69	**Booths**
Silver	Directors Live Ale Courage	£1.69	**Safeway**
Silver	Bishops Finger Kentish Strong Ale Shepherd Neame	£1.69	**Budgens**
Gold	Spitfire Bottle Conditioned Bitter Shepherd Neame	£1.69	**Budgens**
Gold	Rutland Independence Very Strong Ale Ruddles Brewery	£1.70	**Booths**
Silver	Cobbold's 250 Special Year 1996 Beer	£1.70	**Tesco**
Silver	Australian Sparkling Ale Coopers Brewery, South Australia, St Michael	£1.74	**Marks & Spencer**
Bronze	Fuller's 1845 Bottle Conditioned Celebration Strong Ale	£1.75	**Tesco**
Bronze	Fuller's 1845 Bottle Conditioned Celebration Strong Ale	£1.75	**Waitrose**
Bronze	Fuller's ESB Export Extra Special Bitter	£1.75	**Budgens**
Gold	Spitfire Bottle Conditioned Bitter Shepherd Neame	£1.76	**Morrisons**
Gold	Spitfire Bottle Conditioned Bitter Shepherd Neame	£1.76	**Safeway**
Gold	Spitfire Bottle Conditioned Bitter Shepherd Neame	£1.76	**Tesco**
Silver	Bishops Finger Kentish Strong Ale Shepherd Neame	£1.76	**Morrisons**
Silver	Bishops Finger Kentish Strong Ale Shepherd Neame	£1.76	**Tesco**
Silver	Bishops Finger Kentish Strong Ale Shepherd Neame	£1.76	**Waitrose**
Silver	Bishops Finger Kentish Strong Ale Shepherd Neame	£1.76	**Safeway**
Silver	Bishops Finger Kentish Strong Ale Shepherd Neame	£1.81	**Londis**
Gold	Spitfire Bottle Conditioned Bitter Shepherd Neame	£1.81	**Londis**
Bronze	Fuller's 1845 Bottle Conditioned Celebration Strong Ale	£1.85	**Budgens**
Bronze	Edinburgh Strong Ale Caledonian Brewery	£1.87	**Waitrose**

	Pete's Wicked Ale	£1.90	**Waitrose**
Silver	Boddingtons Export	£1.91	**Safeway**
Silver	Worthington's White Shield Fine Strong Ale	£1.96	**Booths**
Bronze	Jenlain Bière de Garde Ambrée Brasserie Duyck	£2.03	**Tesco**
Bronze	Norman's Conquest Extra Strong Ale	£2.05	**Tesco**
	Sainsbury's Bière de Garde Brewery Castelain	£2.10	**Sainsbury's**

Bitter or Traditional Ale Style

With widgets

Widgetized bitter is nowhere near as successful as widgetized stout, for the simple reason that the head on a pint of traditional pulled real ale is air, not nitrogen. You could put a widget in an air-flushed can or bottle of bitter containing little CO_2, but the beer would go off before it reached the shelf. These products should not be regarded as bitters, but judged as a completely separate category of smooth, creamy beer (which many people like, judging by the Caffrey's phenomenon). In which case they should not bear the same name as the brew you can get by the pint or bottle. Even so, the brewers are missing out on a large group of consumers who would bridge the gap between those who are happily hooked on creamy widget beers and those who would not touch the stuff with a barge pole. There are many beer drinkers who would drink a widgetized beer if it had some real bitterness coming through. Bitterness in beers – all beers, including lagers, stouts and so on – is measured in EBUs, and it strikes me that the brewers should have 30 to 50 per cent more EBU in a widgetized beer to get a similar taste coming through the creamy mask of nitrogen bubbles. Prices ranged from the equivalent of 80p per pint to £1.91.

Bronze	Portland Draught Ale Traditional Style Asda	£0.85	**Asda**
	Asda Chesters Draught Ale Samlesbury Brewery	£0.96	**Asda**
	Theakston Draught Best Bitter	£1.09	**Asda**
Silver	Wethered's Draught Bitter St Michael	£1.13	**Marks & Spencer**

	Tetley's Draught Yorkshire Bitter	£1.16	**Kwik Save**
	Draught Premium Bitter Somerfield	£1.20	**Somerfield**
Bronze	John Smith's Extra Smooth Bitter	£1.24	**Kwik Save**
Bronze	Boddingtons Draught	£1.26	**Co-op Pioneer**
Bronze	Boddingtons Draught	£1.27	**Somerfield**
Bronze	John Smith's Extra Smooth Bitter	£1.29	**Budgens**
Bronze	John Smith's Extra Smooth Bitter	£1.38	**Safeway**
Bronze	John Smith's Extra Smooth Bitter	£1.38	**Somerfield**
	Tetley's Draught Yorkshire Bitter	£1.40	**Safeway**
Bronze	Brains S.A. Draught Best Bitter	£1.45	**Safeway**
	Tetley's Draught Yorkshire Bitter	£1.45	**Somerfield**
Bronze	Boddingtons Draught	£1.47	**Safeway**
Bronze	Boddingtons Draught	£1.47	**Littlewoods**
Bronze	Marston's Pedigree Bitter Draught	£1.50	**Tesco**
Bronze	Brains S.A. Draught Best Bitter	£1.54	**Londis**
Gold	Boddingtons Manchester Gold	£1.59	**Co-op**
Bronze	Caffrey's Draught Irish Ale	£1.61	**Co-op Pioneer**
Bronze	Caffrey's Draught Irish Ale	£1.61	**Littlewoods**
Bronze	Caffrey's Draught Irish Ale	£1.61	**Safeway**
Bronze	Caffrey's Draught Irish Ale	£1.61	**Somerfield**
Bronze	Caffrey's Draught Irish Ale	£1.61	**Tesco**
Bronze	Kilkenny Draught Irish Beer Guinness	£1.61	**Littlewoods**
Bronze	Kilkenny Draught Irish Beer Guinness	£1.61	**Morrisons**
Bronze	Kilkenny Draught Irish Beer Guinness	£1.67	**Londis**
Bronze	Caffrey's Draught Irish Ale	£1.67	**Budgens**
Silver	Boddingtons Export	£1.91	**Asda**

Dark Beers

Milds, stouts and porters: without widgets

Most mild is dark brown, although lighter examples do exist. It should be a soft-tasting ale with a sweetness that devotees enjoy for its lingering quality – although most bitter drinkers would find this cloying. Classic stout is bitter stout, and Guinness, Murphy's and Beamish are all first-rate examples, although they are all Irish, of course, whereas stout is a derivative of old English porter. A plethora of English and Scottish stouts and porters have emerged in the last year or so. Mild is 2.7–3.2 per cent, porter around 5 per cent and stout 4.5–5 per cent, although bottled versions exported to the tropics can be as high as 8 per cent.

Prices ranged from an equivalent of 48p per pint to £2.22.

Bronze	Cains Dark Mild	£0.65	**Kwik Save**
Silver	Brady's Traditional Stout Kwik Save	£0.84	**Kwik Save**
Bronze	Guinness Original	£1.29	**Co-op Pioneer**
Bronze	Guinness Original	£1.29	**Safeway**
Bronze	Guinness Original	£1.29	**Somerfield**
Silver	Scottish Oatmeal Stout Broughton Ales	£1.47	**Booths**
Gold	Robert Cain's Superior Stout	£1.58	**Booths**
Bronze	Samuel Smith's The Celebrated Oatmeal Stout Old Brewery Tadcaster	£1.61	**Co-op Pioneer**
	Marston's Oyster Stout Bottle Conditioned Head Brewers Choice	£1.65	**Booths**
	Marston's Oyster Stout Bottle Conditioned Head Brewers Choice	£1.65	**Morrisons**
	Marston's Oyster Stout Bottle Conditioned Head Brewers Choice	£1.65	**Sainsbury's**
Gold	Guinness Foreign Extra Stout	£2.01	**Co-op Pioneer**
Gold	Guinness Foreign Extra Stout	£2.01	**Safeway**

Dark Beers

Stouts: with widgets

This could, and should, include widgetized porters and mild, but no brewery has had the nerve to make one yet. The startling difference between bitter bottled stout and creamy draught stout is due to gas: the bottled version, like all bottled beers, contains CO_2, which is coarse on the tongue and accentuates the extreme bitter character of a stout, whereas the head on the draught version is principally nitrogen, an inert gas that is smooth on the tongue, and the creamy effect of this subdues the bitter elements. Most beer writers are very sniffy about the widget, but without it draught stout drinkers would go thirsty at home. The widget in a can replicates the creamy effect by pushing nitrogen and beer through a tiny hole to create millions of minuscule, long-lasting bubbles. Draught stout is about 4–4.5 per cent ABV. Prices ranged from the equivalent of £1.08 per pint to £1.81.

Silver	Gillespie's Draught Malt Stout	£1.08	**Asda**
Silver	Genuine Irish Stout Somerfield	£1.20	**Somerfield**

Silver	Beamish Draught	£1.28	**Londis**
Silver	Beamish Draught	£1.29	**Co-op Pioneer**
Gold	Draught Guinness	£1.29	**Budgens**
Silver	Gillespie's Draught Malt Stout	£1.29	**Somerfield**
Gold	Draught Guinness	£1.48	**Co-op Pioneer**
Gold	Draught Guinness	£1.51	**Somerfield**
Silver	Murphy's Draught Irish Stout	£1.51	**Waitrose**
Gold	Draught Guinness	£1.52	**Littlewoods**
Silver	Murphy's Draught Irish Stout	£1.65	**Londis**
Silver	Murphy's Draught Irish Stout	£1.69	**Co-op Pioneer**
Silver	Murphy's Draught Irish Stout	£1.69	**Safeway**
Silver	Murphy's Draught Irish Stout	£1.69	**Somerfield**
Silver	Murphy's Draught Irish Stout	£1.81	**Budgens**

Lager and Pilsner Styles

Without widgets

The name lager comes from the German *Lager* or storehouse, as this beer should be aged for up to six months at a very cold temperature to precipitate the finest suspended matter, rendering the lager star-bright. Most commercial brews of lager will, however, be aged for fewer than six weeks. Pils, Pilsener and Pilsner are all much-abused designations that are now applied to lager-type beers of any strength, quality or age, although they were originally restricted to lagers brewed in the Czech town of Pilsen. As Pilsener caught on, the name of the Czech town was used for any top-quality, well-hopped lager of at least 5 per cent ABV brewed from Pilsener malt to give the very long and delicate, almost floral-perfumed, flavour for which this beer was justifiably famous. Only one Ice Beer made the cut. From my notes there is nothing to suggest that Ice Beer is any better than ordinary lager styles. If anything, it is less distinctive: it's just more expensive. Prices ranged from an equivalent of 48p per pint to £2.22.

Silver	Bavaria Dutch Lager	£0.64	**Londis**
Silver	Bavaria Lager Beer	£0.66	**Safeway**
Silver	Bavaria Lager Beer	£0.68	**Londis**
	Strasbourg Lager Bière d'Alsace	£0.68	**Asda**
	Spar Extra Lager	£0.76	**Spar**

	Schonbrau Pilsner Lager St Michael	£0.76	**Marks & Spencer**
	Pilsor Première Bière de Luxe Brasserie Jeanne d'Arc	£0.84	**Kwik Save**
	Ceres Royal Export	£0.85	**Morrisons**
	Ceres Royal Export	£0.85	**Co-op**
Bronze	Asda German Pilsener Premium Strength Export Lager	£0.85	**Asda**
Bronze	Spar Premium Gold Bier	£0.89	**Spar**
	Biere d'Alsace Premium Strength French Lager, Morrisons	£0.91	**Morrisons**
Silver	San Miguel Export Premium Lager	£0.93	**Kwik Save**
Bronze	Asda French Bière de Luxe Premium Strength Export Lager, Meteor Brewery	£1.04	**Asda**
	Faxe Premium Danish Export Lager	£1.11	**Somerfield**
Bronze	Waitrose Czech Lager	£1.12	**Waitrose**
	Faxe Premium Danish Export Lager	£1.13	**Morrisons**
	Faxe Premium Danish Export Lager	£1.13	**Londis**
	Faxe Premium Danish Export Lager	£1.13	**Safeway**
	Original Premium Pilsener Lager St. Pauli, St Michael	£1.13	**Marks & Spencer**
	Biere d'Alsace Brasserie Fischer, M&S	£1.13	**Marks & Spencer**
Bronze	Premium German Pilsener Lager St Michael	£1.13	**Marks & Spencer**
	French Premium Lager Bière d'Alsace, Somerfield	£1.13	**Somerfield**
	Waitrose German Lager	£1.14	**Waitrose**
Bronze	Sainsbury's German Pilsener Premium Lager	£1.16	**Sainsbury's**
Silver	DAB Original German Pilsener Lager Dortmunder Actien-Brauerei	£1.18	**Budgens**
	Grolsch Premium Lager	£1.19	**Londis**
	Co-op Super Strength Lager	£1.22	**Co-op**
Bronze	Vratislav Lager Tesco	£1.24	**Tesco**
	Amstel Bier Lager	£1.27	**Kwik Save**
Gold	Pilsner Urquell	£1.27	**Asda**
Bronze	Bavaria 8.6 Holland Beer	£1.29	**Kwik Save**
Bronze	Sainsbury's Nazdravi	£1.29	**Sainsbury's**
Bronze	Spanish Lager Export Tesco	£1.29	**Tesco**
Silver	Waitrose Westphalian Lager	£1.29	**Waitrose**

	Asda Italian Birra Premium Strength Export Lager	£1.29	Asda
Silver	Asda German Pilsener Premium Strength Export Lager	£1.29	Asda
Bronze	Kronenbourg 1664 Courage	£1.29	Co-op Pioneer
Bronze	Kronenbourg 1664 Courage	£1.29	Safeway
Bronze	Kronenbourg 1664 Courage	£1.29	Somerfield
Bronze	German Pilsener Somerfield	£1.29	Somerfield
	Waitrose Very Strong Lager	£1.29	Waitrose
Silver	German Pilsener Bier Tesco	£1.35	Tesco
Silver	Budweiser Budvar	£1.47	Budgens
Silver	Budweiser Budvar	£1.47	Somerfield
	'33' Export	£1.47	Co-op Pioneer
	'33' Export	£1.47	Safeway
Silver	DAB Original German Beer Dortmunder Actien-Brauerei	£1.48	Tesco
Bronze	Kronenbourg 1664 Premium Bière	£1.51	Tesco
Bronze	Kronenbourg 1664 Premium Bière	£1.51	Safeway
Silver	Budweiser Budvar	£1.53	Safeway
Silver	Carlsberg Ice Beer	£1.54	Asda
Bronze	HB Original Hofbräuhaus München Premium Lager	£1.58	Sainsbury's
Silver	Budweiser Budvar	£1.58	Co-op Pioneer
	Amstel Bier Lager	£1.59	Co-op Pioneer
	Stella Artois Premium Lager Beer	£1.63	Co-op Pioneer
	Stella Artois Premium Lager Beer	£1.63	Safeway
	Stella Artois Premium Lager Beer	£1.63	Somerfield
	Budweiser Anheuser-Busch Inc	£1.64	Littlewoods
	Stella Artois Premium Lager Beer	£1.66	Budgens
Bronze	San Miguel Export Premium Lager	£1.70	Budgens
Bronze	San Miguel Export Premium Lager	£1.70	Co-op Pioneer
Bronze	San Miguel Export Premium Lager	£1.70	Safeway
	Fosters Export Australia's Famous Beer Courage	£1.70	Co-op Pioneer
Bronze	Moretti Birra Friulana Italian Pilsner Beer	£1.70	Tesco
Silver	Carlsberg Ice Beer	£1.70	Londis
Silver	Carlsberg Ice Beer	£1.70	Safeway
Silver	Staropramen Beer	£1.70	Somerfield
	Alsace Gold Fischer, St Michael	£1.72	Marks & Spencer

Silver	Bitburger Premium Pils Klassisch Herb	£1.72	**Asda**
	Budweiser Anheuser-Busch	£1.72	**Asda**
	Beck's	£1.72	**Budgens**
Silver	Sainsbury's Bière de Prestige Premium French Lager, Fischer	£1.74	**Sainsbury's**
	Fischer Tradition Bière Blonde Spéciale d'Alsace	£1.74	**Tesco**
	Beck's	£1.91	**Kwik Save**
	Beck's	£1.92	**Co-op Pioneer**
	Beck's	£1.92	**Littlewoods**
	Beck's	£1.92	**Safeway**
	Beck's	£1.92	**Somerfield**
	Stella Artois Dry Premium Beer Export Strength	£1.96	**Co-op Pioneer**
	Beck's	£1.96	**Londis**
	Stella Artois Dry Premium Beer Export Strength	£1.96	**Safeway**
Silver	Staropramen Beer	£1.98	**Co-op Pioneer**
Gold	Staropramen Dark Lager	£1.98	**Sainsbury's**
Silver	Staropramen Beer	£1.98	**Sainsbury's**
Silver	Staropramen Beer	£1.98	**Tesco**
Silver	Staropramen Beer	£1.98	**Safeway**
Bronze	Samuel Adams Boston Lager	£2.05	**Co-op**
Gold	Grolsch Premium Lager	£2.13	**Sainsbury's**
Gold	Grolsch Premium Lager	£2.13	**Safeway**
Gold	Grolsch Premium Lager	£2.13	**Somerfield**

Lager and Pilsner Styles

With widgets

The widget seems even less successful when applied to lager styles than it does when applied to bitter ales. Prices ranged from the equivalent of £1.19 to £1.29.

	Carling Premier Draught Lager	£1.29	**Asda**
Bronze	Enigma Draught Lager Guinness	£1.29	**Waitrose**

Pale Ale

Pale Ale is the name applied to a particular bottled version of draught bitter. First brewed in London in the mid-eighteenth century, it did not become famous until Bass produced this style of beer at its Burton-on-Trent brewery, since when Burton has become synonymous with Pale Ale. This is because the Burton water contains gypsum, which precipitates the most ultra-fine sediments suspended in a beer, giving it a much paler colour: hence Pale Ale, thus Burton Pale Ale. Prices ranged from an equivalent of 75p per pint to £2.03.

Silver	Samuel Smith's Old Brewery Strong Pale Ale	£1.47	**Booths**
Silver	Samuel Smith's Old Brewery Pale Ale	£1.52	**Co-op Pioneer**
Bronze	India Pale Ale Original Export Shepherd Neame	£1.53	**Booths**
Silver	Bottle Conditioned India Pale Ale Tesco Select Ales, Marston Thompson Evershed	£1.58	**Tesco**
Bronze	'Old Speckled Hen' Strong Pale Ale Morland	£1.62	**Tesco**
Silver	Deuchars Export Strength IPA India Pale Ale Caledonian Brewery	£1.65	**Morrisons**
Silver	Marston's India Export Pale Ale Head Brewers Choice	£1.65	**Booths**
Silver	Marston's India Export Pale Ale Head Brewers Choice	£1.69	**Morrisons**
Bronze	'Old Speckled Hen' Strong Pale Ale Morland	£1.76	**Morrisons**
Bronze	'Old Speckled Hen' Strong Pale Ale Morland	£1.76	**Safeway**
Bronze	'Old Speckled Hen' Strong Pale Ale Morland	£1.76	**Somerfield**
Bronze	'Old Speckled Hen' Strong Pale Ale Morland	£1.81	**Londis**
Bronze	'Old Speckled Hen' Strong Pale Ale Morland	£1.92	**Co-op Pioneer**
Bronze	'Old Speckled Hen' Strong Pale Ale Morland	£2.03	**Budgens**

Speciality Beers

A hotchpotch of brews, but mostly Trappist ales and wheat beers. The Desperado is not really recommended (*see* **Tesco**). Prices ranged from £1.01 to £3.43 per pint.

Bronze	Bavarian Wheat Beer Weizenbier, Somerfield	£1.01	Somerfield
Silver	Bavarian Wheat Beer Tesco	£1.47	Tesco
	Thurn und Taxis Kristall Bavarian Weizen Beer	£1.53	Tesco
Bronze	Hoegaarden White Beer	£1.70	Safeway
Bronze	Hoegaarden White Beer	£1.70	Tesco
	Desperados Tequila Beer Brasserie Fischer	£2.05	**Tesco**
Bronze	La Trappe Koningshoeven Trappiste Brune	£3.40	**Waitrose**
Silver	Chimay Pères Trappistes 1996 Scourmont Abbey	£3.43	**Tesco**

SPIRIT GUIDE

Although *SuperBooze* does not taste spirits, it does provide a price comparison of own-label and common major brands. This illustrates what the street price is, and reveals how much over the odds you may be paying.

Spirit prices are subject to almost continuous change as supermarkets try to maintain a competitive edge, thus this price guide can only be regarded as a snapshot of the market at one particular point in time – in this case July 1996. Although this yo-yo effect prevents the price guide from being used daily on a shop-by-shop basis, it does provide the reader with the means to save a considerable amount of money when purchasing spirits. For although the supermarkets claim to keep their spirit prices competitive, this snapshot proves that many do not, or are caught out when others drop their prices. The cheapest figures, highlighted in bold, indicate the going street price, while the column on the right reveals how much you could be paying over the odds.

Comparing prices for own-label spirits can result in misleading differentials, as you will not necessarily be comparing like with like, but the table demonstrates that it pays to shop around. Note that not every supermarket stocks every product.

	Asda	Booth's	Budgens	Co-op	Co-operative Pioneer	Kwik Save	Littlewoods
Brandy							
Own-Brand Armagnac	–	–	–	–	–	–	–
Own-Brand Cognac	**11.79**	15.69	–	–	12.99	–	–
Own-Brand Grape	7.89	8.39	8.15	–	8.49	**6.75**	–
Asbach German	–	15.99	–	**14.99**	15.19	–	–
Courvoisier ***	17.69	17.89	17.69	17.69	17.69	**15.95**	17.49
Janneau Armagnac	–	–	**15.69**	16.19	**15.69**	–	–
Martell ***	17.69	17.75	17.69	17.69	17.69	17.65	–
Metaxa Greek	**13.49**	14.89	–	14.89	–	–	–
Rémy Martin VSOP	25.69	**24.39**	25.59	25.99	–	–	–
Three Barrels	11.99	11.99	11.99	**11.49**	**11.49**	11.95	11.99
Gin							
Own Brand	8.29	7.99	9.29	8.49	8.25	**6.74**	8.49
Beefeater	12.99	12.99	12.99	11.69	12.99	–	–
Gordons	10.99	10.99	10.99	10.99	10.99	**10.95**	10.99
White Satin	9.99	9.95	9.99	9.99	9.99	**9.95**	9.99
Rum							
Own-Brand White	8.19	7.99	–	8.59	8.25	**6.74**	8.75
Own-Brand Dark	9.49	7.99	–	8.59	8.25	**7.69**	8.75
Bacardi	11.79	11.79	**11.29**	11.79	11.79	11.69	11.79
Captain Morgan Black	11.95	–	11.95	11.95	11.95	**11.59**	–
Lambs Navy	**10.99**	11.69	11.99	11.69	11.99	11.65	11.99
Woods Navy 100°	–	–	–	–	16.89	–	–
Vodka							
Own-Brand	7.69	7.89	7.99	7.69	7.69	**6.74**	8.49
Smirnoff Blue	**12.39**	13.99	–	13.89	–	–	–
Smirnoff Red	10.69	10.69	10.69	10.69	10.69	10.65	**9.99**
Stolichnaya	–	**11.99**	–	–	–	–	–
Vladivar	9.19	9.49	9.29	9.29	9.19	**9.09**	9.19
Whisky							
Own-Brand Scotch	8.99	8.89	9.39	8.25	8.99	**7.49**	7.99
Jim Beam Bourbon	–	–	–	15.49	15.49	15.29	–
Bells	11.99	11.99	11.99	11.99	11.99	**11.95**	11.99

Londis	M&S	Morrisons	Safeway	Sainsbury's	Somerfield	Tesco	Waitrose	Max. Difference
–	–	–	15.65	15.19	–	**14.65**	15.15	1.00
–	–	11.99	13.55	13.25	13.25	13.19	16.45	4.66
8.49	12.49	8.29	–	–	9.69	9.49	–	5.74
–	–	–	–	**13.19**	–	–	–	2.80
16.99	–	17.69	17.69	17.69	17.69	17.69	17.65	1.94
–	–	15.72	–	–	–	–	–	0.50
17.19	–	**15.69**	17.69	17.69	17.69	17.69	17.65	2.06
–	–	–	–	14.55	–	–	–	1.40
–	–	24.49	25.99	25.99	–	25.65	26. 00	1.61
11.99	–	11.99	11.99	11.99	11.99	11.99	–	0.50
7.99	9.99	8.49	9.19	7.69	9.19	9.19	9.19	2.25
12.99	–	**10.99**	12.99	12.99	12.99	12.99	12.95	2.00
10.99	–	10.99	10.99	10.99	10.99	10.99	10.99	0.04
9.99	–	9.99	9.99	**9.69**	9.99	9.99	9.99	0.30
8.79	–	8.29	8.99	8.95	8.59	8.65	8.89	2.25
8.49	–	8.49	10.19	9.89	9.59	9.89	9.89	2.50
11.79	–	11.79	11.79	11.79	11.79	11.79	11.79	0.50
11.99	–	11.65	11.95	11.65	11.95	11.95	–	0.40
11.99	–	11.95	11.99	11.95	11.99	11.99	11.99	1.00
–	–	16.65	**14.99**	–	16.89	16.89	–	1.90
7.99	9.99	7.69	7.79	7.59	7.69	7.79	7.79	3.25
–	–	–	**12.39**	13.89	13.89	13.89	–	1.60
10.99	–	10.69	10.69	10.69	10.69	10.69	10.69	1.00
–	–	–	12.49	12.49	–	12.49	12.49	0.50
9.19	–	9.19	9.19	9.19	9.19	9.29	–	0.40
8.59	12.49	8.95	7.95	9.19	9.29	9.29	9.29	5.00
14.99	–	15.49	15.49	15.49	15.49	15.49	–	0.50
11.99	–	11.99	11.99	11.99	11.99	11.99	11.99	0.04

	Asda	Booth's	Budgens	Co-op	Co-operative Pioneer	Kwik Save	Littlewoods
Canadian Club	13.99	13.99	–	13.99	–	–	–
Chivas Regal	–	24.99	–	–	24.65	–	–
Claymore	9.99	9.99	8.99	9.99	8.99	**8.95**	9.99
Jack Daniels Bourbon	16.99	16.99	–	16.99	16.69	16.59	16.99
Famous Grouse	12.99	**12.19**	12.99	12.29	12.29	**12.19**	12.29
Glenfiddich	19.49	19.49	19.49	19.49	19.49	**19.45**	19.49
Glenlivet	19.99	20.39	–	19.99	19.99	–	–
Glenmorangie	**21.19**	22.49	21.49	21.49	21.49	–	21.49
Grants	11.49	**10.49**	11.29	11.49	11.49	11.39	10.99
J&B Rare	–	**14.69**	14.99	**14.69**	–	–	–
Jameson Irish	13.69	**13.49**	13.69	13.69	13.99	13.59	13.99
Macallan	21.99	–	–	21.99	21.99	–	21.99
Mackinlay	–	–	**9.99**	–	–	–	–
Teachers	11.69	11.69	11.69	11.69	11.69	**10.95**	11.69
Vat 69	9.99	–	9.99	**9.49**	9.99	9.75	–
Johnnie Walker Black	18.69	18.99	18.99	18.69	**16.99**	–	–
White Horse	10.99	10.99	10.75	10.99	**9.99**	10.95	10.99
Whyte & Mackay	11.25	11.49	11.39	11.29	11.29	11.19	11.29
Liqueurs etc							
Baileys Irish Cream	11.69	11.99	11.79	11.79	11.65	**11.59**	11.79
Cadburys Cream	–	**9.99**	10.79	10.99	–	–	–
Carolans Irish Cream	6.99	**4.99**	–	7.59	–	–	7.85
Cointreau	15.99	15.99	15.79	15.99	15.99	15.89	17.29
Drambuie (50cl)	12.79	12.79	**12.69**	–	–	**12.69**	12.99
Grand Marnier	–	19.29	**18.49**	18.95	–	–	–
Malibu	14.99	11.99	10.99	10.99	10.99	10.79	10.99
Pernod	13.59	12.75	**9.79**	13.89	13.89	13.49	13.99
Southern Comfort	14.99	15.49	14.99	14.99	15.19	**14.95**	–
Terry's Orange Chocolate	–	11.75	–	**9.99**	**9.99**	–	–
Tia Maria	13.99	13.99	–	13.99	13.99	13.95	**13.79**
Warninks Advocaat	9.89	10.15	–	9.89	9.89	**9.29**	9.89

Note All prices for 70cl unless otherwise stated.

Londis	M&S	Morrisons	Safeway	Sainsbury's	Somerfield	Tesco	Waitrose	Max. Difference
12.99	–	**11.99**	12.49	–	13.99	13.99	–	2.00
–	–	–	–	–	–	**24.64**	–	0.35
9.99	–	9.99	9.99	9.99	9.99	9.99	–	1.04
16.99	–	**14.69**	16.99	16.99	16.99	16.99	16.95	2.30
12.29	–	12.29	12.29	12.29	12.29	12.29	12.29	0.80
19.49	–	19.49	19.49	19.49	22.29	19.49	**19.45**	2.84
–	–	19.99	19.99	19.99	19.99	19.99	**19.95**	0.44
21.99	–	21.49	21.49	21.49	21.49	21.49	21.50	1.30
10.99	–	11.49	11.49	11.49	11.49	11.49	11.49	1.00
14.99	–	–	**14.69**	–	–	**14.69**	–	0.30
13.69	–	13.69	13.99	13.69	13.69	13.69	13.65	0.50
–	–	**19.99**	–	21.99	21.99	21.99	22.00	2.01
–	–	–	–	–	–	10.68	–	0.69
11.79	–	11.69	11.69	11.69	10.99	11.69	11.69	0.74
–	–	9.99	9.99	9.99	9.99	9.99	9.99	0.50
19.49	–	18.69	18.69	18.69	18.69	18.69	–	2.50
10.99	–	10.99	10.99	10.99	10.99	10.99	10.99	1.00
11.19	–	**10.99**	11.29	11.29	11.29	11.29	11.29	0.50
11.79	–	11.69	11.89	11.79	11.79	11.79	11.79	0.40
–	–	–	–	–	10.99	10.99	–	1.00
–	–	6.59	7.59	7.59	–	7.59	–	2.86
15.99	–	**14.42**	15.99	15.69	15.99	15.99	15.95	2.87
–	–	12.79	12.79	12.76	–	–	12.95	0.30
–	–	–	–	**13.99**	–	–	–	5.30
10.99	–	10.99	10.99	**10.99**	**9.99**	10.99	10.99	5.00
13.49	–	13.99	13.99	13.99	13.89	13.99	13.95	4.20
15.19	–	–	15.15	14.99	14.99	15.19	14.95	0.54
–	–	–	10.75	–	–	–	–	1.76
13.99	–	13.99	13.99	13.99	13.99	13.99	13.95	0.20
–	–	9.49	9.89	9.89	9.69	–	9.89	0.86

GLOSSARY OF TECHNICAL AND TASTING TERMS

I have tried to make the descriptions of wines and beers self-evident wherever possible, but every subject from house-building to fly-fishing has developed its own jargon to express concepts more precisely, and booze is no exception. I hope the following will clarify the meaning of terms the reader may not be familiar with.

ABV This stands for Alcohol By Volume and is expressed in percentage terms. For those who remember the Degrees Proof system, a typical spirit of 70° Proof would be equal to 40 per cent ABV.

Accessible Literally means that the wine is easy to approach, with no great barriers of tannin, acidity or undeveloped extract to prevent enjoyment and drinkability. This term is often used for young, fine-quality wine where the tannin is supple and thus approachable, although it will undoubtedly improve with age.

Acidity Essential for the life and vitality of all wines. Too much will make wine too sharp (not sour – that's a fault), but not enough will make it taste flat and dull, and the flavour will not last in the mouth.

Aftertaste The flavour and aroma left in the mouth after the wine has been swallowed. When attractive, this adds a pleasurable dimension to a wine, and could be the reason why you prefer it to a similar wine with no aftertaste as such.

Ages gracefully A wine that retains finesse as it matures, and sometimes even increases in finesse.

Aggressive The opposite of soft and smooth.

Alcohol It may sound obvious, but alcohol is essential to the flavour and body of alcoholic products. Because wines contain a greater percentage of alcohol than beers, a de-alcoholized wine is intrinsically more difficult to perfect than a de-alcoholized beer.

Aldehyde The midway stage between an alcohol and an acid, formed during the oxidation of an alcohol. Acetaldehyde is the most important of the common wine aldehydes, forming as wine alcohol oxidizes into acetic acid (vinegar). Small amounts of acetaldehyde add to the complexity of a wine, but too much will make a table wine smell like sherry.

Amylic The peardrop or banana aroma of amyl acetate, a volatile compound created in the vinification process. Particularly dominant in cool-fermented white wines and red wines produced by *macération carbonique* such as Beaujolais Nouveau. Also possible in wines of any colour that have undergone a cold, pre-fermentation maceration.

AOC *Appellation d'Origine Contrôlée* is the top rung in the French wine classification system, although in practice it includes everything from the greatest French wines to the absolute pits. If I have learned anything, it is that it is better to buy an expensive *vin de pays* than a cheap AOC. A £4.99 white Burgundy can be rubbish, but a £4.99 *vin de pays* Chardonnay will often be delicious.

Appellation Literally 'name', this usually refers to an official, geographically based designation for a wine.

Aroma This should really be confined to the fresh and fruity smells reminiscent of grapes, rather than the more winey or bottle-mature complexities of bouquet; but it is not always possible to use this word in its purest form, hence aroma and bouquet may be read as synonymous.

Attack A wine with good attack is one that is complete and readily presents its full armament of taste characteristics to the palate. The wine is likely to be youthful rather than mature, and its attack augurs well for its future.

Auslese A sweet, botrytis-affected, German wine that can be sublime, but beware of cheap versions, as they are seldom bargains and you would be better advised paying a top price for a Spätlese.

Australian, Typically It is dangerous to allude to styles on a geographic basis, particularly one as all encompassing as an entire continent, but I must conclude from a great many blind tastings that an unmistakable Australian signature often comes through, even when the wines do not actually come from Down Under, but are made by Australian flying winemakers in all four corners of the globe. What this Oz or Ozzified character is, therefore, has nothing to do with Australia as such, but with the methods its winemakers habitually employ, which include how the juice is handled, prior to and during fermentation, the yeast strains applied and the use of new oak.

Balance Refers to the harmonious relationship between acids, alcohol, fruit, tannin and other natural elements. If you have two similar wines but you definitely prefer one of them, its balance is likely to be one of the two determining factors (length being the other).

Beerenauslese A luscious German botrytis wine, the sweetness of which falls between that of an Auslese and a Trockenbeerenauslese.

Big vintage/year Terms usually applied to great years, because the exceptional weather conditions produce bigger (that is, fuller, richer) wines than normal. May also be used literally, to describe a year with a big crop.

Big wine A full-bodied wine with an exceptionally rich flavour.

Bio-dynamic Wines or beers produced bio-dynamically are made from raw materials (grapes, barley, hops, etc.) grown without the aid of chemical or synthetic sprays or fertilizers, and are vinified with natural yeast and the minimum use of filtration, SO_2 and chaptalization.

Biscuity A desirable aspect of bouquet found in some Champagnes, particularly a well-matured, Pinot Noir-dominated blend (Chardonnay-dominated Champagnes tend to go toasty).

Bite A very definite qualification of grip. Usually a desirable characteristic, but an unpleasant bite is possible.

Bitterness Can be good or bad! (1) An unpleasant aspect of a poorly made wine. (2) An expected characteristic of an as-yet undeveloped concentration of flavours that should, with maturity, become rich and delicious.

Blanc de Blancs Literally 'white of whites', a white wine made from white grapes, a term that is often, but not exclusively, used for sparkling wines.

Blanc de Noirs Literally 'white of blacks', a white wine made from black grapes, a term that is often, but not exclusively, used for sparkling wines. In the New World the wines usually have a tinge of pink, often no different from that of a fully fledged rosé, but a classic *blanc de noirs* should be as white as possible without using artificial means.

Blind, blind tasting An objective tasting where the identity of wines is unknown to the taster until after he or she has made notes and given scores. All competitive tastings are blind.

Blowzy An overblown, exaggerated fruity aroma, such as fruit jam, that may be attractive in a cheap wine, but would indicate a lack of finesse in a more expensive product.

Blush An Americanism conjured up to sell rosé wines to people who think that rosé is cheap and nasty. Zinfandel is the most popular blush wine style, and there is even such a thing as Blush Chardonnay!

Bodega Literally a wine cellar in Spanish and can mean a wine shop, but in this book solely refers to a winery.

Body The extract of fruit (in a wine) or malt (in a beer) and alcoholic strength that together give an impression of weight in the mouth.

Botrytis Literally 'rot', which is usually an unwanted disorder of the vine. But *botrytis cinerea* or 'noble rot' is necessary for the production of the finest quality of sweet wines and, perhaps confusingly, is commonly contracted to botrytis or botrytised grapes when discussing such wines.

Bottle-age The length of time a wine or beer spends in bottle before it is consumed. A wine that has good bottle-age is one that has had sufficient time to mature properly. Bottle-ageing has a mellowing effect.

Bottle-conditioned A beer that is either unfiltered or has been bottled with a small yeast solution. In both instances, the fermentation process continues in the bottle, adding a touch of fizz, a certain plumpness and a fruitiness to the beer. It also creates some sediment, which is why a bottle-conditioned beer must be poured with extreme care if you are to avoid the dregs and keep the ale star-bright – unless, that is, it happens to be a wheat or white beer.

Bouquet This should really be applied to the combination of smells directly attributable to a wine's maturity in bottle – thus, aroma for grape and bouquet for bottle. But it is not always possible to use these words in their purest form, hence aroma and bouquet may be read as synonymous.

Bourgeois growth A Bordeaux château classification beneath *cru classé*.

Breathing Term used to describe the interaction between a wine and the air after a bottle has been opened and before it is drunk.

Breed The finesse of a wine that is due to the intrinsic quality of grape and *terroir* combined with the skill and experience of a great winemaker.

Breezy A fruitiness that is so fresh that it feels and tastes not just lifted, but as if the very freshness is actually breezing around the mouth.

Brut Normally reserved for sparkling wines, Brut literally means raw or bone-dry, but in practice there is always some sweetness and so the wine can at the most only be termed dry.

Buttery Normally a rich, fat and positively delicious character found in many white wines, particularly if produced in a great vintage or warm country.

Carbon gas This is naturally produced in the fermentation process, when the sugar is converted into almost equal parts of alcohol and carbon dioxide or carbonic gas. Carbonic gas is normally allowed to escape during fermentation, although a tiny amount will always be present in its dissolved form in any wine, even a still one, otherwise it would taste dull, flat and lifeless. If the gas is prevented from escaping, the wine becomes sparkling.

Chaptalization The practice of adding sugar to fresh grape juice to raise a wine's alcoholic potential. The term is named after Antoine Chaptal, a brilliant chemist and technocrat who served Napoleon as Minister of the Interior from 1800 to 1805 and instructed wine-growers on the advantages of adding sugar at the time of pressing.

Charm A subjective term: if a wine charms, it appeals without blatantly attracting in an obvious fashion.

Chewy An extreme qualification of meaty.

Citrus Citrussy indicates aromas and flavours of far greater complexity than mere 'lemony' can suggest.

Clean Straightforward term applied to a wine devoid of any unwanted or unnatural undertones of aroma and flavour.

Closed Refers to the nose or palate of a wine that fails to open or show much character. It also implies that the wine has some qualities, even if they are hidden – these should open up as the wine develops in bottle.

Cloying The sickly and sticky character of a poor sweet wine, where the finish is heavy and often unclean.

Coarse A term that should be applied to a rough and ready wine; not necessarily unpleasant, but certainly not fine.

Coconut An attractive if very obvious characteristic that almost invariably applies to American oak, particularly if it is part of the bouquet as well as the palate, although a certain coconutty character can develop from honeyed, bottle-aged aromas of fruit on the finish or aftertaste of a wine.

Commercial A diplomatic way for experts to say, 'I don't like this, but I expect the masses will'! A commercial wine is blended to a widely acceptable formula; at its worst it may be bland and inoffensive, at its best it is probably fruity, quaffable and uncomplicated.

Complete A wine that has everything (fruit, tannin, acidity, depth, length, etc.) and thus feels satisfying in the mouth.

Complexity An overworked word that implies a wine has many different nuances of smell or taste. Great wines in their youth may have a certain complexity, but it is only with maturity in bottle that a wine will eventually achieve full potential in terms of complexity.

Concoction Usually a derogatory term, but when found in a guide to exclusively exciting wines or beers like this it will at the very least be tongue in cheek, if you will excuse the pun. I might be referring to a literal concoction of component parts (as in a cocktail wine) or to what tastes like a medley of fruits or flavours in a less expensive wine.

Contrived Wines can either be made in a hands-on or hands-off way. Those who employ the hands-off method seek to make the most natural wines and are content to let the grapes express themselves. Winemakers who use a more hands-on approach are more willing to interfere when, say, the fermentation is not going to plan. Good and bad exist under both regimes and at best a good hands-on wine is just as individual as a good hands-off wine, it is just more expressive of the winemaker – more of a hand-crafted product, if you like. Some hands-on wines, however, are crafted not so much to reflect their individual makers as some sort of preconceived type or style (e.g., upfront, oak-matured, fruit-driven). These are basically contrived wines and some are more cleverly contrived than others.

Cool-fermented An obviously cool-fermented wine is very fresh, with simple aromas of apples, pears and bananas.

Corked This does not imply that there is anything inherently wrong with the wine, but that there is a penicillin infection inside the cork which gives an unpleasant musty character, spoiling an otherwise good wine. It should be highly improbable to find two consecutive corked bottles of the same wine, but every day scientists are discovering corky-smelling compounds that have nothing to do with the cork, so it is quite possible for entire batches of wine to smell or taste corked. No wine buyer should, however, put such wines on the shelf.

Correct A wine with all the correct characteristics for its type and origin. Not necessarily an exciting wine, therefore no wine in *SuperBooze* should be merely correct.

Creamy A subjective term used to describe a creamy flavour that may be indicative of the variety of grape or the method of vinification. I tend to use this word in connection with the fruitiness or oakiness of a wine.

Crémant Traditionally ascribed to a Champagne with a low pressure and a soft, creamy mousse, this term has now been phased out in Champagne owing to its use for other French Méthode Champenoise appellations such as Crémant de Bourgogne and Crémant d'Alsace.

Crisp A clean wine, with good acidity showing on the finish, yielding a fresh, clean taste.

Cru Literally a 'growth', *cru* usually refers to a single named vineyard that has been defined and delimited over the centuries by one or more elements of *terroir* that are markedly different from those of the surrounding vineyards. This forms the basis of official classifications, such as *grands crus* of Burgundy and the *crus classés* of Bordeaux.

Cru Bourgeois An official Bordeaux classification ranking below Bordeaux's *cru classé* system.

Cru classé An official classification in Bordeaux, established in 1855, whereby the best châteaux are graded in a five-tier hierarchical system from *premier cru classé,* or first growth, down to *cinquième cru classé,* or fifth growth.

Cuvée Originally the wine of one *cuvé* or vat, but now refers to a specific blend or product which, in current commercial practice, will be from several vats.

Definition A wine with good definition is one that is not just clean with a correct balance, but also has a positive expression of its grape variety and/or origin.

Delicate Describes the quieter characteristics of quality that give a wine charm.

Demi-sec Literally 'semi-dry', but actually tastes quite sweet.

Depth Refers first to a wine's depth of flavour and secondly to its depth of interest.

Disgorgement This is part of the process of making a bottle-fermented sparkling wine such as Champagne. After fermentation the yeast forms a deposit, which must be removed. To do this the bottles are inverted in freezing brine just long enough for the sediment to form a semi-frozen slush that adheres to the neck of the bottle. This enables the bottle to be returned to an upright position without disturbing the wine. The temporary cap used to seal the bottle is removed and the internal pressure is sufficient to eject or disgorge the slush of sediment without losing very much wine at all. The wine is then topped up and a traditional Champagne cork used to seal the bottle.

Dirty Applies to any wine with an unpleasant off-taste or off-smell, probably the result of poor vinification or bad bottling.

Distinctive A wine with a positive character. All fine wines are distinctive to some degree, but not all distinctive wines are necessarily fine.

DO This stands for Spain's *Denominación de Origen*, which is theoretically the equivalent of the French AOC. *See* **AOC**.

DOC Confusingly, this stands for both Italy's *Denominazione di Origine Controllata* and Portugal's *Denominaçao de Origem Controlada*, which are theoretically the equivalent of the French AOC. *See* **AOC**. It also stands for Spain's *Denominación de Origen Calificada*, which is the equivalent of the Italian DOCG. *See* **DOCG**.

DOCG Italy's *Denominazione di Origine Controllata e Garantita* is theoretically one step above the French AOC. Ideally it should be similar to, say, a *Premier* or *Grand Cru* in Burgundy or a *Cru Classé* in Bordeaux, but in reality, it is almost as big a sop as Italy's DOC itself.

Dosage When the sediment is removed from a sparkling wine, a little sugar dissolved in wine is added to balance the acidity, which would taste harsh otherwise, as all bubbly must be made from relatively high-acid wines.

Easy Synonymous to a certain extent with accessible, but probably implies a cheaper, value-for-money wine, whereas accessible often applies to finer wines.

Elegant A subjective term applied to wines that may be described as stylish or possessing finesse.

Expansive A wine that is big, but open and accessible.

Expressive A wine true to its grape variety and area of origin.

Extract The term covers all the solids in a wine or beer that literally give the drink its body.

Fat A wine full in body and extract.

Fermentation All beers and wines are the result of fermentation, where yeast cells convert sugar (or maltose in the case of beer) into alcohol and carbonic gas.

Filter, filtration There are various methods of filtration, which essentially involve the passing of wine or beer through a medium that removes particles of a certain size.

Finesse That elusive, indescribable quality that separates a fine wine from those of lesser quality.

Fine Wine Quality wines, representing only a small percentage of all wines produced.

Finish The quality and enjoyment of a wine's aftertaste.

Firm Refers to a certain amount of grip. A firm wine is one of good constitution, held up by a certain amount of tannin and acidity.

Flabby The opposite of crisp – a wine lacking in acidity and consequently dull, weak and short.

Flat (1) A sparkling wine that has lost all its mousse. (2) A term interchangeable with flabby, especially when referring to a lack of acidity on the finish.

Fleshy Refers to a wine with plenty of fruit and extract and with a certain underlying firmness.

Flor A scum-like yeast film that occurs naturally and floats on the surface of some sherries as they mature in part-filled wooden butts. It is the *flor* that gives Fino Sherry its inimitable character.

Flying winemaker The concept of the flying winemaker was born in Australia, where consultants like Brian Croser (now Petaluma) and Tony Jordan (now Green Point) would hop by plane from harvest to harvest practising their skills across the entire Australian continent. Riding on the success of Australian wines in the UK market, other Oz wine wizards began to stretch their wings, flying in and out of everywhere from Southern Italy to Moldova, usually at the behest of British supermarkets. Like the spread of Chardonnay and Cabernet, the flying winemakers were at first welcomed by the wine press, then turned upon for standardizing wine wherever they went. The truth is that before the arrival of international grapes and international winemakers, the peasant co-operatives in these countries had no idea that they could even produce wines to compete on the international market. Now that they have established a certain standard with known grape varieties and modern technology, they are beginning to turn to their roots, to see whether indigenous varieties might have the potential to produce more expressive wines. But for the ubiquitous international grapes and winemakers, they would still be producing dross in wineries not fit to hold a party in.

Food wine Although wine is generally perceived to be the natural accompaniment of food, not all wines are ideal for the purpose. Some wines are so light and delicate in style that they are overwhelmed by strongly flavoured or spicy food, but there are equally light and delicate dishes that make ideal partners and, generally, the inability of lighter styles of wine to accompany food has been grossly exaggerated. Put simply there are two basic styles that do not make good food wine: those that are very pure and fruity and, surprisingly, those that are massively structured and flavoured. Both these styles have something in common with, I suspect, every non-food wine ever produced – they are so complete on their own that food can only detract from their enjoyment. Food wines, on the other hand, rarely reveal all their characteristics and qualities in a pure-drinking or clinical-tasting environment. They require coaxing with a meal and provide increasing pleasure and interest from glass to glass.

Fresh Wines that are clean and still vital with youth.

Fruit Wine is made from grapes and must therefore be 100 per cent fruit, yet it will not have a fruity flavour unless the grapes used have the correct combination of ripeness and acidity.

Full Usually refers to body, e.g. full-bodied. But a wine can be light in body yet full in flavour.

Fût A wooden cask, usually made of oak, in which some wines are aged, or fermented and aged.

Generic A wine, usually blended, of a general appellation.

Generous A generous wine gives its fruit freely on the palate, while an ungenerous one is likely to have little or no fruit and, probably, an excess of tannin. All wines should have some degree of generosity.

Gluggy Easy to guzzle.

Grande Marque Literally a great or famous brand; in the world of wine, the term *grande marque* is specific to Champagne and applies to members of the Syndicat de Grandes Marques, which of course includes all the most famous names.

Grand vin Normally used in Bordeaux, this applies to the main wine sold under the château's famous name, which will have been produced from only the finest barrels. Wines excluded during this process go into second, third and sometimes fourth wines that are sold under different labels.

Grapy Applied to the aroma and flavour of a wine that are reminiscent of grapes rather than overtly winey.

Grip Applied to a firm wine with a positive finish. A wine showing grip on the finish indicates a certain bite of acidity or, if red, tannin.

Grower Champagne All the *grandes marques* or famous brands of Champagne (Moët, Clicquot, Bollinger *et al*) are produced by houses or *négociants*, which may purchase grapes to supplement their own-grown raw materials, although some *cuvées* – particularly vintage or deluxe Champagnes – will often be exclusively from the producer's own estate. A grower Champagne, on other hand, is made by one of the thousands of growers in region and will always be produced entirely from that grower's own estate, which might be restricted to just one village, although many own vineyards in several villages.

Gutsy A wine full in body, fruit, extract and, usually, alcohol. Normally applied to ordinary-quality wines.

Guzzly Synonymous with gluggy.

Hollow A wine that appears to lack any real flavour in the mouth compared to the promise shown on the nose. Usually due to a lack of body, fruit or acidity.

Honest Applied to any wine, but usually those of a fairly basic quality, honest implies it is true in character and typical of its type and origin. It also suggests that the wine does not seem to have been souped up or mucked about with in any unlawful way. The use of the word honest is, however, a way of damning with faint praise, for it does not suggest a wine of any special or memorable quality.

Hops The flower of the hop, either dried or in the form of a concentrate, is widely used to flavour – or, to be more precise, season – a beer during the brewing process.

Jammy Literally means tastes of jam, and there is good and less good (probably more cloying) jamminess, although the term 'preserve' might be used if the jam has a particular finesse. Everything is relative, so whereas jammy is generally a derogatory term, it is possible to find a really enjoyable jamminess, especially if the wine is inexpensive. As all the wines in *SuperBooze* are very strongly recommended (because those that do not make the grade are excluded), jammy will be used in a positive sense nine times out of ten in this book.

Kabinett Usually a touch drier than basic QbA, a Kabinett from a good producer often represents the best value and most expressive example of its area of origin. The first level of QmP before Spätlese, Auslese, Beerenauslese and Trockenbeerenauslese, each of which represents a significant step-up in sweetness and, of course, price.

Landed-age Most Champagnes of old had good landed-age, a period of ageing in the importer's cellar prior to being released on to the market, and it is during this time that the toasty and biscuity post-disgorgement bottle-aromas begin to emerge. Few importers today bother or can afford to give Champagne any sort of regimented ageing, thus when the term is applied to current wines, the landed-age will almost invariably be inadvertent – either the importer has not actually sold the stock or it has stuck on the retailer's shelf.

Late-harvest In a perfect world grapes are normally harvested when they are ripe, early-harvested grapes when they are less than ripe (as often happens for sparkling wines, when acidity is more crucial than sugar) and late-harvested are more than ripe or overripe. In the real world, however, some late-harvest wines such as most of the cheaper German Spätlesen are merely ripe and lower grades are underripe and over-chaptalized.

Lees The sediment that accumulates in the bottom of a vat during the fermentation of a wine.

Leesy Some wines, notably Muscadet, are aged on their lees, whereas a number, including barrel-fermented Chardonnay, are subject to a periodic stirring of the lees, which adds a certain leesy character or yeasty fullness and complexity.

Length Indicates that the flavour of a wine lingers in the mouth a long time after swallowing. If two wines taste the same, yet you definitely prefer one but do not understand why, it is probably because the one you prefer has a greater length.

Light vintage/year A year that produces relatively light wines. Not a great vintage, but not necessarily a bad one either.

Lingering Normally applied to the finish of a wine – an aftertaste that literally lingers.

Liquorous Liqueur-like or *liquoreux* in French, this term is often applied to dessert wines of a certain viscosity and unctuous quality.

Live beer Synonymous with bottle-conditioned.

Liveliness A term that usually implies a certain youthful freshness of fruit owing to good acidity and a touch of carbonic gas.

Longevity Potentially long-lived wines may owe their longevity to a significant content of one or more of the following: tannin, acidity, alcohol and sugar.

Maceration A term usually applied to the period during the vinification process when the fermenting juice is in contact with the grape skins. This traditionally applies in red wine-making, but it is on the increase for white wines utilizing pre-fermentation maceration techniques.

Macération carbonique or **maceration style** Generic terms for several similar methods of initially vinifying wine under the pressure of carbonic gas, and identifiable by an aroma of peardrops, bubblegum or nail-varnish. Beaujolais Nouveau is the archetypal *macération carbonique* wine.

Malt and **Malting** Malt is the biscuity-smelling germinated grain of cereal (usually barley), and malting is the application of warmth and moisture that germinates the grain.

Mellow A wine that is round and nearing its peak of maturity.

Méthode Champenoise Process whereby an effervescence is induced through secondary fermentation in bottle, used for Champagne and other good-quality sparkling wines.

Mid-palate (1) The centre-top of your tongue. (2) A subjective term to describe the middle of the taste sensation when taking a mouthful of wine. Could be hollow if the wine is thin and lacking, or full if the wine is rich and satisfying.

Must Unfermented or partly fermenting grape juice.

Négociant French for trader or merchant, this term is commonly used to describe larger wine-producing companies and is derived from the traditional practice of negotiating with growers to buy grapes and wholesalers or other customers to sell the wine produced.

Nitrogen flushed The non-widgetized method of producing the newfangled creamy beers (albeit less creamy than the fully fledged widgetized brews), the tins are flushed with nitrogen prior to filling.

Nose The smell or odour of a wine, encompassing both aroma and bouquet.

Oak Many wines are fermented or aged in wooden casks, and the most commonly used wood is oak. There are two main categories of oak, French and American, and they are both used the world over. The French always use French oak, and the greatest California wines are also usually made in French oak barrels. American oak is traditional in Spain, particularly Rioja, and Australia, although both these countries make increasing use of French oak. Oak often gives a vanilla taste to wine because it contains a substance called vanillin, which also gives vanilla pods their aroma. French oak is perceived to be finer and more refined (guess who started that one), while American oak is generally considered to have a more upfront, obvious character. The reason for this is not because one is French and the other American (although the latter grows quicker and has a bigger grain, which does have some influence), but because French oak is traditionally weathered in the open for several years, which leeches out the most volatile aromatics, and is split, not sawn, whereas American oak is kiln-dried, thus not leeched, and sawn, which ruptures the grain, exposing the wine to the most volatile elements in a relatively short time. If French oak were to be kiln-dried and sawn, and American weathered and split, I suspect our perception of the two forms of oak might well be reversed. American oak is highly charred in the construction of a barrel (wine makers can order it lightly toasted, medium toast, or highly charred), and this too has an effect, adding caramel, toffee, and smoky-toasty aromas to a wine. The toastiness in oak is different to the toastiness derived from the grape itself (usually Chardonnay). Strangely, oak can have a cedary taste, although this is probably confined to older wood and spicy red grape varieties. If you get a very strong impression of coconut, it's a good bet that the oak used was American. Oak barrels are very expensive to buy and labour-intensive to work with, so if you find a very cheap wine with obvious oak character, it will inevitably be due to the use of oak chips or shavings, which are chucked into a huge, gleaming stainless-steel vat of wine. Cheating maybe, but legal, and if people like the taste of oak-aged wine but cannot afford to pay very much for a bottle, why not?

Off vintage/year A year in which many poor wines are produced owing to adverse climatic conditions, such as insufficient sunshine during the summer, which can result in unripe grapes, or rain or humid heat at the harvest, which can result in rot. Generally a vintage to be avoided, but approach any opportunity to taste the wines with an open mind because there are always good wines made in every vintage, however poor, and they have to be sold at bargain prices because of the vintage's bad reputation.

Openknit An open and enjoyable nose or palate; usually a modest wine, not capable of much development.

Opulent Suggestive of a rather luxurious varietal aroma, very rich but not quite blowzy.

Overripe-style A late-harvest style the French call *passerillé* where the grapes are overripe and have possibly started to shrivel like a raisin, but not botrytis-affected.

Overtone A dominating element of nose and palate, often one that is not directly attributable to the grape or wine.

Oxidative A wine that openly demonstrates the character of maturation on the nose or palate. An extremely oxidative wine will have a sherry-like aroma.

Ozzified The curious ability of Australians to stamp their mark on almost every wine they make, anywhere in the world (*see* **Australian, Typically**).

Palate The flavour or taste of a wine.

Peacock's tail Used to describe the elegant fanning-out of flavours on the finish of a wine. This often occurs in wines with a tightly focused concentration of mid-palate fruit, which leads the taster to expect an intense finish, but surprisingly unfolds into a medley of different flavours, possibly indicating the potential complexity the wine may possess if aged a little longer.

Peak The so-called peak in the maturity of a wine depends upon the preferences of the consumer. Those liking fresher, crisper wines will perceive an earlier peak (in the same wine) than 'golden oldie' drinkers. A rule of thumb that applies to all extremes of taste is that a wine will remain at its peak for as long as it took to reach it.

Peardrop *See* **Macération carbonique**.

Pétillant A wine with enough carbonic gas to create a light sparkle.

Petit château Literally small château, this term is applied to any wine château that is neither a *cru classé* nor a *cru bourgeois*.

Phylloxera A native American bug that wiped out European vineyards in the late nineteenth century. The remedy was (and still is, because it still exists in almost every vineyard) to graft vines on to native American rootstocks, which have a natural resistance. There are, however, a few tiny plots dotted here and there where Phylloxera failed to penetrate, and the vines are still grown on their own rootstock. These are usually referred to as pre-Phylloxera vines and the wines they produce are highly prized.

QbA Germany's *Qualitätswein bestimmter Anbaugebiete* is theoretically the equivalent of the French AOC. *See* **AOC**.

Reserve Wine Still wines from previous vintages that are blended with the wines of one principal year to produce a balanced, non-vintage Champagne.

Reticent Suggests that the wine is holding back on its nose or palate, perhaps through youth, and may well develop with a little more maturity.

Rich, richness A balanced wealth of fruit and depth on the palate and finish.

Ripe Grapes ripen, wines mature. The term ripe should refer to richness that only ripe grapes can give, although a certain amount of residual sugar can fool even an experienced taster into mistaking sweetness for ripeness.

Ripe acidity The main acidity in ripe grapes (tartaric acid) tastes refreshing and fruity, even in large proportions, whereas the main acidity in unripe grapes (malic acid) tastes hard and unpleasant.

Robust A milder form of aggressive, which may often be applied to a mature product: i.e. the wine is robust by nature, not aggressive through youth.

Rustic Possibly plain and simple, definitely unrefined, but not necessarily lacking a certain basic appeal.

Sassy A less cringing version of the cheeky, audacious character found in a wine with bold, brash, but not necessarily big, flavour.

Sediment Wine and beer are both natural products that are subject to a continuous evolution through a series of complex chemical and biochemical changes that can in time result in a harmless deposit or sediment. Some beers, however, are bottled live – that is to say with active yeast – and this yields a sediment that should be avoided when pouring (unless it is a wheat or white beer).

Sharp In wine, this term applies to acidity, whereas bitterness applies to tannin and, sometimes, other natural solids. An immature wine might be sharp, but this term, if used by professional tasters, is usually a derogatory one. Good acidity is usually described as ripe acidity, which can make the fruit refreshingly tangy.

Sherbetty A subjective term to indicate the ultra-fresh fruit found in some wines.

Sherry-like Undesirable in low-strength or unfortified wines, this refers to the odour of wine in an advanced state of oxidation.

Short Refers to a wine that may have a good nose and initial flavour, but falls short on the finish, its taste quickly disappearing after the wine has been swallowed.

Skin-contact The maceration of grape skins in must or fermenting wine can extract varying amounts of colouring pigments, tannin and various aromatic compounds.

Sleepy-hop aroma The powerful, resinous aroma reminiscent of hop-pillows.

Smooth The opposite of aggressive and more extreme than round.

Soapy A very fresh characteristic often (but not solely) found in Riesling, soapiness wears off after time in bottle and usually indicates a degree of potential finesse in a wine.

Soft Interchangeable with smooth, although it usually refers to the fruit on the palate, whereas smooth is more often applied to the finish. Soft is very desirable, but 'extremely soft' may be derogatory, inferring a weak and flabby wine.

SO_2 Chemical term for sulphur dioxide. *See* **Sulphur dioxide**.

Solera A system of continually refreshing an established blend with a small amount of new wine (equivalent to the amount extracted from the *solera*) to effect a wine of consistent quality and character. Some *soleras* were laid down in the nineteenth century, and whereas it would be true to say that every bottle sold now contains a little of that first vintage, it would not even be a teaspoon. You would have to measure it in molecules, but there would also be infinitesimal amounts of each and every vintage from the date of inception to the year before bottling.

Soupy or **Souped-up** Implies that a wine has been blended with something richer or more robust. A wine may well be legitimately souped up, or it could mean that the wine has been played around with. The wine might not be correct, but it could still be very enjoyable.

Spätlese Semi-sweet to sweet German wine made from late-harvested grapes. Spätlesen is the plural of Spätlese.

Spicy A varietal characteristic of certain grapes such as Gewurztraminer. The Tokay-Pinot Gris and Auxerrois also definitely have some spiciness.

Spritz or **spritzig** Synonymous with pétillant.

Straw wine Complex sweet wine produced by leaving late-picked grapes to dry and shrivel in the sun, originally on or over straw mats. Known in France as *vin de paille*.

Structure The structure of a wine is composed of its solids (tannin, acidity, sugar, and extract or density of fruit flavour) in balance with the alcohol, and how positive is its form and feel in the mouth.

Stylish Wines possessing all the subjective qualities of charm, elegance and finesse. Wines might have the style of a certain region or type, but a wine is either stylish or it is not. It defies definition.

Subtle Although this should mean a significant yet understated characteristic, it is often employed by wine snobs and frauds who taste a wine with a famous label and know that it should be special, but cannot detect anything exceptional, and need an ambiguous word to talk their way out of the hole they have dug for themselves.

Suck-a-stone A note of freshness detected on Sauvignon Blanc that is reminiscent of the effect of sucking a smooth pebble (for anyone old and poor enough to remember – or anyone who has done any survival training), the suck-a-stone quality can usually be picked up on the nose as well as the palate and is an indication of the wine's finesse.

Sulphur dioxide This is added to help prevent oxidation and bacterial spoilage. Sulphur should not be noticeable in the finished product, but for various reasons a whiff may be detected on recently bottled wines, which a good swirl in the glass or a vigorous decanting should remove. With a few months in bottle, this whiff ought to disappear. The acrid odour of sulphur in a wine should, if detected, be akin to the smell of a recently extinguished match. If it has a rotten egg aroma, the wine should be returned to the retailer, as this means the sulphur has reduced to hydrogen sulphide. All good winemakers try to use as little sulphur as possible, but some people worry about its use in wine when there are far higher concentrations in orange juice, packets of ham and virtually any preserved commodity, which many of the same people consume without thought, let alone worry, every day.

Supple Indicates a wine easy to drink, not necessarily soft, but suggesting more ease than simply 'round' does. With age, the tannin in wine becomes supple.

Supple tannins Tannins are generally perceived to be harsh and mouth-puckering, but the tannins in a ripe grape are supple, whereas those in an unripe grape are not.

Tannin Generic term for various substances found naturally in wine from the skin, pips and stalks. It can also be picked up from wooden casks. The tannins in unripe grapes are not water-soluble and will remain harsh no matter how old the wine is, whereas the tannins in ripe grapes are water-soluble and drop out as the wine matures. Ripe grape tannin softens with age, is indispensable in the structure of a serious red wine, and is useful when matching food and wine. Tannin is essential for the preservation of red wines.

Tart Refers to a noticeable acidity, coming somewhere between sharp and piquant.

Terroir Literally 'soil' in French, but in a viticultural sense *terroir* refers to the complete growing environment, which also includes altitude, aspect, climate and any other factor that may affect the life of a vine.

Thin A wine lacking in body, fruit and other properties.

Tight A firm wine of good extract and possibly significant tannin that seems to be under tension, like a wound spring waiting to be released. Its potential is far more obvious than that of reticent or closed wines.

Toasty A bottle-induced aroma commonly associated with the Chardonnay grape and/or oak.

Trockenbeerenauslese A great, rare and extremely expensive German botrytis wine that is as sweet and concentrated as Sauternes, but with much higher acidity, which makes it much more tangy and less of a food wine.

Typical An over-used and less than honest form of 'honest'.

Typicity A wine that shows good typicity is one that accurately reflects its grape and soil.

Undertone Subtle and supporting, not dominating like an overtone. In a fine wine, a strong and simple overtone of youth can evolve into a delicate undertone with maturity, adding to a vast array of other nuances that give it complexity.

Ungenerous A wine that lacks generosity has little or no fruit and far too much tannin (if red) or acidity for a correct and harmonious balance.

Upfront Suggests an attractive, simple quality immediately recognized, which says it all. The wine may initially be interesting, but there would be no further development and the last glass would say nothing more than the first.

Vanillin An aldehyde with a vanilla aroma found naturally in oak to some degree or another.

Varietal, varietal character The character of a single grape variety as expressed in the wine it produces.

Vinification Far more than simply fermentation, this involves the entire process of making wine, from the moment the grapes are picked to the point it is bottled.

Vin ordinaire Literally an ordinary wine, this term is synonymous with the derogatory meaning of table wine.

Vintage (1) A wine of one year. (2) Synonymous with harvest.

Vivid The fruit in some wines can be so fresh, ripe, clean-cut and expressive that it quickly gives a vivid impression of complete character in the mouth.

Warm, warmth Suggestive of a good-flavoured red wine with a high alcoholic content or, if used with cedary or creamy, well matured in oak.

Weight, weighty Refers to the body of a wine.

Wheat beer A beer fermented from a mix of wheat malt (usually a minimum 50 per cent) and barley malt, which usually produces a very pale beer with a fruity-biscuity flavour (distinctive brews often have a spiced-apple character) and a substantial sediment (those prefixed with *Hefe* labour this point). Unlike most bottle-conditioned ales, the sediment in a wheat beer is supposed to be poured into the glass to produce the desired cloudy effect. It gives the beer its special fruity roundness and, of course, makes the beer fizzy to one degree or another, which when poured often throws such a vast, fluffy, voluminous head that it requires the use of a special glass to contain.

White beer Synonymous with wheat beer.

Widget Nickname employed by Boddingtons for their version of the Draughtflow system developed by Guinness to replicate the creamy head of a draught stout. Guinness may have invented this simple but clever plastic device, but the widget was unknown before cult comedian Jack Dee sang the immortal words, 'It's got a widget, a widget it has got'.

Wow! wine A commonly used term in the wine trade, it was first employed by buyers at Victoria Wine. As they tasted down a row of wines being considered for purchase, they would make comments in passing about one product, or fiercely debate the merits of another, but occasionally they would come across a wine that stood out so far from the rest of the pack that no one would think of questioning its selection and everyone would instinctively say 'Wow!' when they first took a sniff. It got to the point that a taster arriving late would ask 'Any wow! wines?' or the others would pre-empt him with 'No wow! wines today.'

Yield There are two forms of yield: how much fruit is produced from a given area of land, and how much juice you press from it. Confusingly, wine people in Europe tend to talk about hectolitres per hectare (hl/ha), which is literally how much juice has been squeezed from an area of land. This is more than a bit daft and open to abuse, but generally white wines can benefit from a higher yield than red wines, although sweet wines should be the lowest of all yields. Sparkling wines can get away with relatively high yields. For example, Sauternes averages 25hl/ha, Bordeaux 50hl/ha, and Champagne 80hl/ha.

Zesty A lively characteristic that suggests a zippy, tactile impression combined, maybe, with a hint of citrussy aroma.

Zing, zingy, zip, zippy Terms all indicative of something refreshing, lively and vital, resulting from a high balance of ripe fruit acidity.